Gone for Good?

Gone for Good?

*Church-Leaving and Returning
in the Twenty-First Century*

Leslie J. Francis
and
Philip Richter

 EPWORTH

Scripture quotations taken from the HOLY BIBLE, NEW INTERNATIONAL VERSION. Copyright © 1973, 1978, 1984 by International Bible Society. Used by permission of Hodder & Stoughton Ltd, a member of the Hodder Headline Ltd.

British Library Cataloguing in Publication data

A catalogue record for this book is available from the British Library

978 0 7162 0633 0

First published in 2007
by Epworth
4 John Wesley Road
Werrington
Peterborough PE4 6ZP

Typeset by Regent Typesetting, London
Printed and bound in Great Britain by
William Clowes Ltd, Beccles, Suffolk

Contents

Preface

In our earlier volume *Gone but not Forgotten* we tested the strength of the perspectives and methods proposed by empirical theology to assess and to illuminate the implications of church-leaving for the vitality of the churches in England and Wales. Bishop John Finney provided an encouraging Foreword, suggesting that research of this nature should be seen as an essential part of the Christian Church's response to the command of its Master to 'keep watch . . . keep awake' (Mark 13.33–37). We share his view and have continued to develop this line of research.

During the decade since the earlier volume was completed, we have continued to review the relevant literature, to increase our pool of empirical data and to reflect theologically on our findings. As a consequence *Gone for Good?* goes beyond *Gone but not Forgotten* in a number of ways, but three are of particular importance to us. First, we have refined our typology of the reasons or motivations underpinning church-leaving to identify 15 discrete themes. Second, we have expanded our database to a size that is able to test a series of hypotheses about ways in which reasons or motivations for church-leaving vary across clearly defined groups, including differences between the sexes, between age groups and between denominations. Third, reviewing our data we have tried to discern what God is saying to the churches in contemporary Britain through the voices of church-leavers. What we have heard encourages us to develop a new model of church life characterised as 'the multiplex church'. As we develop it, this model is grounded in a strong doctrine of creation and supported by a theology of individual differences.

In his Foreword to our earlier volume, Bishop John Finney also drew attention to the way in which industry and commerce generally support relevant empirical research with up to 15% of their turnover. The churches are yet to be convinced that such activity is worth the investment. Our research has, therefore, remained largely unfunded and been relegated to those twilight zones where hobbies and matters of real concern are allowed their proper place. Without two significant sources of support, however, this work would never have emerged from the twilight zones into the bright light of day. First, we wish to express our gratitude to the Bible Society, which awarded a grant to Philip to cover the cost of conducting the telephone interviews, distributing the postal questionnaires and analysing the quantitative data. Second, we wish to express our gratitude to the Welsh National Centre for Religious Education for supporting Leslie's contribution to the project.

We have also appreciated the assistance and support offered by a number of colleagues, including Káren North (conducting many of the interviews), Kevin Bales (recruiting the telephone survey team), Mandy Robbins (managing the data), Andrew Village (commenting on our conclusions), Susan Thomas (shaping the manuscript), Diane Drayson (proofreading and providing the indices) and Natalie Watson (Head of Publishing at Epworth).

Leslie J. Francis
Welsh National Centre for Religious Education

Philip Richter
Southern Theological Education and Training Scheme
March 2007

1

Introduction

If I don't worry about the one that strays and gets lost, even the one that is strong will think it is rather fun to stray and get lost. I do indeed desire outward gains, but I am more afraid of inner losses.

Augustine of Hippo, *Sermon* 46.15

Setting the scene

Millions of people have stopped going to church in Britain. Many church-leavers have firmly shut the door against church-going. But some keep the door open and claim that one day they might return. Why do people leave churches, sometimes after years of involvement? Is there one common reason or do different people leave for different reasons? And who is most likely to come back? Where should our energies be targeted as churches if we are to encourage people to begin coming to church again? Burying our heads in the sand is not an option. As the Letter to the Hebrews puts it: 'Let us not give up meeting together, as some are in the habit of doing, but let us encourage one another' (Hebrews 10.25a, *NIV*). There is plenty of popular wisdom in most churches about why people leave. Everyone tends to put forward his or her own pet hunch, ranging from, say, the competing attractions of Sunday shopping to the undermining of people's faith by such critics as Professor Richard Dawkins. But how do we find out which hunches are right? In order to get beyond pure guesswork and speculation, in this book we are using some well-tried tools from the world of social science to find out more about church-leavers. Our aim is to help make sure that, as far as leaving is concerned, churches are able to develop well-informed and properly focused strategies. So we invite you to join us in our investigation, in order better to understand, and respond to, church-leavers.

Some claim that it is a matter of trying to 'shut the stable door after the horse has bolted': during the last thirty years of the twentieth century church attendance in England plummeted from 12% to just 7.5% of the population (Bruce, 2002: 64). Others claim that energy exerted in studying church-leavers is misdirected: is it not more important to find out what attracts individuals to church-going in the first place? Perhaps churches are better off without those who have left: if the uncommitted have defected, then this should leave a more committed core. However, many churches in Britain have witnessed substantial decline in even their committed core. Those who are newly attracted through the 'front door' have not made up for those lost through death and through the 'back door'. While churches, given their present age-composition, can do little to stem mortality-related decline, it is important that churches and their leaders are aware of the factors influencing church-leaving and church-returning.

From the churches' own internal perspective there are good reasons, therefore, for studying church-leaving, if only to put flesh on the bones of church decline. Rather than encouraging church leaders to shelter behind generalised explanations, such as pervasive secularisation or the expansion of alternative things to do on Sundays, good quality research can sharpen churches' perceptions of the reasons behind church-leaving in particular social and ecclesiastical contexts.

There are also good reasons for studying church-leaving from a wider perspective. Society at large has become increasingly interested in the fate of religious organisations. Across the developed world, there is a growing public policy concerned with the role of the local church as a generator of human and social capital and as a provider of welfare and educational services. The British government and other British political parties are keen to unlock the social capital represented by faith communities. Local churches have an important part to play in sustaining civil society, by 'facilitating social integration, self-identity, self-realization and interest in wider civic engagement' (Harris, 1998b: 199). The government has expanded the role of religious organisations as partners in the provision of state-maintained education by increasing the number of religiously based and 'voluntary' schools within the state-maintained sector. There is also interest in the potential of faith-based social welfare initiatives to provide economical, well-targeted care and support, although congregations are more successful in sustaining less 'organised' types of welfare, such as 'mutual aid, social integration and various kinds of informal care', rather than formal or large-scale welfare projects (Harris, 1998b: 194–5). John Battle MP was appointed in December 2001 as the government's 'Faith Envoy' to act as an informal contact point between the government and faith communities. As the Chief Rabbi, Dr Jonathan Sacks, claimed, in a Radio 4 *Thought for the Day* broadcast:

> I love our congregations, because they're almost the only place nowadays where rich and poor, old and young, meet in equal dignity and mutual responsibility. For me, community is the place where they know your name and where they miss you when you're not there. It's society with a human face, and that's a source of welfare no government can reproduce. (19 June 2000)

Most churches engage in some form of community service, social justice or welfare activities. The 2001 English Church Life Profile found that 94% of churches were engaged in activities of this kind and that more than one in five church-goers were involved in these activities (Churches Information for Mission, 2001: 25). This is not just a case of churches providing support for their own memberships. Church-goers also tend to be disproportionately involved in voluntary service within the wider community. The English Church Life Profile found that 24% of church-goers were involved in community service, social action or welfare groups unconnected to their local church (Churches Information for Mission, 2001: 25). It is also increasingly recognised that religious participation can contribute to social well-being in a more indirect sense, in that it promotes individual well-being and good health.

Church-leaving is referred to by a variety of terms in the literature, including 'disengagement', 'disaffiliation', 'deconversion', 'drifting', 'dropping out', 'exiting' and 'distancing'. Some of these terms presuppose a relatively high level of commitment to the religious institution; others make no such prior assumptions. Some terms presuppose that church-leaving is predominantly an activity initiated by the church-leaver; others allow for the fact that the institution may share responsibility for the exit. One of the most neutral terms is 'les distancés de l'Eglise' (those who are distanced from the church). This is the preferred term in Félix Moser's study, *Les Croyants Non Pratiquants* (1999: 20). Here Moser plays on the ambiguity of the term, which can be taken either in an active or passive sense. On the one hand, if the term is taken in an active sense, 'les distancés' refers to individuals who voluntarily take, or keep, their distance from the church. On the other hand, interpreted in a passive sense, the term refers to distancing due to external factors and circumstances: for example, the religious institution may have alienated leavers, or distanced itself from them. Unfortunately, there is no straightforward English translation of this term that is able to retain this necessary ambiguity. So we have generally opted for the relatively neutral term, 'church- leavers', while taking account of the range of types of church-leaving described in the literature.

4

It has sometimes been claimed that studies into church-going and church-leaving must, necessarily, be biased. Respondents to surveys, it has been argued, tend to give misleadingly positive responses, out of a sense of guilt or a desire to please the interviewer. This means that they over-estimate their levels of church participation or choose to conceal the real reasons why they have disaffiliated. So, for example, instead of owning up to having lost their faith, they attribute their church-leaving to contextual factors, such as removal to a new area. Steve Bruce criticised our earlier study, *Gone but not Forgotten* (Richter and Francis, 1998), along these lines, suggesting that the responses were 'shaded by politeness and guilt' (Bruce, 2002: 197). However, one might equally argue that those who have left churches would not want to be too encouraging to an interviewer, for fear that they might be seen as 'easy prey' for recruitment back into the church (Moser, 1999: 136, 225). In any case, such a critique is less justified if the survey is carried out in an academic context: here there is no reason for the respondent to imagine that a misleadingly positive answer will necessarily please the interviewer, who may, or may not, be religiously sympathetic. Provided that the interviewer is properly trained to ask probing questions, and displays appropriate curiosity, tenacity and sensitivity, there is little reason to suppose that in-depth face-to-face interviews will be open to the bias introduced by pleasing the interviewer (Richter, 2000). In the case of the quantitative survey on which we will be reporting in this book, the data were collected by anonymous questionnaire, from an academic source, completed by the respondents independently and without the help of an interviewer.

The study of church-leaving, both professionally by sociologists and, sometimes on a more amateur basis, by churches themselves, can be broken down historically into the five main phases, which we have characterised as follows: charting decline – counting the missing; post-war decline – profiling the leaver; new religious movements – their entrances and exits; the baby-boomer factor; and digging down further.

Charting decline – counting the missing

In this phase, covering, broadly, the early nineteenth to mid-twentieth centuries, attention was focused on the numerical decline of the churches, in the context of their exposure to urbanisation and the breakdown of traditional, more close-knit communities. Perhaps the most well-known of the earliest theorists was Thomas Chalmers, who became Professor of Divinity in Edinburgh in the 1820s and who linked decline in working-class church-going to the growth of new industrial towns and the demise of 'close paternalistic ties between social ranks' (Brown, 2001: 20). One of the main questions driving studies of church-leaving during this phase was: 'is it true that fewer individuals are attending church, and is this linked to urbanisation?'

Robin Gill has identified a wide range of studies of church attendance in this period, many quite locally focused (Gill, 1993, 2003a, 2003b). He describes four main sources of data dealing with this period: the 1851 Religious Census; independent newspaper censuses, mostly from the 1880s; occasional censuses by statistical societies and individuals, mostly from the 1830s; and local clergy returns, Catholic records and Free Church records (Gill, 2003a: 15). Urban census data, of these various types, suggest that Sunday attendances in the Church of England continuously declined after the 1851 Religious Census, while Free Church attendances began continuous decline in the 1880s, initially among the older Free Churches (Gill, 2003a: 57, 94). Sometimes commentary and analysis accompanied the statistical findings. *The Nonconformist and Independent*, for instance, reviewed the 1881 newspaper censuses and concluded that:

whatever the reasons – and they are manifold – the masses of the population remain outside our places of worship, and the public ministrations of religion are, to a great extent, regarded by the working people in our towns as a matter which concerns the classes that are higher in social position, but has no particular relation to them. (*The Nonconformist and Independent*, 2 February 1882: 106)

At the beginning of the twentieth century, Charles Booth's seminal study, *Life and Labour of the People in London* (Booth, 1902a), gave a richly detailed account of generally declining churches and chapels in the capital. He noted that churches and chapels were often largely empty in working-class areas: 'the vast majority attend no place of worship' (Booth, 1902b: 4). Women and children predominated in most congregations, and church-going among working-class men would have 'appeared as exceedingly odd' (Gill, 2003a: 130). Children, even those of the working classes, tended to go to Sunday school, but then failed to become church-goers as adults: 'The desire to put away childish things comes very early; much sooner than St Paul intended. Great efforts are made to retain some hold on the children at this time; everywhere the efforts are of the same kind and nowhere are they particularly successful' (Booth, 1902b: 15).

At the end of the Great War, army chaplains conducted a unique survey of men of all ranks, which revealed that, while most soldiers believed in God, prayer and the afterlife, albeit not necessarily in specifically Christian terms, only 11.5% of English soldiers were 'in vital relationship with any of the churches'. Although 80% of the soldiers had attended Sunday school, 80% of the Sunday school attendees had failed subsequently to attend church as an adult (Cairns, 1919; Gill, 2003a: 132). The survey summarised its findings in these terms:

We seem to have left the impression upon them that there is little or no life in the church at all, that it is an antiquated and decaying institution, standing by dogmas expressed in archaic language, and utterly out of touch with modern thought and living experience . . . they believe that the churches are more and more governed by the middle-aged and the elderly; they think ministry professionalised and out of touch with the life of men, deferring unduly to wealth . . . They say they do not see any real differences in the strength and purity of life between the people who go to church and the people who do not. (Cairns, 1919: 220–21)

In the late 1920s Arthur Black contributed a series of reports to *The British Weekly* about the 1927/8 sample surveys of London church-going. He was particularly surprised to discover that average attendances at churches and chapels had dropped significantly in his middle-class suburban sample area, as well as in the other two (working-class) areas surveyed. He speculated that decline in this suburban area was:

partly due to causes beyond the control of the churches . . . [that is, the war, and distractions such as] the gramophone, cinema, wireless . . . [improved social conditions and travel opportunities] and, last, the intellectual unsettlement, within the church and outside, consequent upon modern biblical scholarship and the new scientific explanations of man's place in the universe. (Black, 1928)

But, even earlier, at the turn of the century, Charles Booth had also detected decline in church-going beyond the ranks of the working classes: 'as a pervading spiritual force capable of uplifting the mass of its adherents, the Church of England fails even among the rich' (Booth, 1902b: 44); in Westminster he discovered that 'fashionable dwellers in flats are seldom seen at church . . . flat-dwellers are continually on the move in and out of town, and cannot be relied on to share in either the worship or work of the churches' (Booth, 1902c: 80).

Post-war decline – profiling the leaver

After the Second World War, there was in Britain an unexpected, but temporary, increase in church participation, in the period between 1945 and 1956 (Brown, 2001: 188). However, this reversal of church decline did not last and there followed a very rapid drop in the level of church participation. Predictably, declining churches wanted to do more than simply chart their own decline. They needed to find out who were dropping out and why they were leaving. In 1964, John R. Butler analysed the aetiology of lapsing in a single Methodist District, applying 'the techniques of social investigation and analysis to an important contemporary problem in Methodism – that of declining membership' (Butler, 1966: 236). The explanations for lapsing adduced by Butler included class tensions and work pressures. The 1950s were also a heyday of church-going in the United States of America; but, similarly, there was a significant decline thereafter, from the 1958 peak of 49% of all Americans attending church or synagogue in any given week (Gallup Jr, 1990: 45). In the United Methodist Church, for instance, after membership peaked in 1964, there was a net loss of over one million members in the following decade. There was, therefore, a similar interest across the Atlantic in explaining why people drop out of church involvement. Warren J. Hartman's analysis of United Methodist Church membership trends focused on those who dropped out in early adolescence or when they moved (Hartman, 1976: 4–6). Hartman attributed church-leaving to four main reasons: loss of sense of belonging; changes in personal circumstances; perceived irrelevance; or rejection of the church as too liberal or too conservative (Hartman, 1976: 7). John S. Savage's study, also of those who had dropped out of United Methodist congregations, analysed the psychological and theological dynamics of the drift into 'inactivity'. Savage attributed church-leaving typically to unrelieved anxiety, especially in relation to 'conflict with the pastor, with other church members, and with members of one's family' (Savage, 1976: 67). David A. Roozen's analysis of national survey data profiled the 'unchurched' – a category that included church-leavers, but also included those who had never been church-goers. His study explicitly sought to make sense of the dramatic decline of church membership since the mid-1960s (Roozen, 1978: 1–2). Roozen detailed the social background of the unchurched, their religious characteristics, their quality of life and their social attitudes.

Most of the research on church-leaving in the English-speaking world was conducted, and continues to be conducted, in North America, rather than in Great Britain. Church-going is the norm in the United States of America, whereas in Britain it is much less normal. In Britain, church-leaving has been seen largely within the context of the secularisation thesis, which among some sociologists of religion has become uncritically revered. The puzzle has been: 'Why do individuals bother to go to church at all, in a secularised society?' However, this has rarely been translated into empirical studies of British church-goers. Sociologists in the United States of America were also interested in abnormal behaviour, but in the North American context it was church-leaving that cried out for explanation. So sociologists tended to ask a different set of questions, such as 'Why are some dropping out?' and 'Who is dropping out?'

During this period, it became fashionable to develop typologies of church-leavers. J. Russell Hale's qualitative survey placed the unchurched into ten different categories, of which several included sub-categories: i) the anti-institutionalists; ii) the boxed in; iii) the burned out; iv) the floaters; v) the hedonists; vi) the locked out; vii) the nomads; viii) the pilgrims; ix) the publicans;

x) the true unbelievers (Hale, 1980: 100–108). Hale admitted that his taxonomy might need to be refined further; indeed, an earlier version of the taxonomy had twelve categories (Hale, 1977: 39–44). As David A. Roozen reflected, 'the reasons articulated for non-affiliation [were] so varied and complex as to defy easy and/or useful summation' (Roozen, 1978: 3). Hale sought to describe and categorise non-affiliation and disaffiliation, but made little attempt to set these phenomena within broader explanatory frameworks, simply suggesting that 'unchurched-ness may be linked to . . . alienation' (Hale, 1980: 175).

Dean R. Hoge, Kenneth McGuire and Bernard F. Stratman's study of Catholic converts, dropouts and returners placed drop-outs into five categories, based on the predispositions for the change (Hoge, McGuire and Stratman, 1981): i) family-tension dropouts; ii) weary dropouts; iii) life-style dropouts; iv) spiritual-need dropouts; and v) anti-change dropouts. Their study was theoretically informed by Lofland and Stark's (1965) theory of recruitment to religious organisations (Hoge, McGuire and Stratman, 1981: 13) and also supported by quantitative analysis. C. Kirk Hadaway's (1989, 1990a, 1990b) study of 'apostates' was, in his terms, concerned with individuals who had rejected a prior religious identity. Using cluster analysis of a national social survey, Hadaway placed apostates into five clusters: i) successful swinging singles; ii) sidetracked singles; iii) young settled liberals; iv) young libertarians; and v) irreligious traditionalists (Hadaway, 1989: 206–13). Hadaway claimed that this typology did proper justice to the diversity among apostates and avoided treating apostates as a homogeneous population. However, although the typology described who apostates were, it offered inadequate explanation of why individuals became apostates, as Hadaway himself recognised (Hadaway, 1989: 214).

New religious movements – their entrances and exits

Within the sociology of religion, from the 1970s onwards, attention tended to shift from mainstream conventional religion to new religious movements (NRMs), which appeared to be burgeoning and, in some cases, attracting those who had given up on mainstream churches. Sociologists of religion became less interested in 'priestly religion' and more interested in 'prophetic religion', which 'contest[ed] the established order and sacralize[d] resistance [to conventional society]' (Bromley, 1998b: 4). Study of new religious movements included attention to processes of defection, both voluntary or, in the case of forcible 'rescue' and deprogramming, involuntary. The focus was on 'how', as well as 'why', individuals defected. For example, Stuart A. Wright's analysis of the dynamics of defection, based on a survey of defectors from the Children of God, Hare Krishna and the Unification Church, identified four primary precipitating factors in the defection process: i) breakdown in social insulation; ii) unregulated development of dyadic relationships; iii) perceived failure in achieving world transformation; and iv) inconsistencies between leaders' actions and ideals (Wright, 1987: 25–50). He identified three different patterns of leave-taking: i) covert; ii) overt; and iii) declarative. Wright suggested that the defection process was 'analogous to marital separation and divorce' (Wright, 1987: 5, 91) and was best studied within the 'conceptual framework and language of commitment' (Wright, 1987: 5).

David G. Bromley found that members' commitment tended to be undermined by problems endemic to the new religious movement organisational structure (Bromley, 1997: 56). Bromley identified five key categories of 'organizational destabilisation and tension which give rise to disaffiliation': i) disruption of internal solidarity; ii) destabilisation of leadership authority; iii) erosion of organisational totalism; iv) diminished spiritual authority; and v) prophetic deconfirmation (Bromley, 1997: 43–8).

12

Several collected volumes of research in this field have been published, including two edited by David G. Bromley (1988, 1998b). The writers in *The Politics of Religious Apostasy* (Bromley, 1998b) focused on the social construction of the apostate role, and the impact of apostates within conflicts between so-called 'subversive' new religious movements and wider society. Bromley distinguishes 'apostates' from 'defectors', on the one hand, and 'whistleblowers', on the other hand. He uses 'apostate' to refer to those leave-takers 'who are involved in contested exit and affiliate with an oppositional coalition' (Bromley, 1998b: 5); by contrast, church-leavers normally fall into the category of 'defectors' (Bromley, 1998b: 27–31). Given that church-leaving differs significantly from new religious movement leave-taking, in this and other ways, while some of this literature can shed light on church-leaving, it is seldom directly transferable.

The baby-boomer factor

In the last three decades of the twentieth century, attention also began to be focused on the baby-boomer generation, which appeared to be quite different from previous generations, in many ways. Baby boomers' patterns of religious involvement did not necessarily reproduce those of their forebears. Sociologists of religion began to ask why baby boomers were breaking the earlier mould. Attention began to focus on generation-specific factors associated with church-leaving. Baby boomers began to investigate themselves and to take account of the effects of the immense social and cultural upheavals of the 1960s and early 1970s on patterns of affiliation and disaffiliation. One of the earliest studies to take account of the influence of shifting cultural values was that of Carl S. Dudley (1979). Like the theorists represented in the phase concerned with post-war decline above, Dudley was responding to 'unexpected, unprecedented, and most upsetting' mainline Protestant membership decline (Dudley, 1979: x), but the explanation he gave for the decline was quite different. He found that the primary cause of membership decline was 'the churches' inability to attract and hold young members' (Dudley, 1979: 33). The events of the late 1960s and early 1970s had diverted young people away from institutional religion and toward more individualistic, personally integrative forms of faith (Dudley, 1979: 10–11). The 'new believers', as Dudley termed them, prioritised personal religious experience, spiritual mystical faith, non-institutional sources of faith, and fulfilment in community (Dudley, 1979: 12–17). Dudley claimed that, because mainline denominations had become increasingly privatised and accommodated to the American Dream, their response to these new cultural shifts was already attenuated (Dudley, 1979: 18–32).

The most sustained and comprehensive treatment of the religious involvement of baby boomers is to be found in a set of studies by Wade Clark Roof (1993, 1999), which included analyses of their church-leaving and church-returning. Roof's studies were based on survey data, in-depth interviews and field observation. He claimed that 'the boundaries of popular religious communities are now being redrawn, encouraged by the quests of the large generations following the Second World War, and facilitated by the rise of an expanded spiritual marketplace' (Roof, 1999: 10). Roof suggested that those most affected by the value shifts of the 1960s and 1970s were more likely to have dropped out of church-going and least likely to return (Roof, 1993: 56, 171).

Other theorists have criticised this strong focus on generation-specific factors. Dean R. Hoge, Benton Johnson and Donald A. Luidens, in their study of the religion of mainline Protestant baby boomers, suggested that mainline Protestant decline was being fuelled by multiple forces, including not only changes in American culture, but also 'the gradual weakening of mainline

14

churches . . . and the churches' policy of openness to change'
(Hoge, Johnson and Luidens, 1994: 202).

Digging down further

Alongside the two phases concerned with new religious movements and with the baby-boomer factor, and in the period since
those phases were dominant, there has also been increasing
interest in the specifics of church-leaving, fuelled by reports of
continuing church decline, especially in Britain, and by the sense
that previous studies had been over-generalised. Sociologists of
religion have begun to ask 'What is the detailed picture?' This has
taken a variety of different perspectives.

The first perspective is concerned with differentiation by
geographical context. Much church-leaving theory has been
developed on the basis of data from the United Sates of America.
Given that church-going is a quite different phenomenon in the
United States of America than in Europe (Davie, 2002), some
aspects of church-leaving theory may not necessarily be transferable elsewhere. Hence, nationally based studies of church-leavers
have been developed, located, for example, in Australia (Lovat,
1997; Hughes, Bellamy, Black and Kaldor, 2000), Canada
(McTaggart, 1997), Denmark (Iversen, 1997), England (Fanstone,
1993; Richter and Francis, 1998; Partridge and Reid, 2006),
Germany (Henkys and Schweitzer, 1997), Israel (Bar-Lev, Leslau
and Ne'eman, 1997) and New Zealand (Jamieson, 2002, 2004).

The second perspective is concerned with differentiation by
denomination. A growing recognition of the cultural and other
differences between denominations (Carroll and Roof, 1993;
Richter, 2004) has helped to promote studies of church-leaving
within specific denominations and types of church. Studies have
related to, for example, Evangelical, Pentecostal and Charismatic
churches (Jamieson, 2002), Protestant fundamentalism (Babinski,

1995), Presbyterian churches (Hoge, Johnson and Luidens, 1995), and Methodism (Field, 2000).

The third perspective is concerned with the study of different variables. One of the problems associated with large-scale, broad-canvas studies is that the degree of variation among church-leavers is understated. The factors affecting church-leaving by children and adolescents are, for example, somewhat different from those affecting the departures of those who are older (Kay and Francis, 1996). Church-leaving patterns can vary according to: the generation to which individuals belong; their sex; the period during which they left; their denomination; the age at which they left; their length of association; the type of area in which they live; the size of their church; their upbringing; their beliefs, or lack of beliefs; the speed with which they leave; their sense of personal well-being, or lack of well-being; and whether they see their departure as permanent or temporary. Single variables of this sort are sometimes covered within more broad-canvas studies of church-leaving, but attention often has to turn to journal articles or edited volumes to find more in-depth treatment of these factors.

The fourth perspective is concerned with differentiation by congregation. If the large-scale, broad-canvas way of studying church-leaving is too catch-all and imprecise, an alternative approach is to focus on individual congregations or local churches. Each congregation is a 'complex particular world' (Wind, 1995: 178) with its own unique cultural identity (Ammerman, 1998: 78). As James P. Wind has claimed: 'Part of the problem in our previous attempts to understand congregational and denominational affiliation patterns . . . is that we have failed to fathom just how much is going on in the life of any individual who approaches a congregation, in any congregation itself, and in any interaction between the two' (Wind, 1995: 179). Local contextual and institutional factors need to be taken into account, as well as, and alongside, broader trends. Indeed, the growth or decline of individual congregations may owe most to local factors, such as 'satisfaction with leadership, amount of conflict in the congregation, and program emphases and strengths', rather than national factors (Hoge, Johnson and Luidens, 1994: 10–11). A good example of a micro-level study of church-leaving is Gary Dorsey's account of his return to church-going in his semi-journalistic, semi-ethnographic work, *Congregation: the journey back to church* (Dorsey, 1998). Dorsey provides an engaging 'thick description' of life in one particular congregation, although he makes little reference to wider trends. The current renaissance of local church studies (see, for example, Guest, Tusting and Woodhead, 2004) should offer new opportunities to take proper account of the effects of differences between congregations on church-leaving patterns. In time, new typologies of congregations may be developed that could explicitly relate different types of congregation to different patterns of church-leaving: this would help to make micro-level studies of this sort more generalisable and less idiosyncratic.

Methods and motives

Studies of church-leavers are conducted for different reasons and by different types of investigator. Broadly speaking, studies by church personnel tend to be motivated by concern at church decline and the desire to find out what factors might retain those at risk of leaving or attract them back. For example, John S. Savage, as an ordained minister, undertook his research into church-leaving because he had become uncomfortably aware that large numbers within his Methodist parish had become 'completely inactive and disinterested' (Savage, 1976: i, 91). Academic studies, on the other hand, tend to leave open the question as to whether church decline is a welcome, or unwelcome, phenomenon and typically relate church-leaving to wider social trends (for example, Roof, 1993).

A range of different methods is used for studying church-leavers. Typically, a 'snapshot' is offered of a particular set of church-leavers, or, sometimes, a series of snapshots from different periods. All too rarely, individuals and sets of leavers are studied 'longitudinally', over an extended period of time (for example, Wilson and Sherkat, 1994; Dudley, 1999). Sometimes quantitative survey methods are used, sometimes qualitative are used, and sometimes a powerful combination of both (for example, Richter and Francis, 1998: 168–74). J. Russell Hale's approach was to use unstructured interviews, probing 'the attitudes of everyday life as it is lived and articulated in simple, vulgarised, deintellectualized rhetoric' (Hale, 1980: 175). One of his most candid items of qualitative survey data goes as follows: 'A topless waitress working at a tavern outside Sarasota City came to my table after I had arranged with the owner for an interview. She opened her makeshift sarong. "Just look at me, sir, (take) a good look! Now, do I look like a choir girl to you?"' Most instances of church-leavers 'baring their souls' are somewhat less dramatic. Other studies, by contrast, are statistically driven and do not involve personal interviews (for example, Roozen, 1978).

The present study, presented in the remainder of this book, is an attempt to dig deeper into the phenomenon of church-leaving. We shall be examining the effects of seven different variables on church-leaving, testing out our own and others' theories as to how these variables influence church-leaving. Although both authors are ordained ministers, the study has been conducted within the academic context. Compared with our previous work about church-leaving and church-returning, *Gone but not Forgotten* (Richter and Francis, 1998), this book is driven to a greater extent by quantitative data. Since 1998, we have doubled our database of church-leavers and extended its geographical spread. We shall, however, also be drawing on our original qualitative survey.

2

Listening to leavers

Setting the scene

The Church Leaving Applied Research Project was established during the 1990s to take seriously the specific problem of church-leaving within the social context of England and Wales. The project was conceived as an initiative in empirical theology.

Empirical theology is now a well-established methodological perspective within practical theology. Within the Catholic University of Nijmegen the foundations of empirical theology were put in place during the 1980s by Professor Hans van der Ven (see for example, van der Ven, 1993, 1998). The international face of empirical theology was established through the *Journal of Empirical Theology* launched in 1987.

Van der Ven takes the view that the tools and techniques developed by the social sciences have a proper place within the activity of theology. In this sense, methods developed within the social sciences are used in an intra-disciplinary way within theology. An important implication deriving from this perspective is that the Church Leaving Applied Research Project was not conceived as a social scientific study of church-leaving looking at the church from the outside. As a study in empirical theology, the Church Leaving Applied Research Project was firmly grounded in the theological and practical concerns of practical theology.

Alongside van der Ven's pioneering and foundational work in empirical theology in the Netherlands, a second and distinctive strand in empirical theology has been shaped in the United Kingdom by Leslie J. Francis' research group working within the University of Wales (first at Trinity College, Carmarthen and later at Bangor). Francis is in total agreement with van der Ven's understanding of empirical theology employing the tools of the social sciences in an *intra*-disciplinary manner. He qualifies van der Ven's perspective, however, by arguing that empirical theology should be understood not only as an intra-disciplinary activity but also as an inter-disciplinary activity (see Francis, 2002). The point here is that, on Francis' understanding, empirical theologians have a responsibility to test their work not only in the area of theology but also in the area of the social sciences. The debate between these perspectives has been well rehearsed by Cartledge (1999).

The collaboration between Philip Richter and Leslie J. Francis in the Church Leaving Applied Research Project brought together differing ecclesiastical perspectives and differing social scientific methodologies. Richter is a Methodist minister; Francis is an Anglican priest. Richter is a sociologist; Francis is a social psychologist. Richter is grounded in qualitative methodologies, using interviews; Francis is grounded in quantitative methodologies, using questionnaires.

As the name implies, the quantitative approach is concerned with the collection, organisation and analysis of statistical data. This approach often results in the design of surveys, conducted either face-to-face through interviews, or by means of self-completion questionnaires. The types of questions asked by such surveys need to be well focused and to generate the kind of responses that can be counted. Providing the group of people surveyed has been randomly selected and is sufficiently large and representative, and providing there is a reasonable response rate, it is possible to generalise from the sample surveyed to the wider population that sample has been chosen to represent. Newspapers, for instance, will adopt this approach when they want to gauge public opinion on a contentious issue. For data generated by quantitative surveys to be really useful it is crucial that the questions have been well shaped, and that they are clear and unambiguous. The quantitative approach can provide high quality information over a narrowly focused area, but it does so at the expense of not doing complete justice to the richness and complexity of people's behaviour.

By way of contrast, the qualitative approach prefers to survey fewer people in greater depth. While the quantitative approach will generally use a series of 'closed' questions, allowing for a limited range of possible responses, the qualitative approach prefers to use broader 'open-ended' questions. Such questions can be raised either through the self-completion questionnaire, which invites people to respond discursively, through written responses, or through an in-depth semi-structured interview. The real advantage of the interview is that the interviewee's responses can be probed and followed up in greater depth. Although such interviews are generally guided by a clear inter-view schedule, the conversations may suddenly cover quite un-expected territories that bring further rich insights to the study.

Clearly, both approaches have their own strengths and weak-nesses. The qualitative approach yields much richer and better-nuanced data and avoids imposing preconceived categories on the material, but it remains very difficult to generalise on the basis of such data. The quantitative approach provides a good basis for testing clearly defined hypotheses and for providing a good descriptive overview, but disguises some of the rich depth and diversity among individuals. There remain considerable advan-tages, therefore, in research projects that are able to draw on the diverse strengths of both quantitative and qualitative research methodologies.

The Church Leaving Applied Research Project recognises the advantages of combining qualitative and quantitative methods. The qualitative approach concentrated on conducting a number of in-depth semi-structured interviews. The quantitative approach concentrated on designing a self-completion questionnaire survey.

Shaping definitions

The idea of studying church-leavers seems both simple and attractive, until fundamental questions are asked concerning what is meant by the description 'church-leavers' and concerning ways in which individuals who are representative of church-leavers can be identified and contacted. The problem of defining church-leavers is, in part, derived from the wider problem of recognising the multidimensional nature of religiosity in contemporary society. Even in a church-related context individuals may be defined as religious in a variety of ways, in terms, for example, of affiliation, belief, membership or practice. Each of these constructs will be examined in turn.

Affiliation

Religious affiliation is perhaps the most widely affirmed definition of religion as the term is employed in the United Kingdom today. The introduction of a religious question in 2001 to the national census in England, Wales and Scotland, for the first time ever, refocused attention on the importance of self-assigned religious affiliation for the people of these nations. In England and Wales 72% of the population were included, by those who completed the census forms, in the category 'Christian'. According to this operational definition, the Christian churches in England and Wales have retained the allegiance of nearly three-quarters of the population. According to this definition, a church-leaver would be someone who once checked the category 'Christian' on the census return and then in a subsequent census redefined himself or herself by checking either the category 'none' (indicating movement away from the category of being religious), or one of the other faith groups listed (indicating switching from one religious category to another religious category). The Church Leaving Applied Research Project was not concerned with church-leaving in this sense, since this is far too nebulous a definition and largely unrelated to actual church-going.

Belief

Religious belief is perhaps the second most widely affirmed definition of religion within the United Kingdom today. Although the national census considered it inappropriate to explore the religious beliefs of the population, the British Social Attitudes Survey has collected this kind of data over a number of years, although these data have not been routinely published for each year in which they have been collected. The findings from the British Social Attitudes Survey published by de Graff and Need (2000: 125) show that 52% of the population of Britain in 1998 believed in God.

This statistic is both potentially useful and potentially misleading in trying to understand the strength of the Christian churches in England and Wales and in trying to define church-leavers. If belief in God could be regarded as synonymous with belief in the Christian God, then we could argue that 52% of the population were church-related through belief in God, and church-leavers could be defined as those who had formerly believed in God and then subsequently lost their faith in God. Such an argument is, however, clearly flawed by the fact that the Christian tradition has no monopoly over belief in God.

If religion is defined in terms of belief, perhaps belief in Jesus Christ as the Son of God might have a stronger claim for helping to define church-leavers. According to this definition, a church-leaver would be someone who once had professed belief in Jesus as the Son of God and then subsequently ceased to hold that particular belief. The Church Leaving Applied Research Project was not concerned with church-leaving in this sense, since belief does not necessarily presuppose actual church-going.

Membership

Church membership is perhaps the most elusive definition of religion as the term is employed in the United Kingdom today. The notion of church membership is elusive for a number of reasons. Not only does the notion of church membership vary widely from one denomination to another, but there can be multiple definitions of membership even within one denomination.

The Church of England provides a particularly intriguing example of how membership can be defined in a variety of ways. There is one sense in which everyone in England is a member of the Church of England, as the established church of the nation, unless they deliberately choose to opt out. Everyone lives within a Church of England parish and has a legal right to be married in their parish church, provided that they fulfil the formal criteria of the legal provision. Theologically within the Church of England it seems that baptism is regarded as the gateway into church membership. Infant baptism rates at Church of England fonts have dropped steeply from 60% of live births in 1956 to 17% in 2004 (Church of England, 1959: 24; 2006: 13). According to this definition of a church member, a high proportion of people living in England must be able to produce a baptism certificate to demonstrate church membership. According to this definition of membership, a church-leaver would be someone who actively renounced his or her baptism.

A third definition of membership within the Church of England might be based on confirmation. At the time of the 1662 Book of Common Prayer, confirmation was seen as the completion of the sacramental rite of initiation begun in infant baptism.

Confirmation provided an opportunity for adult ratification of promises made vicariously by godparents and opened the gateway to Communion. Changing theological perspectives on baptism as a complete sacramental rite of total initiation and on admission to Communion prior to confirmation have further eroded the usefulness of confirmation as an indicator of church membership or as a potential mechanism for identifying church-leavers.

A fourth and frequently cited definition of membership within the Church of England is derived from a rubric in the 1662 Book of Common Prayer. This rubric specifies that 'every parishioner shall communicate at least three times in the year, of which Easter to be one'. Here membership becomes closely identified with conformity to practice. According to this definition of membership, a church-leaver would be someone who formerly received Communion at Easter, but then subsequently ceased to do so.

A fifth definition of membership within the Church of England is based on the system of the electoral roll. Once Anglicans reach the age of 16, they are eligible to be placed on the electoral roll of the parish church where they live or where they habitually attend. It is those individuals enlisted on the electoral roll who can elect candidates to serve on the Parochial Church Council and who form the basis for the whole representative system of synodical government at deanery, diocesan, and national levels. According to this definition of membership, a church-leaver would be someone who either removed his or her name from the local electoral roll or who failed to re-register when the electoral rolls were remade every six years and has not at the same time transferred to the electoral roll of another church.

For the Roman Catholic Church in England, the concept of membership may be almost as elusive as it is for the Church of England. Once an individual becomes a Catholic he or she remains a Catholic for life, unless a sin has been committed grave enough to warrant excommunication. Entry to the Roman

Catholic Church takes place through baptism, either as an infant or as an adult. Infant baptism is followed by first Communion (at about seven years old) and confirmation (at about 14 years old). Catholics are then expected to attend Mass every Sunday and on major feast days, unless they are prevented by unavoidable circumstances. Those who do not attend Mass regularly would often be described as 'lapsed Catholics', although there is a tendency to prefer the description 'resting Catholics' in the hope that this state will not be permanent. Each local Roman Catholic parish might then carry two informal membership lists: a list of those known to be practising their faith through regular reception at Mass and those known to have been baptised into the faith but who are not currently practising. There is, however, no formal register of members.

Free or Nonconformist Churches tend to have a much more developed membership system in comparison with the Church of England. Indeed, the concept of 'church membership' is very much a Free Church concept. It was the Methodist Church that first attempted to count its members accurately (Bruce, 1996: 28). Its methodological approach to keeping track of its members has persisted. Methodists become members of the church through baptism and confirmation. Confirmation is also known as being 'received into full membership'. Their names are then held on the membership roll of their local Methodist Church. Should they move away from their local area, say to a new home elsewhere, their membership is meant to be transferred to their new church. Every three years detailed statistics of membership are presented to the Methodist Church's governing body, the Methodist Conference. Methodist members receive membership tickets at least once a year, which include a printed reminder of their obligations as members. Within the Methodist Church, members commit themselves to 'worship, Holy Communion, fellowship of service, prayer and Bible study, and responsible giving'. In the wider world there is a commitment to work out their faith in daily life, to offer 'personal service in the community, the Christian use of resources, and the support of the church in its total world mission'. If Methodist members fail to satisfy these obligations, their membership may be rescinded and they may be classified as 'ceased to meet'. According to this definition of membership, a church-leaver would be someone who had 'ceased to meet' or whose name was no longer on a membership roll.

Moreover, Methodists are expected to take part in what is known as the Covenant Service, a special annual opportunity to 'renew their Covenant with God'. This service, usually held early in January, contains a profound reaffirmation of commitment, not unlike the vows a person would make at ordination or upon reception into a religious community.

> I am no longer my own but yours. Your will, not mine, be done in all things, wherever you may place me, in all that I do and in all that I may endure; when there is work for me and when there is none; when I am troubled and when I am at peace. Your will be done when I am valued and when I am disregarded; when I find fulfilment and when it is lacking; when I have all things and when I have nothing. I willingly offer all I have and am to serve you, as and where you choose. (Methodist Church, 1999: 288–99)

As well as denominational differences, there are also variations according to the theological style of a given church or local congregation, in the way in which membership is discussed and defined. Conservative, more sect-like, churches tend to have much tighter membership expectations than liberal churches. Although many churches expect some degree of doctrinal orthodoxy from their members, among conservative churches a high premium is placed on theological and moral orthodoxy; there is a strongly defined boundary between the church and the secular world; the threshold level for entry into the church is high; and sacrificial giving, for example in the form of tithing disposable income, is often the norm. Where people fail to meet these expectations their continued membership is in doubt. Paradoxically, conservative churches do not necessarily get all that concerned about the phenomenon of church-leaving. There are two main reasons for this. First, they tend to prefer to channel their energies into evangelising the unchurched, and may feel that worrying about the back door can divert attention from the front door. Second, if the less committed choose to leave, then, by definition, this means that those who remain are more committed. It may seem better to lose people on the periphery of the church, if this leaves a more committed core.

For this variety of reasons the notion of church membership does not provide a helpful basis on which to define and operationalise research concerned with church-leaving. The Church Leaving Applied Research Project was not concerned with church-leaving in this sense.

Practice

The research literature has tended to focus the study of church-leaving on the easily recognised marker of religious practice as observable through church attendance. Such a definition is consistent with wider debates on what defines contemporary church-related religiosity. For example, the Gallup Organization defines the 'unchurched' American as someone who has 'not attended services in the previous six months other than for special religious holidays, weddings, funerals or the like' (Gallup, 1988: 2). The decision to base empirical research on church-leavers defined in terms of religious practice is not, however, unproblematic, either conceptually or operationally.

The conceptual problem has two roots. The first root concerns the way in which practice is regarded somewhat differently in different church traditions, and as a consequence different church traditions may regard reduction or cessation of practice in different ways. For example, the strict conservative sect may regard individuals who reduce Sunday attendance to once a month as de facto church-leavers. The Roman Catholic Church may regard occasional non-attenders as remaining within the fold of the church. The Anglican Church may regard individuals who stop attending but continue with covenanted subscriptions as far from being church-leavers. The second root concerns the self-understanding of church-related people themselves. The widespread belief, documented, for example, by Edward Bailey (1997) in his studies of implicit religion, that 'you can be a perfectly good Christian without going to church' could well justify many people who have stopped attending church denying the description of being church-leavers.

The operational problem concerns finding ways of specifying with precision how church attendance can be counted, both to define church-goers and to identify church-leavers. For example, with what frequency do individuals need to attend church in order to qualify for the description as 'church-goers'? Do those who attend just at Christmas, or for weddings and funerals, qualify as church-goers, or do people have to attend every week in order so to qualify?

For its operational definition of church-goers and church-leavers the Church Leaving Applied Research Project built on the pioneering work of Dean R. Hoge (see Hoge, Johnson and Luidens, 1993). Their operational definition defined church-goers as individuals who attended church at least six times a year, not including Christmas, Easter, weddings, or funerals. Then church-leavers were defined as individuals who had formerly engaged in this level of religious practice and subsequently reduced their practice below that level.

Shaping research

Having agreed on the operational definition of church-leavers, the research was conducted in two phases. The first phase of the research adopted a qualitative approach, involving a series of in-depth interviews with church-leavers and with clergy. On the basis of the themes that emerged from these interviews, the questionnaire was developed and refined for use in the second phase of the research. The second phase adopted a quantitative approach. Having identified a sample of church-leavers in the population at large by means of a random telephone survey, an extensive postal questionnaire was mailed to those who indicated a willingness to participate in the project.

Qualitative data

For the qualitative component of our study we conducted 27 in-depth interviews with a range of people who had left or, in a few cases, switched between Anglican, Roman Catholic, Methodist and 'New Churches'. Sometimes known as 'House Churches' or 'Restorationist Churches', New Churches often meet in hired halls for neo-pentecostalist-style worship. We felt it was important to understand why people dropped out of even these apparently thriving churches and 'fellowships'. All interviewees were encouraged to tell their own stories and to talk in detail about the factors underlying their dropping out.

Our aim was to interview a broad range of church-leavers from each of the four denominations, especially people within the age-groups and gender categories statistically least likely to attend church. We conducted in-depth interviews with 15 males and 12 females. Nine of our interviewees were Anglican, seven Roman Catholic, seven Methodist, and four were associated with New Churches. Four of our interviewees were in their teens; seven were in their twenties; four were in their thirties; nine were in their forties; and the remaining three were over fifty years old, including one over seventy. The tape-recorded interviews, each approximately one hour in length, were subsequently fully transcribed and analysed.

For reasons of economy, most of our interviews took place in the south-east of England. We did, however, conduct two interviews elsewhere in England and four in Northern Ireland. It was not easy to contact church-leavers in Northern Ireland, since virtually everyone claims to be a Protestant or a Roman Catholic. We even met the phenomenon of a 'Protestant atheist'! Given the strong political and cultural reasons for church-going in Northern Ireland we were especially keen to explore the motivations of those who had defied the tide and dropped out. Although the majority of our interviewees lived in the south-east of England, some had left church earlier in their lives when living elsewhere in the country. Most of our interviewees lived in suburban areas (16), although some lived in the inner city (1), council estates (2), small towns (5) or villages (3). We were keen to set up interviews with members of ethnic minority communities but, in the event, only two in-depth interviews – with a young female of African-Caribbean origin and a young African male – fell into this category.

By definition, church-leavers are not the easiest people to contact. Unlike church-goers they do not congregate on Sundays with other like-minded people. We considered a number of possible ways of contacting church-leavers. We ruled out the use of newspaper advertisements, inviting church-leavers to contact us, on the basis that we might simply attract those who had especially strong feelings against the church and who might have a particular 'axe to grind'. We considered contacting those churches that had reported an above average number of leavers in a given year, but concluded that this might be attributable to a single idiosyncratic factor, such as a local scandal or local theological disagreement, and that such church-leavers might not be properly representative. In the end, we decided to contact church-leavers through the following channels. The majority (17 interviewees) were contacted via clergy. Other church-leavers were contacted via university chaplains (2 interviewees), our own contact networks (4 interviewees), 'snowballing' when further contacts were suggested by our initial contacts (2 interviewees), and a youth group (2 interviewees).

Altogether, over 200,000 words were spoken in the interviews. Most of the interviews were conducted in the relaxing and familiar environment of people's own homes. Most people were prepared to speak at considerable depth about their reasons for disengaging from church. We sensed that in some cases this was the first opportunity the interviewee had ever taken to talk about this transition in his or her life. Sometimes the interview appeared to take on a therapeutic function, with tears or verbal violence coming to the surface. In one case, the interviewee found the conversation so personally valuable that she recorded her address and the date at the end of the interview. Several interviewees announced that they would now be giving the church 'another try'.

These 27 in-depth interviews with church-leavers were supplemented by interviews with 11 clergy, exploring their perceptions of why people leave, and 37 short interviews with Methodist young people associated with the Methodist Association of Youth Clubs (MAYC). These young people were drawn from all over Britain. Altogether, then, 75 individuals were interviewed.

Each interview was tape-recorded, transcribed and analysed in detail by several colleagues. Every interviewee was given an appropriate pseudonym and in some cases personal details were altered, to preserve his or her confidentiality. We found recurrent themes and categories beginning to crystallise from the interview data. These formed the basis for key parts of the questionnaire we used in our postal survey.

Quantitative data

For the quantitative component of our study we conducted a postal survey of church-leavers in the general population, using our own extensive questionnaire. As well as eliciting demographic details and information about people's previous church-going and disengagement, it included a battery of nearly 200 possible reasons for their church-leaving, to which they were asked to express their agreement or disagreement on a five-point Likert scale (with the following options: 'agree strongly', 'agree', 'not certain', 'disagree', or 'disagree strongly'). The content of the questionnaire was based both on our own qualitative data and also on items from previous surveys, conducted in Britain and the United States of America. Our questionnaire was designed to be as comprehensive as possible, while not exceeding the length of some consumer surveys.

In order to identify a sample of church-leavers among the general population, we conducted a random telephone survey which focused on three areas: London (50%), Exeter (25%), and York (25%). The primary aim of the survey was to identify 1,600 individuals living at addresses within these three areas, who would be willing to receive postal questionnaires, and who met the following two criteria. The first criterion was that they had once attended any denomination of church at least six times a year (not including Christmas and Easter). The second criterion was that, having attended church at least six times a year, they had subsequently lapsed to less than six times a year. For some, these two criteria meant that currently they were not classified as regular church-goers. Others, however, may have resumed regular church attendance after a period of lapsing from attendance.

People were phoned on an entirely random basis. The phone numbers used were taken at regular sampling intervals from the latest edition of the relevant postal area residential phone books. Altogether 7,195 live calls were made, not including calls to unobtainable numbers and unattended answerphones. Callers were carefully supervised and an automatic computer-log kept of the numbers called. The survey continued until 1,611 questionnaire recipients had been identified. While 3,149 telephone subscribers declined to take part in the telephone survey, 4,046 agreed to take part. Of these 4,046 telephone interviewees, 2,437 either fell outside the categories in which we were interested or declined to take a questionnaire. A wide social mix was achieved. The only age category that was under-represented was those under twenty years old. The questionnaire recipients comprised 40% males and 60% females, which is quite similar to the sex ratio of church-goers, as measured by the survey undertaken by Brierley (1991) under the title *Prospects for the Nineties* (42% males and 58% females); the percentage in the general population being 49% males and 51% females. It is, perhaps, not surprising that the sex ratio among church- leavers should reflect so closely the sex ratio among church-goers.

A total of 1,604 questionnaires were successfully mailed. Thanks to telephone follow-up of tardy respondents, we achieved a response rate of 56%. Through the use of a unique reference number on each reply-paid envelope it was possible to log which questionnaires had been returned, while preserving complete confidentiality. The questionnaires were coded and analysed using the SPSS statistical package. Our analysis of the questionnaire data was intended both to map the field of church-leaving and also to test out a range of hypotheses deriving from our interview data and the findings of previous studies.

The data from the completed questionnaires make a very important contribution to our study. It is essential, therefore, to say something about the people who responded, in terms of their sex, ages, and experience of church-going. Two-fifths (39%) of the questionnaires were returned by men and three-fifths (61%) were returned by women. Very few of the respondents (2%) were under the age of twenty, 10% were in their twenties, 15% in their thirties, 25% in their forties, 20% in their fifties, 17% in their sixties and 12% were aged seventy or over. Among this sample of church-leavers, three-fifths (64%) had once attended an Anglican congregation more than six times a year, one-fifth (21%) had once attended a Roman Catholic congregation more than six times a year, and nearly one-fifth (18%) had attended a Methodist congregation more than six times a year. A Baptist congregation had once been attended more than six times a year by 6% of the respondents, a United Reformed Church congregation by 4%, a Salvation Army citadel by 2%, a Society of Friends meeting by 1%, and a New Church fellowship by 1% of the respondents. Other denominations were mentioned by 8% of the respondents. This list of denominations adds up to well over 100% since a number of the respondents had left more than one denomination at different stages in their lives.

Gone but not Forgotten

The first book to be published from the Church Leaving Applied Research Project was *Gone but not Forgotten* (Richter and Francis, 1998). *Gone but not Forgotten* provided an interim perspective on the Church Leaving Applied Research Project in two senses. First, at the stage when the first book was prepared we had completed only the first tranche of the quantitative survey. Second, at the stage when the first book was prepared we had developed a typology of church-leaving which identified eight basic themes.

Since the publication of *Gone but not Forgotten*, the Church Leaving Applied Research Project has progressed in two important ways. First, our close analysis of what we have heard from listening to church-leavers has expanded our typology from eight basic themes to fifteen. This expanded typology enables us to distinguish more carefully between different causative or precipitative factors leading to church-leaving, and also to discern more accurately those reasons for church-leaving which nonetheless keep open the possibility of returning. Second, the analysis of a further stage of the questionnaire survey has strengthened the quantitative database to the point that a whole range of more nuanced questions can be posed about the correlates of church-leaving in terms of factors like the differences between men and women and the differences between individuals shaped by various denominational traditions. It is these developments which lead to the originality and richness of the second volume, *Gone for Good?*

Gone for Good?

Building on our earlier discussion in *Gone but not Forgotten*, the analysis presented in this sequel, *Gone for Good?*, has been structured by two major principles: the first principle has been employed to shape the titles of the chapters; the second principle has been employed to shape the structure of the chapters. Each of the main 15 chapters discusses one of the discrete causes for church-leaving identified by the Church Leaving Applied Research Project.

The first cause for church-leaving, discussed in Chapter 5, is described as 'matters of belief and unbelief'. The aim of this chapter is to examine the extent to which church-leavers explain their distance from the church in terms of matters of belief and matters of unbelief. Four specific themes have been identified within this area: the general notion of loss of faith; the life experiences that lead to loss of faith; problems with religious belief; and ways of dealing with doubt.

The second cause for church-leaving, discussed in Chapter 6, is described as 'growing up and changing'. The aim of this chapter is to examine the extent to which church-leavers explain their distance from the church in terms of life's developmental trajectories. Three specific themes have been identified within this area: the general demands of growing up and feeling constrained by the church; the influences of parents and rebellion against such influences; and the inevitability of accepting changes in perspectives and commitments.

The third cause for church-leaving, discussed in Chapter 7, is described as 'life transitions and life changes'. The aim of this chapter is to examine the extent to which church-leavers explain their distance from the church in terms of major transitions and changes that have taken place in their lives. Four specific themes have been identified within this area: leaving home and going away, say to higher education; moving house and going to live in a new area; responding to increased family commitments from growing children or ageing parents; and changing status, say through divorce, illness or bereavement.

The fourth cause for church-leaving, discussed in Chapter 8, is described as 'alternative lives and alternative meanings'. The aim of this chapter is to examine the extent to which church-leavers explain their distance from the church in terms of significant tensions between their commitment to church and the demands of their ordinary everyday lives. Three specific themes have been identified within this area: tensions generated by the pattern and demands of work; tensions generated by the expectations of partners who are not themselves church-goers; and tensions generated by the ever-growing demands of personal and social lives.

The fifth cause for church-leaving, discussed in Chapter 9, is described as 'incompatible life-styles'. The aim of this chapter is to examine the extent to which church-leavers explain their distance from the church in terms of an awareness that their lifestyle or world-view was incompatible with the norms and expectations of the church. Four specific themes have been identified within this area: a growing self-awareness which makes church-going seem hypocritical; a clash between personal values and the values modelled by the church; a clash between personal beliefs and church teachings; and life-style choices which seem out of step with church expectations.

The sixth cause for church-leaving, discussed in Chapter 10, is described as 'not belonging and not fitting in'. The aim of this chapter is to examine the extent to which church-leavers explain their distance from the church in terms of feeling uncomfortable within or marginalised by the local congregation. Four specific themes have been identified within this area: the sense of social exclusion and not being valued by the local church; the issue of personal visibility, either being lost in a large congregation or (more generally) being too conspicuous in a small congregation; the sense of personal marginalisation and not being able to impact congregational life; and the problems of tensions and conflicts in the local church.

The seventh cause for church-leaving, discussed in Chapter 11, is described as 'costs and benefits'. The aim of this chapter is to examine the extent to which church-leavers explain their distance from the church in terms of the benefits of church-going not justifying the effort and costs involved. Three specific themes have been identified within this area: the straightforward recognition that the church was not meeting their personal needs, or the needs of their family; the complaint that the church was not helping their spiritual growth; and the complaint that the church was making too many demands on their time or money.

The eighth cause for church-leaving, discussed in Chapter 12, is described as 'disillusionment with the church'. The aim of this chapter is to examine the extent to which church-leavers explain their distance from the church in terms of the failure of the church to fulfil their expectations. Four specific themes have been identified within this area: disillusionment with fragmented vision, according to which the church seems to say one thing but do another; disillusionment with hypocrisy and factions within the local church; disillusionment with the church's attitude toward justice and power; and disillusionment with the church's attitude toward sex and sexuality.

The ninth cause for church-leaving, discussed in Chapter 13, is described as 'being let down by the church'. The aim of this chapter is to examine the extent to which church-leavers explain their distance from the church in terms of feeling that the church has let them down in some significant way. Three specific themes have been identified within this area: the sense that the church has failed to provide appropriate, expected and deserved care and support; the sense that the church has failed to act with proper professionalism; and the sense that the church has abused its power, physically, psychologically or sexually.

The tenth cause for church-leaving, discussed in Chapter 14, is described as 'problems with relevance'. The aim of this chapter is to examine the extent to which church-leavers explain their distance from the church in terms of the feeling that the church has simply become irrelevant to their life in the contemporary world. Three specific themes have been identified within this area: the complaint that the church's teaching, say in sermons, is irrelevant to everyday life; the complaint that the church fails to connect with the real world; and the view that the personal religious quest can be better pursued outside the institutional church.

The eleventh cause for church-leaving, discussed in Chapter 15, is described as 'problems with change'. The aim of this chapter is to examine the extent to which church-leavers explain their distance from the church in terms of the ways in which the church has itself initiated and pioneered change. Three specific themes have been identified within this area: global dissatisfaction that the church is going in the wrong direction; dissatisfaction with the ways in which the church has introduced new forms of services, new hymns, or new translations of the Bible; and dissatisfaction with the changes that have taken place in the local church, including seating arrangements, service times and the appointment of a new minister.

The twelfth cause for church-leaving, discussed in Chapter 16, is described as 'problems with worship'. The aim of this chapter is to examine the extent to which church-leavers explain their distance from the church in terms of discontent with the services. Three specific themes have been identified within this area: complaints about the style of service, whether too formal or too informal; matters of taste, when the worship provided fails to fulfil the individual's expectations; and matters of level, when the teaching may be criticised as too complex or as too simple.

The thirteenth cause for church-leaving, discussed in Chapter 17, is described as 'problems with leadership'. The aim of this chapter is to examine the extent to which church-leavers explain their distance from the church in terms of discontent with aspects of leadership. Four specific themes were identified within this area: discontent with the leadership style of the local church, whether too authoritarian or too democratic; discontent with ways in which church leaders handle matters of status and hierarchy; and discontent with the direction of church leadership.

The fourteenth cause for church-leaving, discussed in Chapter 18, is described as 'problems with conservatism'. The aim of this chapter is to examine the extent to which church-leavers explain their distance from the church in terms of rejecting the church as being too conservative. Two specific themes were identified within this area: problems with the church's theological teaching being too conservative; and problems with the church's moral teaching being too conservative.

The fifteenth cause for church-leaving, discussed in Chapter 19, is described as 'problems with liberalism'. The aim of this chapter is to examine the extent to which church-leavers explain their distance from the church in terms of rejecting the church as being too liberal. Two specific themes were identified within this area: the criticism that the boundaries between the church and the world were lacking in clarity; and the criticism that the church was failing to provide clear and firm teaching.

Each of these 15 chapters follows the same pattern. The chapter begins by locating the identified theme within a broad theoretical context and illustrates that theme by drawing on the rich resource of qualitative data generated by the interviews with church-leavers. Then attention is turned to the quantitative data generated by the questionnaire survey. These quantitative data are employed to address eight questions.

The first question concerns the overall importance of the cause identified by the chapter for explaining church-leaving today. All the items included in the questionnaire survey to quantify the identified cause are presented in tabular form and given narrative discussion. Three categories of information are provided in the tables presented in the statistical Appendix: the proportion of the respondents who said 'yes' to the statement by checking the agree strongly or agree categories on the questionnaire; the proportion of the respondents who said 'no' to the statement by checking the disagree strongly or disagree categories on the questionnaire; and the proportion of the respondents who said that they were undecided about the statement by checking the uncertain category on the questionnaire. In these tables the percentages have been rounded to whole numbers without decimal places. As a consequence, the rows may sum to 99%, 100% or 101%. This is common practice.

The other seven questions concern the ways in which the quantitative data can be analysed to illuminate how different patterns of church-leaving occur among different groups of people, defined in terms, say, of sex, age or denomination. The statistical significance of the differences between the specified groups has been calculated by means of chi square. In each case the comparison is based on dichotomising the respondents, distinguishing between those who say 'yes' to the statement, by checking the agree strongly or agree categories in the questionnaire, and those who do not say 'yes' to the statement, by checking the disagree strongly, disagree, or not certain categories in the

41

questionnaire. The theoretical background to these questions is the subject of Chapters 3 and 4.

Each of these 15 chapters then concludes with a section on pastoral implications. The aim of this section is to be suggestive rather than prescriptive, and to stimulate further creative reflection among our readers.

3

Exploring differences 1

Setting the scene

The wider literature on church-leaving has identified a number of factors which help to explain individual differences in the importance given to various reasons and motivations underpinning disaffiliation from church. We have selected the most prominent of these factors as the key framework through which to explore our findings. In this sense the questionnaire responses can be used to examine just how much these factors are influential in shaping the patterns of church-leaving in England and Wales.

Chapters 3 and 4, therefore, organise the research literature around seven main themes which we define as: sex differences, generational differences, cohort differences, age of leaving, denomination, sudden or gradual leaving, and likelihood of returning. In our preliminary analyses of the data we also included other factors, like geographical environment (comparisons between towns, cities, suburbs, and villages), church size, parental example and length of membership. These factors, however, proved to be of less consistent interest, and the scope of one volume forced us to concentrate on publishing only the most important analyses.

Sex differences

Generally speaking, more women than men attend church. The 1998 Australian Church Survey found that '24% of women attend church at least once a month, compared with 18% of men' (Hughes, Bellamy, Black and Kaldor, 2000: 180). In Britain and Northern Ireland, two-thirds of frequent church-goers are women (Bruce, 1995: 42). The English Church Life Profile, conducted in 2001, found that 65% of English church attenders were women (Churches Information for Mission, 2001: 9). This reflects the fact that a smaller proportion of men attend church in the first place and also that women typically live longer than men. To what extent are the sociological factors affecting women and men's joining, leaving, or rejoining of churches gender-specific?

A number of studies have examined the impact of women's different 'structural location' in society, by virtue of both their role in childbearing and rearing and, also, their lower levels of participation in employment: the findings have been summarised by Francis (1997, 2005b). There are two main forms of structural-location theory that seek to account for greater religiosity among women. The first focuses on the fact that men and women have different social roles. This form of the theory claims that women tend to have primary responsibility for children's care and social-isation, and that their role is more family-centred. Men, by contrast, are more likely to have an economic role. Given that churches, in modern society, tend to relate more readily to the private sphere of the family, women are more likely to identify with churches. Also, women are more likely to attend church, in order to encourage their children's involvement and attendant moral training. This would be consistent with the findings of the 1991 British Social Attitudes survey (Greeley, 1992), which found that 'women's devoutness and religiosity are more like those of men . . . *before* they acquire a spouse and children'. 'Once you start "taking care" of people, perhaps, you begin implicitly to assume greater responsibility for their "ultimate" welfare', commented Andrew Greeley (1992: 62). The second main form of structural-location theory, seeking to account for greater religiosity among women, focuses on women's under-representation in the workforce. This form of the theory claims that women are likely to be less secularised than men, because they participate less in the modern secular world. Women are, also, it is claimed, more likely to turn to religion as a means of social support, given their isolation from the social contacts afforded by the workplace. Men, it is claimed, are more likely to be affected by workplace values inimical to church participation. Also, women's lower level of participation in the workforce means that they tend to have more disposable time to devote to church participation (Kay and Francis, 1996: 11–13). Structural-location theories have recently tended to become more carefully nuanced, taking account of a wider range of variables.

Wilson and Sherkat conducted a longitudinal study of over 1,600 individuals and their parents, tracking individuals as they moved from their family of origin to setting up their own family of procreation. The study comprised three sets of interviews, conducted in 1965, 1973 and 1983. They discovered that women were much less likely than men to drop out of church-going; but, if women did drop out, they were no more likely than men to return (Wilson and Sherkat, 1994: 155–6). They interpreted their findings in terms of the differential institutional roles of men and women in society in the United States of America. It has been normative in that society to be affiliated to a denomination and women have traditionally been expected to be carriers of religious tradition to the next generation, nurturing the family in their religious practice. Hence, if they grow up in a religious family, women are under social pressure to perpetuate their parents' religious beliefs. It is less likely that they will, as adolescents, rebel against church-going. Dropping out is, for women, a stronger statement than for men. If women do rebel against church-going their rebellion is more likely to be total and sustained, especially if it extends to a more general rejection of normative expectations: with, for instance, the woman choosing not to have children at all or to delay their onset. Dropping out, therefore, for women is more likely to entail a weakening of ties to church *and* family. By contrast, dropping out by men does not entail rejecting normative expectations relating to their gender role. This means that return to church-going will be, if anything, somewhat easier for men, given these gender differences in institutionalised roles:

> For men . . . the ties between religion and family were never particularly strong in the first place, and, since breaking them is not all that significant, re-forming them is not particularly troublesome either; if the family (of procreation) demands religion, then it will be resumed. (Wilson and Sherkat, 1994: 158)

Clearly, these gender differences will vary in different societies and, even within US society, according to the larger cultural context and changing attitudes toward family formation. As Wilson and Sherkat admit: 'a period of greater "familism" might have yielded different results' (Wilson and Sherkat, 1994: 160).

In recent decades, more women, including mothers of young children, have begun to work full-time. It is conceivable that the impact of 'structural factors' of this sort might make women less willing to assume the traditionally gendered roles associated with church-going and less willing to accept external religious authority. Equally, they might no longer need to rely on the church for 'opportunities to socialise and to make meaningful contributions to society' (Hughes, Bellamy, Black and Kaldor, 2000: 181), now that these opportunities are available to them at work. However, Penny Edgell Becker and Heather Hofmeister, in a survey conducted in upstate New York in 1998, concluded that 'there was no statistically significant relationship between full-time paid employment and any form of congregational involve-ment' on the part of women (Becker and Hofmeister, 2001: 713). Women's church participation was mostly determined by 'their own attitudes, beliefs and religious subculture'; those who had dropped out tended to attribute this to 'a lack of perceived fit between religious institutions and their own lifestyle and values' (Becker and Hofmeister, 2001: 719). Women took a more 'expressive' stance than men toward social institutions in general, and the church in particular, consciously and articulately choosing whether or not to be involved 'based on their own assessments of the relevance of religious institutions in their own lives' (Becker and Hofmeister, 2001: 719).

It would, however, be wrong to deduce that greater individual-ism necessarily makes for church disengagement, or reluctance to return. Becker and Hofmeister report that an individualistic stance toward religious authority was sometimes associated with a *higher* probability of church attendance, at least in the case of young mothers. In-depth interviews helped to explain this appar-ent anomaly: mothers of young children reported that they felt it was important to attend church, so that they could begin to sort out their own religious beliefs, at a time when children would be asking their own questions: also, they wanted their children to experience church-going for themselves, so that they could later make up their own minds, in an informed way (Becker and Hofmeister, 2001: 717). Men's religious participation, by con-trast, was more likely to be associated with structural factors: in their case, marriage and the presence of young children in the family (Becker and Hofmeister, 2001: 717). Men returners were more likely than women to report that they had returned to church, almost without thinking, when they got married or upon the birth of their first child: they reported that 'it simply seemed "appropriate" and "natural" once they had started a family' (Becker and Hofmeister, 2001: 717). Religious involvement, or re-engagement, can help to signify 'increased maturity and social establishment' on their part (Becker and Hofmeister, 2001: 719), especially given that marriage and parenting are currently becoming more important to men. In that sense, Becker and Hofmeister conclude, men are becoming 'more like women' in their religious involvement, rather than women becoming 'more like men' (Becker and Hofmeister, 2001: 718).

Women's participation in the workforce is not per se associated with less religious participation. Indeed, higher occupational status generally tends to be associated with more religious participation. However, this trend seems to be offset, at least for full-time employed women, by the strains of balancing multiple commitments which may take 'a toll on participation' (Ammerman and Roof, 1995: 10).

Michael J. Fanstone, in a largely quantitative survey of 509 United Kingdom church-leavers, found that women were more likely than men to leave church because of 'some kind of domestic tension' (67%) or because they 'felt they didn't belong to some extent' (59%). Men, on the other hand, were more likely to have left because they found church-going 'irrelevant to their everyday life' (60%) (Fanstone, 1993: 272). Fanstone's survey item explicitly attributed the 'domestic tension' to church attendance (Fanstone, 1993: 62). This suggests that women's church-going was more likely to bring them into conflict with their spouse or other family members. Given that proportionately more women than men attend church, it is perhaps unsurprising that domestic tension is less likely to be cited by men as a reason for having left, in that men would be more likely to have a church-going partner.

Although not, strictly speaking, a social scientific approach, John D. Barbour's study of autobiographical accounts of loss of faith offers some valuable qualitative data, demonstrating 'the rich potential of women's autobiographies for illuminating the relationships between one's gendered identity and one's religious views and between deconversion and spiritual searching' (Barbour, 1994: 204). Gender-related conflicts tend to be intrin-

sic to the twentieth-century women's autobiographies cited by
Barbour; women attribute their deconversion to such things as
the desire for intellectual independence; the wish to be liberated
from Christian sexual morality; rejection of perceived sexual
abuse and exploitation on the part of religion; abandonment of
patriarchal religion and its oppression of women; rejection of
habits of uncritical deference to authority; the desire to assert
one's autonomy in relation to parents; the need for individual
self-expression.

While women's autobiographies may reject patriarchal religion, this does not necessarily mean that they give up on religion
entirely: the women can reinterpret and reaffirm the faith they
have rejected, recognising, for instance, that a patriarchal church
has also produced 'many exceptionally strong and independent
women' (Barbour, 1994: 193); or discovering 'dark [empower-
ing] female images' within Catholicism (Barbour, 1994: 195); or
reinterpreting 'innocence, purity, and virginity as symbols that
nourish the imagination' (Barbour, 1994: 199). One woman's
return to religion stems from the desire to express thankfulness
for her new child (Barbour, 1994: 189). This account resonates
with Grace Davie's suggestion that women's differential religiosity tends to be attributable to the proximity of women to birth
and death: for instance, 'very few women give birth without any
reflection about the mysteries of creation' (Davie, 1994: 120);
although Davie subsequently proposed that increase in the new
parent's religiosity was associated with (non-gender-specific)
perception of the vulnerability and dependency of the infant and
that 'having children to look after seems to raise men to the
religious level of women' (Walter and Davie, 1998: 650). Most of
the autobiographies detailed by Barbour 'stress spiritual searching and leave the reader with a sense of the search being still
underway, open-ended, incomplete' (Barbour, 1994: 200).

Callum Brown has pinpointed the 1960s as the point at which,
in Britain at least, women 'cancelled their mass subscription to

the discursive domain of Christianity' (Brown, 2001: 195). During the nineteenth century and earlier twentieth century women's religiosity had come to be seen as privileged and pivotal, placing them 'at the fulcrum of family sanctity' and rendering them 'extra special in the wider reformation of . . . the nation as a whole' (Brown, 2001: 59). The unprecedented church-going levels of this era were associated with a puritan evangelicalism which had 'constructed a highly gendered conception of religiosity' (Brown, 2001: 9). It was much more difficult for a woman to drop religion: 'her respectability as a woman, wife and mother, whether she liked it or not, was founded on religion' (Brown, 2001: 183). It was with the 'simultaneous de-pietisation of femininity and the de-feminisation of piety' (Brown, 2001: 192) in the 1960s that, abruptly, Britons, especially women, 'started to reject the role of religion in their lives' (Brown, 2001: 188). The 'permissive society' 'secularised the construction of [women's] identity, and the churches started to lose them', beginning with the young (Brown, 2001: 192). Men had often simply been 'partners to religious respectability' and when women no longer wished to go to church, 'men no longer had "to keep up appearances" in the pews' (Brown, 2001: 192). 'Before 1800, Christian piety had been a "he". From 1800 to 1960, it had been a "she". After 1960, it became nothing in gendered terms' (Brown, 2001: 196), as women turned their back on the discursive domain of Christianity. Significantly, Brown applies a modified form of his theory to North America: the same 'discursive challenge' emerged there in the 1960s, but has not triumphed: 'piety and femininity are still actively enthralled to each other, holding secularisation in check' (Brown, 2001: 197). While Brown's analysis properly highlights the role played by women as carriers of religious discourse, he fails to set church decline within a wider context of economic and social change impacting male-dominated secular institutions such as political parties and trade unions, as well as the churches (Davie, 2002: 21). He also fails to take account of longitudinal studies demonstrating sharp and continuous decline in church-going from the mid-nineteenth century (Gill, 2002: 93).

Research strategy

In order to test the significance of sex differences for understanding and interpreting the reasons and motivations underpinning church-leaving in England and Wales today, we compared the responses to our questionnaire given by male church-leavers and by female church-leavers.

Generational differences

A generation unit is different from merely an age cohort: 'members of a generation are influenced in their formative years by a particular set of social experiences; and, to an extent, they share a common culture and are self-conscious of themselves as having a distinctive outlook and identity' (Roof, Carroll and Roozen, 1998: xii–xiii).

Seniors

Seniors are those born in 1926 or earlier. Members of the oldest extant generation are very likely to have been to Sunday school as children; many will have become church-goers; and many will have sent their own children to Sunday school, even if they had themselves dropped out of church-going (Brierley, 2000: 103). Seniors are more likely than people born after 1961 to 'think linearly and logically' (Brierley, 2000: 108). They are also more likely than later generations to be discursively articulate about religion (Brown, 2001: 183) in terms of the 'evangelical narrative structure', with its moral bipolarities (Brown, 2001: 181–182).

51

Builders

Builders (or 'boosters' or the 'maturity generation') are those
born between 1926 and the end of the Second World War: those
who helped to rebuild the post-war world and to establish new
economic and social systems (Brierley, 2000: 103). Builders are
more likely to respect status, to attend church out of habit, to
'think linearly and logically' (Brierley, 2000: 108) and to have
attended church consistently in the last twenty years (Brierley,
2000: 102). Their parents are likely to have been less strict and
more liberal about religious upbringing than their forebears
(Brown, 2001: 181).

The baby boomers

The baby boomers are those born between 1946 and 1962 (Roof,
1999: 315). The post-Second World War generation grew up at a
time of economic expansion, allowing for a profound culture
shift away 'from giving top priority to physical sustenance and
safety toward heavier emphasis on belonging, self-expression,
and the quality of life' (Inglehart, 1990: 66). Those who grew up
in the 1960s and 1970s also experienced a time of considerable
social unrest – 'the Vietnam War, East-West tensions, environmental crises, lifestyle and sexual experimentation' (Roof, Carroll
and Roozen, 1998: xiii). Disaffiliation from conventional religion
during that period tended to be associated with plummeting
confidence in established institutions, with 'protest against
middle-class values and lifestyles and against America's involvement in the Vietnam War' (Roof and Landres, 1997: 83) and with
cultural marginality. By contrast, those who reject religion today
tend to be more comfortable with the cultural mainstream. The
baby-boomer generation became the carrier of new cultural and
religious values and of 'an emerging spiritual quest culture'
(Roof, 1999: 49), questing for 'wholeness' in the face of the

rationalisation and differentiation of modernity (Roof, 1999: 59–63); hungering for 'self-realisation' in a consumer culture (Roof, 1999: 66–67); 'picking and mixing' from the vast selection of symbols and discourses offered by the mass media (Roof, 1999: 67–72), within an increasingly globalised, and hence de-traditionalised, context (Roof, 1999: 72–74).

As a generation, baby boomers have been relatively non-involved in established religion (Roof, Carroll and Roozen, 1998: 244–5) and have questioned or rejected many traditional beliefs and moral teachings (Roof, Carroll and Roozen, 1998: 246). According to the 1998 English Church Attendance Survey (Brierley, 2000), church involvement in this generation has continued to decline: with the loss of 'three times as many aged thirty to forty-four ... now than was the case a decade ago ... and four [sic] times as many in their late forties and fifties' (Brierley, 2000: 98). Wade Clark Roof and J. Shawn Landres suggest that the primary reasons for baby boomers dropping out were 'personal concerns', 'dissatisfaction with religious teachings', 'a feeling that one's lifestyle is incompatible with a particular congregation', 'life situation changes' and 'perceived lack of relevance and boredom' (Roof and Landres, 1997: 83–6). Philip Richter's analysis of data collected by the Church Leaving Research Project found that there were significant differences between the types of reasons for church-leaving given by people then under the age of fifty (baby boomers and baby busters) and those given by people then aged fifty and over. Under fifty-year-olds were more likely to become church-leavers for the following reasons: because they wanted to assert their personal authenticity; because they perceived their life style as incompatible with continued church membership; because they were attracted by religious questing and by religious pluralism; because they felt disillusioned by what they saw of other church-goers; because they felt alienated by religious hypocrisy (Richter, 1999: 182–3). Those under the age of fifty were also more likely to place greater emphasis on countercultural values. Richter's findings suggest that church-leaving by those born since 1946 can only be fully understood in the context of the extensive cultural shifts that have affected the baby boomers and later generations.

Church-leavers from the baby-boomer generation tend to be committed to the 'new morality'; that is, life-style values deriving from the 1960s, and to an ethic of 'personal fulfilment', stressing the value of 'self-discovery' and 'self-actualization' (Roof and Landres, 1997: 83). However, by the 1990s there had been a move away from 'extreme expressive individualism' toward 'greater attachment to family and to others' and a greater valuing of 'connectedness with people, institutions, places, nature' (Ammerman and Roof, 1995: 3). This shift had occurred for two main reasons: first, many baby boomers were by this period themselves facing parental responsibilities; and, second, they had become aware that 'genuine personal fulfilment lies in discovery of a vital balance between self and concern for others' (Ammerman and Roof, 1995: 3).

Baby boomers were less likely than those of previous generations to rejoin churches: Wade Clark Roof and J. Shawn Landres found that of the two-thirds of those with a religious background who had dropped out, less than a half returned to active involvement (Roof and Landres, 1997: 86). Dropping out of church does not, however, necessarily entail rejection of a religious orientation altogether: 'spiritual seeking' has increased since the 1960s. Many young and middle-aged individuals, while they have disengaged from institutional religion and 'institutional tutelage', are engaged in a quest for 'personal, authentic experience', by means of an 'à la carte' or 'pastiche-style of spirituality' (Roof and Landres, 1997: 87). The shift has been from 'collective-expressive' forms of religion toward more 'individual-expressive' forms.

The expressive individualism of baby boomers can entail choices for, as well as against, religious participation. Where they do commit themselves to belonging to a local church they will tend to stay in that congregation if its values are consonant with their own: if they become convinced that 'participation . . . is the best way for them to enact the personal values and beliefs they already [hold]' (Reiff, 1996: 97). Wade Clark Roof has described the rise of 'participatory' congregations' – reflecting 'the demand of [boomer] laypeople to participate within them on their own terms' (Roof, 1999: 299). Churches are more likely to retain baby boomers if their approach to membership and commitment 'avoids the false norms of both individualistic autonomous freedom and authoritarian myopic community that destroys rather than transforms individual selves' (Reiff, 1996: 115). Baby boomers are also likely to be attracted and retained by churches that have pioneered 'new and innovative experiments in reconnecting faith, family and work in ways more responsive to the needs of people and their life situations' (Ammerman and Roof, 1995: 13), rather than churches that still promote 'traditional' family values and are intolerant of different life-styles. This is not to suggest that conservative churches do not have strong baby-boomer followings and may, indeed, be especially attractive to those confused by the pluralism of late-modernity (Roof, Carroll and Roozen, 1998: 251), simply that because this generation has been influenced by both individualism and feminism it will tend to be alienated from much organised religion (Ammerman and Roof, 1995: 11).

Where boomers belong to Evangelical churches these are likely to be churches that have accommodated, in various degrees, to boomer culture, tending toward 'a deeply personal, subjective understanding of faith and well-being' (Roof, 1999: 129; Roozen, Carroll and Roof, 1998: 71). This is a generation that is not prepared simply to go through the motions of religious involvement: this would smack of hypocrisy 'to many of those who have felt estranged from institutions and activities that, in their judgement, lack authenticity and credibility' (Roof and Gesch, 1995: 72). Boomers are prepared to commit themselves, but only to 'causes and activities . . . [that] give expression to their deepest understandings of who they are and of their more cherished relationships' (Roof and Gesch, 1995: 78). If individuals choose to relate to mainstream denominations 'there is a further choice of what in the denomination's official tradition to accept and what to reject' (Roozen, Carroll and Roof, 1998: 81).

Wade Clark Roof, Jackson W. Carroll and David A. Roozen have described the baby-boomer generation as 'the principal "carrier" of late- or post-modern spirituality' (Roof, Carroll and Roozen, 1998: 247). They identify several key characteristics of boomers' 'religious style': 1) an emphasis on personal choice: a 'highly selective, instrumental approach to religion' based on its 'life-effectiveness' (Roof, Carroll and Roozen, 1998: 248); 2) code-mixing: the personal eclectic construction of spirituality, drawn from a wide variety of different sources; 3) the valuing of religious experience and personal growth, in, for instance, both New Age spirituality and conservative Christianity; 4) anti-institutionalism and anti-hierarchicalism: boomers prefer 'primarily local [organisational forms] with which they have immediate personal contact and which address their particular needs . . . You belong "if it helps you". You drop out if it doesn't' (Roof, Carroll and Roozen, 1998: 253).

Those baby boomers most influenced by the 1960s and 1970s, and most wedded to an individual-expressive mode of identity, are least likely to follow the typical 'life-cycle' religiosity pattern, whereby individuals tend to be religiously involved as children, rebel and drop out during adolescence and early adulthood, and then take up religious involvement again once they have married and have parental responsibilities (Roof, Carroll and Roozen, 1998: 244–5). Of those who favour individual choices within the family (whom Roof and Gesch call 'religious individualists'), 25% of those who have married have returned to religious involvement, and 41% of those who have had children have returned. By contrast, of those baby boomers who do not support religious individualism, 66% who have married have returned to religious involvement, and 90% of those who have had children have returned (Roof and Gesch, 1995: 70). Roof and Gesch conclude that the life-cycle pattern only holds for some baby boomers and that 'cultural shifts in the relation of individuals to religious institutions' can also be key factors influencing this generation (Roof and Gesch, 1995: 70). 'A culture of choice and spiritual exploration prevails' both outside and within religious organisations (Roof, 1999: 53), despite boomers having aged and settled down. Boomers have not gravitated toward more traditional theistic beliefs as they have aged (Roof, 1999: 54–56). Eileen Barker's analysis of the religiosity of English baby boomers finds no evidence that the life-cycle pattern holds for this generation: 'if a similar [life-cycle return] pattern exists in England, it appears still to be statistically swamped by a continuing exodus from the mainstream churches' (Barker, 1998: 5, 22).

Clearly, it is important to differentiate between different types of baby boomers: not all are religious individualists, for instance, around a half of boomers were more traditionally oriented (Roof and Gesch, 1995: 64). It is also difficult to generalise about boomer religiosity. By its very nature it is dynamic and fluid in character, excepting for those who stick with their church-going or those who remain uninvolved (Roof, 1999: 122). For instance, Roof's panel survey of boomers, conducted in 1988 to 1989 and 1995 to 1996, found that the boundaries between 'believing' and 'seeking' were quite permeable: over a half of Roof's interviewees moved 'easily from a discourse of seeking to one of believing, or vice versa' (Roof, 1999: 131).

It has sometimes been suggested that church-leaving among baby boomers is associated with their exposure to the relativism and liberality of the counterculture during their formative years and/or their greater attainment of liberal higher education relative to previous generations. However, Hoge, Johnson and Luidens have noted that the decline in mainstream Protestantism

cannot be solely attributed to the influence of baby-boomer attitudes, given that the decline began in the early 1960s, before the
earliest boomers went into higher education (Hoge, Johnson and
Luidens, 1995: 60).

Generation X

Generation X (aka the 'baby busters') are the post-baby-boom
generation born between 1961 and 1981 (Flory and Miller, 2000:
3), the children of the baby boomers. GenXers have, as a generation, been impacted by such things as rootlessness in their family
life, saturated exposure to an image-dominated mass media,
diminished economic prospects, advances in communications
technology, and multiculturalism (Flory and Miller, 2000: 3–5,
234, 245). They are a realistic generation, which has experienced
the failure of parental relationships and loss of confidence in
political leadership; they are suspicious of 'hype'. Unlike the
boomers, they do not invest their hopes in large-scale utopian
programmes. They expect 'honesty, realism, and authenticity'
from their leaders (Flory and Miller, 2000: 6) and expect their
religious leaders to act in non-judgemental and non-hypocritical
ways (Flory and Miller, 2000: 240). GenXers tend to embrace
pluralism and prioritise subjective knowing above prepositional
truth: 'GenXers are typically willing to give others their space,
rather than building community that is based on right thinking'
(Flory and Miller, 2000: 9). This is a postmodern generation
which tends to deconstruct claims to absolute truth and to recast
religion in experiential and relational terms, playfully reappro-
priating older traditions.

In contrast to older generations, GenXers seek a more experiential and participatory style of religious involvement. In contrast
to baby boomers, GenXers root their religious identities within
religious communities and are less likely to frame their religiosity
in terms of a 'purely personal religious quest' (Flory and Miller,

2000: 238): 'personal fulfilment comes through commitment to the community' (Flory and Miller, 2000: 244) and the 'belonging' and 'authenticity' that can be found there. Also, while boomers tend to have a rationalistic, more text-based, approach to religious meaning, GenXers focus on religious experience, 'not the properly exegeted text' (Flory and Miller, 2000: 243). There remain, however, some key similarities between boomer and GenX religion: both generations prefer democratic, consensual forms of religious organisation; both shop around for whatever fits their needs and desires; both are 'seekers', looking for spiritual experience and fulfilment (Flory and Miller, 2000: 243). Indeed, given this degree of overlap between busters and boomers, some commentators have suggested that 'Generation X' refers to a distinctive way of understanding life within contemporary culture, rather than to a specific generational cohort (Coupland, 1995: 72; Lynch, 2002: 30).

Levels of defection among those of Generation X are high, though 'no higher than when baby boomers were in college in the early 1970s' (Roof and Landres, 1997: 91). GenXers are less likely than boomers to have actively rebelled against parentally promoted church-going: boomer parents were reluctant to force religion on their children, wanting them to make up their own minds, 'consequently, many children had nothing to rebel against as they moved into their teenage years, and simultaneously no set (life-cycle) path to follow' (Flory and Miller, 2000: 4). Their church-leaving is, however, not necessarily to do with rejection of religious belief: 'many xers seek spiritual fulfilment outside institutions' (Roof and Landres, 1997: 91) and seek a form of religion that is 'both relevant to the world around them and personally meaningful' (Roof and Landres, 1997: 93). When they do join faith groups GenXers are looking for: 'authenticity, community, an abandonment of dogmatism, a focus on the arts, and diversity' (Tapia, 1994: 20) (cited in Roof and Landres, 1997: 92); they are most likely to be attracted to 'born-again' Christian denominations, perhaps because this can offer them 'a little structure in their lives' (Flory and Miller, 2000: 10). However, they will find meaning 'in the quality of their communal practice and experience of the faith, not because of pronouncements by external authorities' (Flory and Miller, 2000: 8). While they value personal choice, GenXers are committed to serving the community, 'with moral and quasi-religious passion', but, unlike the baby boomers, they are less committed to 'large-scale social change': 'we care about the environment, alternative forms of energy, world peace, new politics, and less bureaucratic bullshit' (Ryerson, 1995: 7) (cited in Roof and Landres, 1997: 92). They are also more conservative sexually than their forebears (Roof and Landres, 1997: 93).

Much of the data on generational church-leaving comes from the United States of America and, therefore, must be treated with caution: it may not be directly transferable to other contexts, given that religion is 'all-pervasive' in United States culture and 'not easily left behind', and that there is in the United States of America a 'dynamic and innovative religious market' (Roof and Landres, 1997: 81). Gordon Lynch (2002) has suggested that generational differences in church participation between GenXers and baby boomers may be more pronounced in the United Kingdom than in the United States, given that British GenXers are less likely to have been brought up in a religious household.

Research strategy

In order to test the significance of generational differences for understanding and interpreting the reasons and motivations underpinning church-leaving in England and Wales today, we compared the responses to our questionnaire given by three age groups of the respondents: those at the time of our study under the age of forty, those in their forties and fifties, and those aged sixty or over.

Cohort differences

Grotenhuis and Scheepers, in their study of religious disaffiliation in the Netherlands between 1937 and 1995, found that later cohorts were more likely to disaffiliate, owing to the increased levels of rationalisation to which they were exposed in their formative years: 'people in the 1930s and 1940s experienced much lower levels of rationalization during adolescence compared to people born in the 1970s and 1980s . . . this eventually leads to cohorts with different opinions and behaviour' (Grotenhuis and Scheepers, 2001: 604).

Penny Long Marler (1995) has analysed differences between different cohorts of church members in relation to the concept of the 'family church'. At the church she studied, 'Briarglen', older cohorts, whose own families had grown up, looked back wistfully to the 'large confirmation classes and active youth groups' of the 1950s, when the proportion of married persons with children in the United States population was at its peak (Marler, 1995: 25), and viewed a large-scale youth programme as essential. They were more likely than younger cohorts to see themselves as active 'producers' than 'consumers' (Marler, 1995: 42); they tended to be more institutionally committed and more loyal toward, and optimistic about, the church as an institution (Marler 1995: 37; 41–2); they were more likely to perceive the church as 'one big family' (Marler, 1995: 43); they also tended to be very satisfied with worship and to prefer sermons with 'scholarly illustrations' (Marler, 1995: 43). By contrast, younger cohorts tended to be more interested in being more passive consumers of church programmes – for instance, adult education programmes dealing with the family and parenting, or assistance with their own spiritual development (Marler, 1995: 37). They were more likely than older cohorts to want worship that was 'sensitive to the needs' of the congregation and to be critical of worship that was irrelevant to their everyday life (Marler, 1995: 43); they tended to see the church not as 'one large family', but, rather, as a 'loosely knit association of individuals and groups' (Marler, 1995: 39).

Some of the differences between the older and younger cohorts may be to do with differential time pressure at different stages in the life-cycle: those with young children may have little disposable time to fulfil more active 'producer' roles in the church. However, Marler found that, whether single or married, different cohorts approached the church differently: 'for older members, factors such as institutional tradition and denominational loyalty dictate involvement; for younger members, personal tastes and more immediate needs shape church choices' (Marler, 1995: 45). She concluded that the source of these differences was cultural: the shift from 'a socially integrated to a more personal or individuated paradigm for structuring well-being' and consequent 'church consumerism' which had disproportionately impacted the younger cohorts (Marler, 1995: 45). She also noted that the youngest cohorts would be too young to have had personal exposure to the energetic youth programmes of the 1950s and early 1960s: hence they tend to carry 'little sense of a "group loyalty" that crosses the boundaries of other age and interest groups in the church' (Marler, 1995: 50). While Marler does not explicitly relate these cohort differences to church-leaving patterns, one may infer, for example, that older cohorts might be more likely than younger cohorts to leave if their expectations that the church should be 'one large family' were unfulfilled, and that younger cohorts, who have a more consumerist attitude to their church involvement, might be more likely than older cohorts to leave were they to conclude that the church was not meeting their needs; as Marler notes, these are cohort-based, rather than age-related, differences.

Mark Chaves (1991) has analysed church attendance data, from the General Social Survey conducted in the United States of America, in relation to cohort effects on mainstream Protestant church attendance. He claims that cohort differences cannot merely be reduced to age differences: although Chaves agrees that as individuals grow older and form families they are more likely to attend church and to repeat the life-cycle pattern of their parents (as claimed by Firebaugh and Harley, 1991: 499), he points out that this does not explain *inter*-cohort differences. Chaves concludes that 'both cohort effects and age effects are partially connected to differences in family formation that exist both among cohorts and within cohorts across the life course' (Chaves, 1991: 502). He suggests that Protestant church-going is strongly dependent on the fortunes of the 'traditional' nuclear family: a lower rate of formation of traditional families tends to produce declining church attendance rates. However, different cohorts 'exhibit different propensities to form "traditional" families' (Chaves, 1991: 512): the lowest rates of childlessness – and the highest rates of church attendance – are found among the cohorts born between 1928 and 1947 (Chaves, 1991: 512). Chaves concludes that 'there are substantial differences among cohorts in their aggregate propensity to form the kinds of families which produce the most frequent church attenders' (Chaves, 1991: 506). The biggest cohort differences in church attendance rates, with controls for age and period, were between the oldest and youngest cohorts, on the one hand, and the middle cohort (born between 1928 and 1947), on the other hand (Chaves, 1991: 503).

Steve Bruce, in his analysis of British church attendance figures, suggests that younger cohorts are less likely than their predecessors to return to church attendance in old age, given that, unlike previous cohorts, most young Britons have had no initial Christian socialisation or church involvement and 'hence no acquaintance with an ideology that could provide a solution to . . . anxiety (associated with awareness of their own mortality)' (Bruce, 2002: 66). He concludes that 'age differences in church attendance are a cohort effect rather than an effect of biological ageing' (Bruce, 2002: 66).

Philip Hughes, John Bellamy, Alan Black and Peter Kaldor

63

have analysed data from the 1998 Australian Community Survey relating to church attendance in Australia by different age cohorts. They noted that, across different cohorts, 'church attendance is connected with life stage' and that 'the most common experience in most age cohorts was that they had attended as children, but had not attended frequently after that' (Hughes, Bellamy, Black and Kaldor, 2000: 169). However, they found that younger cohorts were less likely to have attended church regularly during childhood: 'of persons aged forty or more (in 1998), less than 20% had not attended church at least monthly during childhood', whereas 30% of those in their thirties and 41% of those in their twenties had not attended (Hughes, Bellamy, Black and Kaldor, 2000: 169). Younger cohorts were also less likely to have maintained their church-going as children: 'of those now in their sixties, 38% dropped out as children; of those now in their forties, 53% dropped out as children; and of those now in their twenties, 58% dropped out as children' (Hughes, Bellamy, Black and Kaldor, 2000: 169). They concluded that, from the 1960s onwards, 'both children and adults began to drop out of church attendance in much larger proportions' (Hughes, Bellamy, Black and Kaldor, 2000: 169).

Research strategy

In order to test the significance of cohort differences for understanding and interpreting the reasons and motivations underpinning church-leaving in England and Wales today, we compared the responses to our questionnaire given by two cohort groups of the respondents: those whose disengagement from church took place within the previous twenty years and those who left church over twenty years before.

4

Exploring differences 2

Setting the scene

Chapter 3 has organised the research literature around three of seven main themes explored in this study of the reasons and motivations underpinning church-leaving: sex differences, generational differences and cohort differences. Now Chapter 4 organises the research literature around the remaining four themes: age at leaving, denominational differences, sudden or gradual leaving, and likelihood of returning.

Age at leaving

Previous research has helped to clarify the discussion regarding church-leaving by focusing on three different phases of life. We plan to follow this model by discussing in turn: childhood and adolescence, mid-life, and older people.

Childhood and adolescence

William K. Kay and Leslie J. Francis, in their analysis of over 100 studies of attitudes toward Christianity in childhood and adolescence, conclude that there is a steady decline in (favourable) attitude toward Christianity throughout the entire age range of their study, from 8 to 16 years. This suggests that deterioration in attitude toward Christianity by young people is not specifically associated with social or developmental stages or 'crisis points', such as 'the move from primary to secondary school, the transition from concrete to abstract operational thinking, or the preparation to leave school for the adult world' (Kay and Francis, 1996: 5). This decline in attitude toward Christianity is much less pronounced among young people who attend church (Kay and Francis, 1996: 29). Kay and Francis suggest that it is likely that 'most people's attitude toward Christianity levels off after leaving school and remains more or less constant . . . for a large part of their lives' (Kay and Francis, 1996: 30). They attribute the decline in attitude toward Christianity to the effects of socialisation within a society generally characterised by indifference toward religion: 'growing up means becoming indifferent to religion' (Kay and Francis, 1996: 31), unless the young person belongs to a religious reference group. Young people are 'absorbed incrementally into the [post-Christian] world of adulthood' (Kay and Francis, 1996: 144). Church-leaving, for young people, severs their attachment to a religious reference group and is likely to render them more indifferent to Christianity, although they will not necessarily inhabit a totally secular world-view, given that religious experience is widely prevalent among young people (Kay and Francis, 1996: 148). Kay and Francis found that parental church attendance was the strongest contextual influence on young people's attitude toward Christianity and, even more so, on their religious practices, such influence increasing in significance between the ages of eleven and sixteen (Kay and Francis, 1996: 150).

Sometimes church-leaving by adolescents can represent a form of rebellion against parental socialisation, as the young person 'tries to assert an adult self by denying those aspects of life perceived as symbolic of the childhood self and tie to parents or family' (McGuire, 1987: 56), especially if parents have exercised undue pressure to attend church (Richter and Francis, 1998: 86–7). David Caplovitz and Fred Sherrow (1977), in a national study of United States college students, found that disaffiliation from church was a form of rebellion against parents and was attributable to four factors: poor parental relations; maladjustment or neurosis; radical or leftist political orientation; and commitment to intellectualism. However, subsequent research suggests that young people do not, on the whole, leave because they are rebelling against their parents: *socialisation* explanations have been preferred to the *rebellion* explanation (see Brown and Hunsberger, 1984: 355).

Steve Bruce and Tony Glendinning, in their analysis of a module of questions on religion in the 2001 Scottish Attitudes Survey, assumed that those who defected from churches before the age of twenty were likely to have left largely for reasons of 'family dynamics', rather than adult dissatisfaction (Bruce and Glendinning, 2003: 90). However, these assumptions were in the nature of informed guesswork and not derived from the survey data. Factors such as 'irrelevance' or 'boredom' might well also have played a part in the defections of young people. Also, their own findings suggest that atheism, or the implausibility of theistic belief, may have had a larger part than they admit in these defections: Bruce and Glendinning themselves point out that older age cohorts 'who grew up in a church-going culture' are more likely to find belief in a personal God more plausible than do younger people (Bruce and Glendinning, 2003: 93).

Mid-life

The middle years (forty-five to sixty-four) are often associated with increased levels of church attendance. The 1991 British Church Attendance figures indicate that 22% of church-goers are aged forty-five to sixty four, which reflects the percentage in the general population. By contrast, there are a smaller proportion of church-goers in the fifteen to forty-four age category than in the general population (Bruce, 1995: 43). American research suggests that this does not necessarily reflect greater religiosity on the part of the middle-aged, rather it reflects 'changing patterns of involvement in voluntary organisations', with decreased involvement in 'work-related, sport-related, and school service associations' (McGuire, 1987: 60–1).

Mid-life is also, however, typically a time of reflection and review: 'a time of heightened sensitivities and awareness, of thinking through where one has come from and where one is going, the discovery of more of oneself' (Roof, 1993: 135). It can be a time of both reaching out and letting go. Individuals may choose to disengage from religious participation or, conversely, re-engage or engage for the first time. Wade Clark Roof, in his study of the spiritual journeys of baby boomers, found that, as they entered mid-life, baby boomers tended to be reaching out 'to commit themselves to something of importance, yearning for relationships and connections, longing for more stable anchors for their lives' (Roof, 1993: 6). However, they also tend to be 'letting go', which, for this generation, means 'the freedom to let go of old ways of religious thinking that are at odds with a healthy sense of self' (Roof, 1993: 140).

David A. Roozen's analysis of data drawn from the 1978 Gallup survey of unchurched Americans (Roozen, 1980) – of whom most were church dropouts – found that different age groups gave different reasons for their church disengagement, but that the greatest difference lay between those who dropped out in their teens and those who dropped out later. 'For those who dropped out in their teens, maturation and the irrelevance of the church dominate(d)' (Roozen, 1980: 439). 'For those who dropped out after age fifty-four, personal contextual reasons dominate(d)', especially 'poor health' (Roozen, 1980: 439, 446), although, Roozen suggested, such disruptions of one's established life routines might also provide 'the occasion for other factors to have effects' (Roozen, 1980: 443), such as 'the irrelevance of the church' (Roozen, 1980: 446). For those who dropped out between the ages of twenty-five to fifty-four, personal contextual reasons, especially 'moving to a new community' (Roozen, 1980: 446), again dominate, 'but not nearly to the extent as for those over fifty-four'; again, 'the irrelevance of the church is also frequently cited across this age group', as is intrachurch discord, though to a lesser extent (Roozen, 1980: 439).

A number of different models relating age to religious participation have been developed. Four models were described by Howard M. Bahr (1970). The first model (1), the traditional or developmental model, posits a curvilinear relationship between age and disengagement, with increasing disengagement from adolescence until the mid-thirties, and thereafter a steady decrease in disengagement. The second model (2), the family cycle model, posits virtually the converse of (1): a decrease in disengagement from early to mid-adulthood, especially associated with marriage (but not with cohabitation) (Thornton, Axinn and Hill, 1992: 628; Stolzenberg, Blair-Loy and Waite, 1995: 94) and parenthood; followed by increasing disengagement after children leave home. This model suggests that individuals return to, or continue, religious participation for one, or both, of the following reasons: to enable their children to receive a formal religious upbringing; to receive emotional support and to benefit from social contacts with other families (Stolzenberg, Blair-Loy and Waite, 1995: 86). The third model (3), the social disengagement model, like model (2), posits a rise in disengagement following middle age, but attributes this to mutual withdrawal on the part of the ageing individuals from their previous social roles. The fourth model (4), the stability model, posits that there is no correlation between age and rates of church-leaving.

David A. Roozen has added a fifth model (5), which he did not label, but which takes into account generational differences in 'the relationship between age, or the stage in the life-cycle, and religious involvement'. This model takes account of the fact that 'the so-called religious revival of the 1950s and the declines of the

1960s were [both] primarily young adult phenomena' (Roozen, 1980: 429). We have already considered the influence of generational factors.

Stolzenberg, Blair-Loy and Waite (1995) have suggested that models (1) and (2) may be seen as interacting, rather than competing, explanations of religious participation. The family cycle has less influence, for instance, on the religious participation of those who have children at an unconventionally young age, because 'atypical parents are less likely to find others in similar family circumstances by joining a church' (Stolzenberg, Blair-Loy and Waite, 1995: 86). Ainlay, Singleton and Swigert (1992) have plausibly critiqued the disengagement model (3), finding that decrease in older individuals' church participation 'does not reflect a desire on the part of individuals to "distance" themselves from the church' (Ainlay, Singleton and Swigert, 1992: 184). Amy Argue, David R. Johnson and Lynn K. White (1999) have recently provided plausible supporting evidence for the traditional model (1): they found that, having allowed for possible period- and cohort-effects, religiosity, measured by the influence of individuals' religious beliefs on their daily life (which correlates highly with measures of 'frequency of church attendance' and 'participation in church activities'), increases with age, with the greatest increase occurring in the early adult years (Argue, Johnson and White, 1999: 433); this effect is independent of family life-course events, such as parenthood.

Older people

The Sir Halley Stewart Age Awareness Project (SHSAAP) conducted qualitative and quantitative studies of older people (over sixty years old), with and without church connections, in the late 1990s; the qualitative surveys were conducted by means of focus groups and the main quantitative survey, carried out by Christian Research, had a sample size of 2,726, with a 77% response rate

(Jewell, 2001: 13). They also drew on three other sources: a literature review, principally relating to the United States of America, by Kenneth Howse: secondary analysis of Richter and Francis' consolidated church-leaving data; and a twenty-year study of 340 ageing people by Peter Coleman (Jewell, 2001: 14–15).

SHSAAP found that the primary reason why people stop attending church was the death of their spouse: 54% reported stopping for this reason. The next most important cause of leaving was 'family responsibilities', which affected 30% of respondents. The remainder reported that they had 'left for no particular reason, or were disillusioned or [had] moved' or had left for other reasons (Peter Brierley, cited in Moffitt, 2001: 18). Laraine Moffitt has analysed the SHSAAP data relating to life's 'changes and chances', which may 'lead to people losing touch with the church by default rather than intention' (Moffitt, 2001: 19). She groups these circumstances into three broad categories: physical factors, family and illness.

Physical factors include the physical structure of the church, which may be inaccessible for older people with mobility difficulties, and its level of comfort. Old age, especially 'Fourth Age', tends to be associated with physical deterioration. Hearing or visual difficulties may preclude older people taking a full part in church worship, unless their needs are taken into account. Seating may be too close together: 'some older people have joints and limbs that will not bend easily or . . . let them squeeze into . . . restricted areas' (Moffitt, 2001: 21).

Toilet facilities may be insufficiently accessible for those older people who, for reasons of medication or bodily deterioration, may need them regularly or unpredictably. The SHSAAP findings are consistent with those of Ainlay, Singleton and Swigert (1992), who found that decline in church attendance by older people tended to be associated with health problems that entailed 'functional limitation' (Ainlay, Singleton and Swigert, 1992: 186). Those with mobility problems may not even be able to reach the

71

church in the first place: 'they may be unable to drive the distance as low income may preclude owning or using a car. It could be that a partner was the car driver and this mode of transport is lost if the partner dies' (Moffitt, 2001: 20).

The SHSAAP Christian Research survey found that nearly 20% of respondents stopped their church-going because they had moved home. In some cases, moving house may simply give older people the opportunity to stop their church-going, which may have simply 'become a chore for them' (Moffitt, 2001: 25). However, in other cases it can be because older people find it impracticable to hunt around for a new church in the new area to which they have moved. Equally, they may find it hard to cross the threshold into a new church: 'assimilating into a new church is especially difficult for single or elderly people ... maybe because they do not have the excuse of going to "family things"' (Richter and Francis, 1998: 69). Assimilation to a new church takes anything up to five years and 'older people may not have five active years remaining in which to do so' (Moffitt, 2001: 24). In some cases the older person will be unable to attend church, if they become housebound or move into a nursing home, either in their previous area or in a new context. This does not necessarily mean that their church attachment will cease; this will partly depend on how proactive churches are in meeting the needs of those who can no longer attend.

Family factors affecting older people predominantly have to do with bereavement: the main reason for their cessation of church attendance is the death of a spouse. However, cessation may only be temporary: the SHSAAP research found that 'many of those who had ceased attending church because of such bereavement did eventually return following their "wilderness period"' (Moffitt, 2001: 27), having left on average for a period of ten years (Hammond and Treetops, 2001: 58). Divorce may also impede their church-going: 'either because they themselves feel failures or because they expect the church to be condemnatory' (Moffitt,

2001: 28); for older people there is more stigma attached to marital breakdown and divorce. Care responsibilities for family members can also make church-going impracticable, either because Sunday is taken up with caring or because Sunday offers the only available break from care responsibilities. Older people may be full-time carers for their pre-school grandchildren or, thanks to increasing emphasis on care in the community, they may be caring for older family members, who are likely to be highly dependent because of disability or frailty. Two-fifths of long-term carers (42%) are themselves over retirement age (Moffitt, 2001: 30).

Acute or chronic illness can also cause a drift away from church, especially if this causes older people to become housebound and their absence from church passes unnoticed. When older people suffer from dementia, they and their carer may effectively be excluded from church-going, because, for instance, congregations may be intolerant of the patients' challenging behaviour or because of the 'stigma still attached to having dementia and to looking after someone who has it' (Moffitt, 2001: 36). On the other hand, illness can sometimes stimulate a return to church-going, given that it may raise awareness of mortality and of the 'purpose and destiny of our lives' (Moffitt, 2001: 34), and illness was given as a reason for leaving by only 7% of older respondents (Moffitt, 2001: 55).

Three other sets of reasons for church-leaving were identified by the SHSAAP studies: changes in relation to the sense of belonging; changes in worship; and changes in believing. In terms of belonging, nearly half of all church-leavers reported that they 'did not feel part of the church'; this was particularly so for those aged over sixty (Hammond and Treetops, 2001: 39). Twenty-three per cent of church-leavers, of whom over a quarter were aged over sixty, reported that they were disillusioned by 'cliques' or in-groups within the church. Sometimes older people feel devalued and 'de-roled', when, for instance, younger people take on leadership positions or when ill health pushes them to the sidelines. Older men can feel marginalised in churches, where they tend to be in a minority, given that females tend to outlive males, and their needs for same-age sex-specific fellowship are less well met (Hammond and Treetops, 2001: 44). Sometimes pastoral care is perceived as lacking: 'of those leaving church later in life, one in four found the church uncaring, one in five felt let down when they needed support and one in six felt that ministers did not provide sufficient care' (Hammond and Treetops, 2001: 52).

In terms of worshipping, some, but by no means all, older people feel marginalised by changes in worship, in terms of, for example, its degree of spontaneity, the use of new biblical translations, the use of new forms of music, new styles of preaching, and greater congregational involvement. 'Removal of or changes to too many trusted landmarks can lead [older people] to feel bewildered and bereft' (Clarke, 2001: 64); other older people, however, may positively welcome such changes and the SHSAAP research found that 'in terms of their personal expectations of worship, older people demonstrate as wide a variety of views as people of other age groups' (Clarke, 2001: 70). The SHSAAP found that 'a significant number of older people felt that much modern worship was escapist' (Clarke, 2001: 76) and failed to connect with the realities of their lives. Older people spoke of 'sermons that seek to give false reassurance which flies in the face of the realities of life' and a third of church-leavers aged over sixty reported that 'they had found sermons irrelevant to their lives' (Clarke, 2001: 77).

In terms of believing, loss of faith is cited as a reason for leaving church by nearly a third of leavers, of whom the highest proportion is people currently aged over sixty (although loss of faith may have occurred earlier in life) (Harris, 2001: 80–81). For those who retain religious faith, church-leaving can be motivated by a sense of the irrelevance of the church's programme to their own faith and spirituality; if, for instance, the church fails to take into account their spiritual maturity, their need to come to terms with the 'diminishment of advancing years', or their need to die 'at peace' (Harris, 2001: 96–100). Leaving church does not necessarily equate with a decline in personal religious activity: 65% of elderly non-church-goers reported that they prayed daily (Harris, 2001: 81); this is consistent with Meridith McGuire's suggestion that 'while physical limitations might prevent an older person from attending church-related activities, it is possible that the person might pray more frequently, remember religious experiences or events more intensely, or base more everyday activity upon religious values' (McGuire, 1987: 61; also, Ainlay, Singleton and Swigert, 1992: 177–178).

Research strategy

In order to test the significance of age of leaving for understanding and interpreting the reasons and motivations underpinning church-leaving in England and Wales today, we compared the responses to our questionnaire given by three groups of the respondents: those who disengaged before their twentieth birthday, those who left church in their twenties or thirties, and those who left church after their fortieth birthday.

Denominational differences

We are using 'denomination' in a non-technical sense here, to describe any grouping of Christian congregations within a common polity. Hence, the term would encompass, for instance, the Roman Catholic and Orthodox Churches, as much as Free Churches.

There is significant denominational variation in terms of rates of decline in membership. Among Trinitarian churches the steepest decline has been experienced by the Presbyterian, Methodist, Anglican and Roman Catholic Churches, which have lost 27%, 27%, 25% and 23% of their members, respectively, between 1975 and 1995. But, by contrast, Pentecostal, Orthodox and Independent Churches have grown by 176%, 146% and 142%, respectively (Francis and Brierley, 1997: 163). However, membership does not necessarily equate with church attendance, except, in this case, for Roman Catholics whose membership is indicated by weekly Mass attendance figures (Francis and Brierley, 1997: 169): large numbers of individuals claim to belong to mainstream churches but never actually attend (Bruce, 1995: 38).

Rates of church attendance also vary between denominations. According to the findings of the 1998 English Church Attendance Survey, attendance at Anglican churches dropped by 23% between 1989 and 1998; Roman Catholic attendance dropped by 28%; Orthodox attendance increased by 105%; and Free Church attendance dropped by 15% (Brierley, 2000: 34, 37). The decline in Roman Catholic attendance in the 1990s was twice as great as its rate of decline in the 1980s; Peter Brierley has suggested that this greater rate of decline was 'partly due to less strict application of the teaching by the Catholic church that a mortal sin is . . . committed if a person does not attend mass' (Brierley, 2000: 34). Anglican church decline had remained at a steadily high rate over both decades. Within the Free Church category, there was considerable variation. On the one hand, attendance at the Methodist Church had declined by 26% between 1989 and 1998; on the other hand, attendance at New Churches and Independent Churches had increased by 38% and 46%, respectively (Brierley, 2000: 37). Sunday attendance figures do not necessarily, however, give a true indication of church-going and may mask trends toward less frequent attendance and weekday, rather than Sunday, attendance. Brierley has attributed a third of the apparent decline in attendance in the 1990s to 'change in frequency of attendance' (Brierley, 2000: 90); his conclusions have been re-inforced by the 2000 Anglican national attendance and member-ship figures, which, it was claimed, demonstrated that the Church has been under-counting its worshippers by almost a third (Church of England, 2002: vi).

Decline in church attendance can adversely affect the morale of those who continue to be church-goers and, hence, indirectly influence church-leaving. However, differences in *perceived* rates of church decline are likely to be more significant than differences in absolute rates of decline. The 1998 English Church Attendance Survey found that, according to local church leaders, 'between one in seven and one in nine Roman Catholic, Methodist or United Reformed Church churches are expecting to decline in the twelve years 1998 to 2010' (Brierley, 2000: 213), while only one in fourteen of Anglican churches expected to decline and no Pentecostal churches expected to decline (Brierley, 2000: 212–13). Methodist churches were much more likely than those of other denominations to expect to close in this period: just over one in every six churches (Brierley, 2000: 212); as Brierley commented, this represents 'a situation where morale may well be difficult to change to prevent this becoming reality' (Brierley, 2000: 213).

Dean R. Hoge, Benton Johnson and Donald A. Luidens, in their study of the religiosity of mainstream Protestant baby boomers (Hoge, Johnson and Luidens, 1994), found little evidence that denominational factors influenced individuals' church-leaving. They considered three possible institutional explanations for membership decline, with particular reference to the Presbyterian Church: adverse response to shifting denominational policies, such as the reformatting of worship or introduction of new Sunday school curricula; rejection of the institutional church as socially irrelevant, and insufficiently active in struggles for peace and justice, by baby boomers; rejection of denominations that have become over-involved in social action programmes, to the detriment of spiritual nurture and evangelism (Hoge, Johnson and Luidens, 1994: 176–7). However, they concluded that 'all three institutional theories should be abandoned' (Hoge, Johnson and Luidens, 1994: 177). The downturn in Presbyterian membership was long-term and continuous and unaffected by particular controversial 'denominational events'. A very similar trend was found in other denominations, in spite of their different programmes and institutional priorities. Furthermore, denominational issues rarely surfaced in the interviews conducted by Hoge, Johnson and Luidens: 'criticisms . . . were directed almost exclusively at *local congregations* rather than at the Presbyterian Church or at mainline Protestantism as a whole' (Hoge, Johnson and Luidens, 1994: 178).

David A. Roozen, Jackson W. Carroll and Wade Clark Roof, in their assessment of religious change in the late twentieth century, agreed that the commitment of mainstream Protestant denominations in the United States of America to social action, in the 1960s and early 1970s, did not lead to a 'mass withdrawal from membership' (Roozen, Carroll and Roof, 1998: 68). However, ecumenical mergers and proposals of mergers 'generated stronger reactions, and more opposition and alienation' (Roozen, Carroll and Roof, 1998: 69): grass-roots members increasingly perceived central denominational agencies as remote and impersonal and as setting less store by 'personal piety and spirituality', and this led, they claimed, to 'significant decreases in membership' (Roozen, Carroll and Roof, 1998: 70). They concluded that church-leaving in relation to the Roman Catholic Church was associated with different factors, during the same period. The defection of young Roman Catholics was because of the 'reaffirmation of traditional Catholic teachings against birth control' in the *Humanae Vitae* encyclical in 1968, which 'blunted much of young adult enthusiasm for the [ecclesiastical reforms of Vatican II], [and] especially their respect for church authority': 'a crisis in authority was provoked by the sudden attempt of the Catholic hierarchy to place limits on personal choice at a time when the larger trends in this direction . . . were gaining momentum' (Roozen, Carroll and Roof, 1998: 73). The differential denominational factors that Roozen Carroll and Roof associate with church-leaving in the 1960s and early 1970s may be largely specific to that period and/or the baby boomers. Denominational institutions in the United States of America have restructured and become less centralised, and congregations have become more selective about their participation in the life of the denomination; the steep member-ship declines of the 1960s and early 1970s have lessened, except in the case of the Presbyterians. Catholic strictures on birth control do not necessarily motivate church-leaving: 'an increasing number of Catholics simply choose to defy the papal line' (Richter and Francis, 1998: 46), except in relation to creedal or core beliefs (Hornsby-Smith, 1992: 130, 133).

C. Kirk Hadaway, in his 1990 survey of disaffiliation research, suggested that in the case of denominations with 'very permeable boundaries', such as the Presbyterian Church, 'people drift in and out', given that 'for a large proportion of . . . adherents, commit-ment and identification are low' (Hadaway, 1990b: 120). Hadaway described these drifters as 'mental members', who had typically moved to a new area, 'retained a religious identity, but they never re-affiliated with a new congregation' (Hadaway, 1990b: 110); they tend to have 'drifted away in apathy rather than having stormed out in anger' (Hadaway, 1990b: 120).

Frank Newport, in his study of religious mobility trends in the United States of America, found that individuals raised as Catholics were more likely than those of other denominations to switch out of religion altogether, rather than, say, to another denomination (Newport, 1979: 538). Darren E. Sherkat and John Wilson's theory of religious mobility attributes this denomina-tional differentiation to the 'consolidation of social ties' among Catholics, which 'make it especially difficult for members to join other denominations, since changing faiths would create a strain between conflicting social roles' and make it easier for them to drop out altogether (Sherkat and Wilson, 1995: 1000). By contrast, liberal Protestant churches are, as Rodney Stark has claimed, 'more like theatre audiences than groups, for only small minorities of liberal Protestants report having close personal friends among members of their local congregation' (Stark, 1996: 142). Robert Wuthnow and Kevin Christiano, in their study of the effects of migration on church attendance in the United States of America, found that 'church attendance [was] affected more by residential mobility among Catholics than it is among Protestants'; they suggested that this was because moving to a new area was more disruptive of Catholic religious practice, given that 'Catholics take the communal aspect of their religion more seriously' (Wuthnow and Christiano, 1979: 266).

Different denominations attach different degrees of importance to the family. For Roman Catholics, church and family are 'mutually reinforcing' and 'family and religious obligations are co-terminous' (Sandomirsky and Wilson, 1990: 1214). By contrast, Protestants tend to give greater priority to faith-bonds, rather than family-bonds. For Protestants, the logic of their faith means that ties and obligations to the faith community are ultimately of more importance than family-bonds (Roof and Gesch, 1995: 63, 67). This will tend to weaken the effects of childhood socialisation, in that children growing up in a Protestant household will be expected to make up their own mind and come to a personal faith-decision, rather than simply to follow the faith of their fathers (and mothers).

Wilson and Sherkat's longitudinal study of parents and children, conducted between 1965 and 1983, found that Roman Catholics were no more likely than Protestants to return to church-going after they married and began to rear their own children. Roman Catholics had mostly originally defected because of their opposition to official church teaching on contraception and pre-marital sex (Wilson and Sherkat, 1994: 155).

Lawton and Bures (2001), in their study of the impact of parental divorce on changes in religious identity, found that Catholics reacted more strongly to parental divorce than did Protestants: given that divorce is more problematic for Catholics 'following a parental divorce, Catholics may feel removed from community and therefore be more likely to . . . change religious affiliation' (Lawton and Bures, 2001: 101,108). Catholics whose parents divorced in childhood were 2.2 times more likely to apostatise than they were to remain Catholic (Lawton and Bures, 2001: 106).

Wade Clark Roof, in his study of the spiritual journeys of the baby-boom generation (Roof, 1993), found that Catholic baby boomers tended to have dropped out for a manifold set of reasons: 'unpleasant memories associated with priests, disagreement with the church's position on divorce and marriage . . . preference for a more private spirituality not linked with any religious institution'; that mainline Protestants tended to be rather vague about why they had dropped out, citing reasons such as: 'Church didn't seem relevant', 'I developed other interests', or 'I was bored'; and that conservative Protestants often attributed their leaving to 'lack of relevance' or 'other interests' (Roof, 1993: 175–7).

Roof's on-going study of baby boomers (1999) found that born-again Christians and religious dogmatists were most influenced by early religious socialisation within the family. Roof suggests that this was because parental influence was reinforced by a religious environment of 'strong, coercive moral and religious norms and distinct idioms of religious expression' (Roof, 1999: 227). Mainstream believers, by contrast, were more affected by other influences, such as peer groups, friends and spouses.

Bruce Hunsberger and Bob Altemeyer's study of apostates who had swum 'upstream against the religious socialisation current of their lives' (Hunsberger, 2000: 233) found that Catholics were over-represented in their 'Amazing Apostates' category; that is, those who had rejected religion, despite having been raised in strongly religious homes. While more Catholics than Protestants came from a 'strong religious [home] background', the Catholic Church 'lost more of its "properly raised" children than any other religion' because it alienated them by its 'stand on various issues, particularly those related to gender and sex' (Hunsberger, 2000: 238).

Reginald W. Bibby's study of the impact of geographical mobility on religious involvement, based on Canadian 1990 national survey data (Bibby, 1997), found that the church-going of Roman Catholics and Pentecostals was less likely to be affected adversely by residential movement than that of mainstream Protestants. The socialisation offered by the former churches was 'frequently sufficiently thorough that . . . [a Catholic or Pentecostal would feel] that he or she should attend a Sunday service, regardless of where she or he [happened] to be on a Sunday morning', but 'being a mainline Protestant . . . [did] little in and of itself to motivate a person to attend church' (Bibby, 1997: 302).

Although religious congregations of different denominations have many common organisational features and problems (Harris, 1998a: 315), Roman Catholic and Protestant churches tend to differ in terms of the weight placed upon intra-church community. Gibson Winter has pointed out that the Roman Catholic Church tends to be a 'client-oriented' type of organisation: 'the parish realizes its principal religious activities through the mediation of the priest' (Winter, 1961: 89). By contrast, Protestant churches tend to be 'member-oriented' types of organisation, in which 'priesthood is embodied in a community of believers' and 'considerable weight [is placed] upon relationships among members' (Winter, 1961: 89). Consistent with Gibson's typology, studies of the United Methodist Church in North America have demonstrated the importance of factors relating to relationships within the church for church-leaving from that Protestant denomination (Hartman, 1976: 40; Savage,

1976: 68). In his own study of Catholic dropouts, Dean R. Hoge commented on these Methodist-based studies: 'relationships with other parishioners were more important in these studies (that is, by Hartman and Savage) than they are for typical Catholics' (Hoge, 1988: 12).

The ways in which congregational cultural identity is constructed, by means of 'activities, artefacts, and accounts' (Ammer-man, 1998: 84), also vary between denominations (Richter, 2004). In some cases changes in denominational culture may be a reason for church-leaving. For instance, contemporary British Methodism has moved toward more liturgical worship, which has tended to 'privilege more "high church" traditions within Methodism' (Richter, 2002: 42); this may tend to alienate those who are less liturgically inclined. One of the interviewees in Philip Richter's analysis of denominational cultures reported that another Methodist had complained to him recently that 'We're getting shorter and shorter sermons'. Richter commented that: 'in the context of a denomination where forty-minute sermons were once the norm, this statement implied that something important was being attenuated; interestingly in an Anglican context it might have had quite opposite connotations!' (Richter, 2004: 181).

Research strategy

In order to test the significance of denominational background for understanding and interpreting the reasons and motivations underpinning church-leaving in England and Wales today, we compared the responses to our questionnaire given by three groups of the respondents: those who described themselves as Roman Catholics, those who described themselves as Anglicans, and those who described themselves as members of one of the Free Churches.

Sudden or gradual leaving

The process of moving out of religion has been most intensively studied in relation to new religious movements, which tend to involve more blatant and more extreme exiting processes (Shaffir, 1997: 13) than those associated with mainstream religion. In his study of affiliation and disaffiliation processes relating to Transformative New Religious Movements (TNRMs), David Bromley concluded that exiting TNRMs 'frequently occurs over an extended period that can stretch into months or even years' (Bromley, 1997: 51). Although members may encounter problems with the TNRM, they may still 'believe that the group's creed and way of life are qualitatively superior to anything they have experienced elsewhere' (Bromley, 1997: 51) and believe that the problems will be resolved satisfactorily. Members of TNRMs are likely to be more thoroughly involved in the organisation than church-goers are typically involved in churches. The TNRM tends to integrate 'community, marital, occupational, and religious relationships in a single social network', hence 'the longer the duration of membership, therefore, the more likely it is that disaffiliation means giving up the entire fabric of one's social life' (Bromley, 1997: 51). Understandably, individuals will be reluctant to rush into disaffiliation if it is going to have a dramatic impact on most aspects of their lives. Some, but not all, church-goers will similarly be closely integrated into their churches and be reluctant to disturb these key social relationships. However, Norman Skonovd, in his study of leaving totalistic religious groups, suggests that leave-taking from mainstream religion is typified by a more 'abrupt manner': for instance, 'after becoming upset over the prejudiced or openly hypocritical attitudes of a congregation and/or member of the clergy' (Skonovd, 1983: 95).

David G. Bromley, in his analysis of *contested* exiting from religious organisations, that is, leave-taking involving 'formal or public airing of disputes' (Bromley, 1998a: 146), suggests that defection from mainline churches, such as the Catholic Church, typically takes place over a long period of time. Bromley categorises mainline churches as 'allegiant organisations', which are 'deemed by both participants and outsiders to be exercising legitimate authority, which places the burden of proof squarely on [disputants]' (Bromley, 1998a: 147). Given that the Church was accorded considerable spiritual authority, defectors risked losing the support of their coreligionists. Bromley cites the study of former nuns by Helen Ebaugh (1988), which reported that 'opposition from family members . . . and other Catholics was a significant impediment to nuns exiting their roles. As a result, nuns were likely to struggle with and defer decisions to exit, often for a number of years' (Bromley, 1998a: 149).

Stuart A. Wright, in an analysis of disaffiliation from new religious movements (NRMs), suggested that most disaffiliation is gradual, except in cases of expulsion; however, even expulsion may entail a lengthy process and the expelled member 'may not lose ideological or affectional ties to the movement' (Wright, 1988: 162). Accounts of apparently sudden deconversion do not necessarily 'reflect accurately the preceding events or experiences that weakened commitment' (Wright, 1988: 161), which may involve a (perhaps group-specific) 'sequence of stages or progressive levels of withdrawal' (Wright, 1988: 150). Wright identified three different modes of exit: covert, overt and declarative (Wright, 1988: 152). Declarative departures are sudden and dramatic, often involving 'displays of anger or frustration' (Wright, 1988: 152) and 'performed with marked deliberateness' (Wright, 1987: 69). A declarative mode of leave-taking tends to be utilised 'when doubt, grievances, and frustrations have proved to be insurmountable'; it is typically 'a release of bottled-up sentiments that have not been shared or resolved' (Wright, 1987: 72). Covert departures are also sudden, but, unlike declarative departures, clandestine. Overt departures, on the other hand, usually take place 'after deliberation with a leader or leaders [of the movement]' (Wright, 1987: 69). Overt defectors are likely to be longer-term members 'who become involved in conflicts over explicit policy-related issues which prompt a direct approach to conflict-resolution through open confrontation or negotiation' (Wright, 1987: 73). Defectors who had belonged to the group for three or more years tended to make overt or declarative exits, while 'novice' members tended to be covert defectors, wrestling 'with "vague, unfocused discontents or deep emotional attachments" that were difficult to articulate openly' (Wright, 1988: 152). Novice defectors were likely to have 'mixed feelings about defecting because of [continuing] strong attachments to the people and the ideals in the (NRM) community' (Wright, 1987: 68).

Where church-leaving is articulated in terms of loss of faith there may be a tendency for leavers, and sociological analysts, to conform to the autobiographical model of 'a (de)conversion story with a sudden resolved crisis' (Barbour, 1994: 50). The imagination of personal change has been influenced by the ability of the 'crisis scene' to provide 'a coherent way of both apprehending and presenting a transition between two very different world-views, ideological commitments, or ways of life' and to give 'a sense of direction and a clear turning point to the narration of events that may have been experienced as unconnected, confusing, or inconclusive' (Barbour, 1994: 50–51).

Alan Jamieson's study of Evangelical, Pentecostal and Charismatic church-leavers, conducted mostly in New Zealand, between 1994 and 1996, found that 'the vast majority' of their interviewees had gradually drifted away: 'they indicated a gradual process of reflection, questioning and withdrawal which lasted many months or years prior to their decision to leave' (Jamieson, 2002: 32). However, for 41% of leavers this process of review and reflection culminated in an abrupt turning point, triggered by a specific event (Jamieson, 2002: 39–40), which crystallised the decision to leave by, for instance, providing final grounds for leaving or by finally breaching the leaver's 'threshold of tolerance'

(Skonovd, 1983: 94). David G. Bromley reported similar turning points in his study of disaffiliation from new religious movements: 'the precipitating event crystallises unresolved discontent, energizes the individual to move toward exit, and provides at least an initial account that will be used to interpret the now formalized decision to audiences inside and outside the group' (Bromley, 1997: 52). Some of Jamieson's interviewees associated these 'turning points' with having been 'knocked back by church'; the offer to join a 'post-church group'; the effects of 'personal struggle or crisis'; move to a different geographical location; or the 'offer to study theology' (Jamieson, 2002: 40).

Bruce Hunsberger's study of individuals who had 'swum against the current' of their religious socialisation (Hunsberger, 2000) suggested that 'Amazing Apostates' (AAs), that is, those who rejected religion, despite having been raised in strongly religious homes, were likely to display 'some of the characteristics of the classic "gradual convert", although . . . the AAs "converted" to atheism or agnosticism' (Hunsberger, 2000: 245). Hunsberger concluded that the process of becoming an AA was 'strongly intellectual and rational, and seem(ed) to result from a slow, careful search for meaning and purpose' (Hunsberger, 2000: 245–6). However, Hunsberger's research was based on a survey of university students, so his findings may not be generalisable to older leavers.

Research strategy

In order to test the significance of sudden or gradual leaving for understanding and interpreting the reasons and motivations underpinning church-leaving in England and Wales today, we compared the responses to our questionnaire given by two groups of the respondents: those who described their church-leaving as sudden, and those who described their church-leaving as gradual.

Likelihood of returning

The Princeton Religion Research Center's 1988 survey of un-churched Americans, based on a survey of over 2,500 adults, found that 'those most likely to return (to church-going) are members of demographic groups which are already highly churched. For example, women are more likely than men to return, blacks are more likely than whites, and married people are more likely to do so than single people' (Princeton Religion Research Center, 1988: 4).

Dropouts do not necessarily remain dropouts. In the United States of America, up to 80% of dropouts subsequently return to church involvement (Roozen, 1980); although less than half of baby-boomer leavers return (Roof and Landres, 1997: 86). Wade Clark Roof has highlighted the 'dynamic, fluid character' of baby-boomer religiosity: 'loyalists and returnees drop out in sizable numbers while dropouts, some of them inactive for twenty or thirty years, find their way back to the churches' (Roof, 1999: 120). Roof's 1988–89 survey found that baby-boomer returners were generally less committed to their churches than those who had never left, that is, the 'loyalists' (Roof, 1993: 180), and scored lower in terms of 'matters of belief; congregational participation; subjective importance of religion; or religious self-identity' (Roof, 1999: 117). Roof commented that 'in a culture of choice, the meaning of a "returning to the fold" is itself open to new interpretation' (Roof, 1993: 180). However, Roof's later, 1995–1996, survey found that most returners were 'almost as active now in a congregation or some religious group as the religious loyalists' and that 'today the majority of them look[ed] pretty much like other religious people' (Roof, 1999: 119). According to the earlier survey, a third of returners described themselves as 'strong believers', a third as having 'occasional doubts', and a third as 'seekers not always sure what to believe'; in the later survey almost a half described themselves as 'strong believers', 'with the remainder divided about equally between "doubters" and "seekers"' (Roof, 1999: 119).

Wade Clark Roof, in his study of the spiritual journeys of the baby-boom generation (Roof, 1993), noted that baby boomers tended to return to active church involvement for three main reasons. The first reason concerns family life. 'The presence of young, school-age children and feelings of parental responsibility for them drives boomers back to church and to enrol their children in religious education classes' (Roof, 1993: 157). However, this reason is more likely to apply to those who had 'parents with a religious background who took them to church' as children (Roof, 1993: 157). The second reason concerns a personal quest for meaning. The quest for 'something to believe in, for answers to questions about life', motivated by feelings of emptiness and loneliness, drives some leavers to return (Roof, 1993: 158). The third reason concerns a desire for communal belonging. Nostalgia for religious belonging, 'and some guilt because they are not more actively involved' drives some leavers back to church (Roof, 1993: 160).

Roof found that those brought up in a more permissive child-rearing home environment were less likely to return to active church involvement; and that those who did not enjoy close relations with their parents as children were less likely to return (Roof, 1993: 163); as far as baby boomers were concerned, parental religious involvement per se made no difference to whether they returned (Roof, 1993: 162). Those who were most exposed to, and influenced by, 1960s values were, also, less likely to return (Roof, 1993: 57, 171). David A. Roozen and William McKinney's analysis of General Social Survey data from the United States of America relating to the early 1970s and early 1980s suggested that 'increased level of regular worship attendance among older baby boomers [was] largely a matter of renewal among those who never totally left, rather than a recapturing of those who had made a clean break with religious institutions during young adulthood' (Roozen and McKinney 1990: 320).

Wade Clark Roof and Lyn Gesch's study of 536 baby boomers, conducted in four states in the United States of America in 1988 and 1989, found that 'religious individualists' were much less likely than 'family attenders' to return to active church involvement. 'Religious individualists' were those who 'insist[ed] on each person making his or her own decision about religious involvement'; while 'family attenders' were those who felt 'that families as a unit should make such decisions' (Roof and Gesch, 1995: 64). Most 'family attenders' had returned to church involvement, but 'the vast majority of the individualist dropouts (were) *still* inactive: 86% among the mainline Protestants, 76% among conservative Protestants, and 73% among Catholics' (Roof and Gesch 1995: 69). The survey items used by Roof and Gesch to measure religious individualism included: 'An individual should arrive at his or her own religious beliefs independent of any church or synagogue'; 'A person can be a good Christian/Jew without attending church/synagogue'; and 'Church is something freely chosen by each person rather than passed on from generation to generation' (Roof and Gesch, 1995: 65).

Dean R. Hoge, Kenneth McGuire and Bernard F. Stratman's analysis of religious change among Catholics found that most returners were in their twenties or early thirties (Hoge, McGuire and Stratman, 1981: 132); 71% were female and 29% male, while a majority of the dropouts were male (Hoge, McGuire and Stratman, 1981: 84). The key motivations for returning to church involvement were: concern for children's religious upbringing (in 55% of the cases); personal spiritual need (41%); and discomfort or guilt at being away from the church (affecting those who have had a strong Catholic upbringing) (30%) (Hoge, McGuire and Stratman, 1981: 132). The most common facilitating events were: serious illness or personal crisis; birth or baptism of a child; marital or family crisis; a move to a new parish or community; or having a religious experience (Hoge, McGuire and Stratman, 1981: 134).

Káren North's qualitative survey of young adults (between the ages of 18 and 30 years) 'distanced', 'lapsed' or 'resting' Roman Catholics, based largely on data from 15 in-depth interviews conducted mainly in south-east England, found that most interviewees had not decided definitely for or against future church involvement: only two of her interviewees had ruled out further contact with the church (North, 2001: 118). However, most of these young adult Roman Catholic leavers reported that there would need to be a significant prompt for their return, for instance, a crisis, or, especially, the wish to hand their faith on to their children (North, 2001: 118). North found that, while dissatisfaction with liturgy played a minor part in the decision to leave (North, 2001: 105), those most likely to return to churchgoing came from parishes where they had experienced excellent liturgy, together with a good welcome and a sense of spirituality (North, 2001: 5, 115).

Alan Jamieson's study of Evangelical, Pentecostal and Charismatic (EPC) church-leavers, conducted mostly in New Zealand between 1994 and 1996 (Jamieson, 2002), found that different types of leavers had different prospects of returning. Jamieson developed a typology of four different kinds of leavers: *disillusioned followers* (18% of the overall total of leavers, including transition to an alternative faith: 2% to New Age and 5% to agnosticism) had left because of 'grumbles' about the church, but remained 'strongly committed to their faith' (Jamieson, 2002: 56); *reflective exiles* (30%) had left 'because of a more foundational questioning of their underlying faith' (Jamieson, 2002: 62), which involved pushing against 'the previous authority and basis of faith they [had] held to' (Jamieson, 2002: 68), but this did not constitute a rejection of their previous faith commitment, instead it represented 'a realization of its inadequacy in the light of their wider experience' (Jamieson, 2002: 72); *transitional explorers*

91

(18%) had moved on from the deconstruction of their received faith, as reflective exiles, to a 're-appropriation of some elements of Christian faith and . . . a new self-owned faith' (Jamieson, 2002: 77), or in some cases to an alternative non-Christian faith; *integrated wayfinders* (27%) had left because they had begun 'seriously to question the dogmatic confidence and exclusivism of Evangelical Christians and their interpretation of the Bible' (Jamieson, 2002: 92), but had subsequently discovered a wider, more rounded, personally owned faith.

Among 'disillusioned followers', those who were hurt and disappointed with their church were much more open to returning to church than were those who were angry and had left because of areas of disagreement: angry disillusioned followers were 'very reluctant about returning to an institutional church' (Jamieson, 2002: 57). 'Reflective exiles' disconnect themselves more thoroughly from the wider EPC community (Jamieson, 2002: 66). The process within which they are engaged of deconstructing and reflecting on their faith can have one of three possible outcomes: personal appropriation of belief; agnosticism; or rejection of faith (Jamieson, 2002: 71). Many of the 'transitional explorers' expressed the desire to become more fully involved in church in future. However, they may have incorporated new beliefs, values and ways of behaving that are inconsistent with the EPC 'faith package' (Jamieson, 2002: 83). The re-involvement of transitional explorers would need to be on their terms: as independent people, appreciated in their own right, and free to 'challenge others when they [are] accepting things in a way [they feel is] inappropriate' (Jamieson, 2002: 85). Finally, Jamieson found that 'integrated wayfarers' were very likely to have already remade 'some connections with people, groups or churches that hold to similar beliefs and a similar faith', but that their degree of church involvement 'will be dependent on the openness of these communities to people like themselves' (Jamieson, 2002: 104).

C. Kirk Hadaway also found that different types of leavers had different prospects of returning, although he categorised church-leavers differently from Jamieson (Hadaway, 1989). Of his five categories, 'sidetracked singles' and 'irreligious traditionalists' were least likely to return to active church involvement (Hadaway, 1989: 213). 'Sidetracked singles' were young, mostly unmarried, highly educated, extremely liberal on social issues, pessimistic, and characterised by a sense that 'they have been shunted to a side-track, watching the good life pass them by' (Hadaway, 1989: 208). 'Irreligious traditionalists', on the other hand, were older, married, politically and socially conservative, unbelievers (Hadaway, 1989: 212–13).

Everett L. Perry, Ruth T. Doyle, James H. Davis and John E. Dyble developed a typology of unchurched Protestants, based on the 1978 Gallup survey of unchurched Americans (Perry, Doyle, Davis and Dyble, 1980). They found that different types of unchurched Protestants had different prospects of being reached again by the church: they identified three types of unchurched Protestants. The 'estranged' had mostly previously belonged to a church and continued to hold traditional Christian beliefs and attitudes, but had drifted away, mainly for contextual reasons; Perry, Doyle, Davis and Dyble suggested that they could be 'rechurched' 'to the extent that they [could] be convinced that the institutional church [was] relevant to their own faith journey and [was] able to meet their needs' (Perry, Doyle, Davis and Dyble, 1980: 402). The 'indifferent' lacked 'religious commitment or a feeling that religion [was] important': they had tended to '[drift] away to other interests and activities'; Perry, Doyle, Davis and Dyble suggested that only evangelistic outreach might encourage their return (Perry, Doyle, Davis and Dyble, 1980: 402). Finally, the 'nominals' had 'few vestiges of religion, except for the identi-fying label of Protestant'; Perry, Doyle, Davis and Dyble found that this group was much less likely to return – only one in twenty of them 'could even imagine a circumstance when they might become active in a church'; compared with one in five of the estranged, who 'might return to the church, under certain circumstances' (Perry, Doyle, Davis and Dyble, 1980: 402).

Tony Glendinning and Steve Bruce's analysis of a module of questions on religion in the 2001 Scottish Attitudes Survey found that 61% of the Scottish population had once attended church regularly, that is, 'once a month or more often'. Of these, 61% (37% of the general population) had since given up going to church (Glendinning and Bruce, 2006: 402; Bruce and Glendinning, 2003: 89). Of those who had given up church-going, three-quarters had never seriously considered going back (Bruce and Glendinning, 2003: 89). Glendinning and Bruce's findings are in some respects closely similar to those of our own 1996 random telephone survey in the London area (Richter and Francis, 1998: xii). In this survey we found that 62% of the population had once attended church regularly – that is, at least six times a year (not including Christmas and Easter). Of these, 60% had since given up their church-going. Our findings differed, however, in terms of the proportion of ex-church-goers who reported serious interest in the possibility of one day returning to the church. In the case of our survey, 45% of church-leavers were leaving the possibility of returning open. This disparity may derive from the different phrasing of the survey questions. In our case, we asked, 'Are you likely to become actively involved in a church in future?', while the Scottish Attitudes Survey asked whether 'they had ever considered going back' (Bruce and Glendinning, 2003: 89). Arguably, the Scottish Attitudes Survey may have underestimated the proportion of potential returners, given that previous indifference does not necessarily rule out openness to church-going at a future stage of an individual's life.

Glendinning and Bruce found that the religious beliefs of potential returners were much closer to those of regular church attenders than to the beliefs of permanent disaffiliates. 'Few of those who were not raised in a religion, who never attended regularly, or who stopped and have never considered going back, hold a theistic view' (Bruce and Glendinning, 2003: 93). However, potential returners differed markedly from regular church-goers in certain respects: for example, a significantly greater proportion of potential returners believed that they had lived a previous life and claimed contact with the dead (Glendinning and Bruce, 2006: 409). Potential returners, in the phrase popularised by Grace Davie, 'believe without belonging', but their beliefs tend not to be entirely orthodox. Although Glendinning and Bruce suggest that potential returners are 'too much formed by the modern spirit of assertive individualism to be readily brought back into the mainstream of church life' (private correspondence with Steve Bruce, 2002), one could surmise that it might, instead, be the perception on the part of 'stopped-hesitants' that their beliefs are unacceptable within a church context that distances them from the church – a perception that, for whatever reasons, overlooks or is unaware of the heterogeneity of belief exhibited by regular church-goers, who also, though to a lesser degree, share their unorthodox beliefs, according to the Scottish Attitudes Survey (Bruce and Glendinning, 2003: 93). One must also beware of typecasting potential returners as deviant believers, in that less than one third reported unorthodox beliefs of this sort.

Research strategy

In order to examine the link between the reasons and motivations underpinning church-leaving in England and Wales and the likelihood of returning to church at a later stage in life, we compared the responses to our questions given by three groups of the respondents: those who were clear that they would not consider returning to church, those who were clear that they were open to becoming church-returners, and those who remained unclear as to whether or not they would ever return.

5

Matters of belief and unbelief

Setting the scene

The complex relationship between religious belief and church attendance has long been debated in the literature. In his perceptive historical analysis of church decline, published in his book *The Myth of the Empty Church*, Robin Gill (1993) takes the view not only that church-leaving was a precursor to loss of religious faith but that church-leaving promoted the erosion of faith. A very different perspective is taken by Steve Bruce in his book *Religion in Modern Britain* when he concludes that 'those who explain their lack of church involvement by considerations other than a lack of belief are fooling themselves or fooling the researchers' (Bruce, 1995: 47). The aim of the present chapter, therefore, is to examine the extent to which church-leavers themselves explain their distance from the church in terms of matters of belief and matters of unbelief. Listening to our interviewees, four main themes emerged within the broad area of beliefs. We described these themes as: losing faith, life experience, problems with belief, and responding to doubt.

Losing faith

The first theme focused on the way in which some church-leavers came out directly with a statement like, 'I lost my faith'. Others spoke more tentatively about the connection between disengagement from church and the erosion of faith. They said things like, 'I doubted or questioned my faith'. Some people linked ideas of faith and meaning and said, 'church had lost its meaning for me'. Such people, however, were quite often quick to distinguish between faith in God and faith in the church. Many who had lost their faith in the church had not lost their faith in God. Many who found that the church had lost its meaning continued to find meaning in God. The point was made, for example, by Siobhan, a young Roman Catholic church-leaver from Northern Ireland.

In some ways my belief is stronger since having left church . . . I think it was the fact that I was, well I felt as though, I was made to go, beforehand. That, I just didn't even think what it was all about. And now that I have the choice, sometimes like, I might feel guilty that I don't go, and I think, it's made me realise what faith I have, you know, because I'd never thought of what it meant to me beforehand, I just naturally went, and, you know, just did what others expected of me.

A similar point was made by Russell Briggs, a middle-aged ex-minister, who had left a New Church. Russell Briggs had left the church, but he had not left God.

God's never left [my life]. Unfortunately I'm stuck with that. You see, I've had [an experience of God] and 'he that hath an experience is not at the mercy of him that hath an argument'. In fact [when I first moved here] my next-door neighbour came to me and . . . I kept it quiet that I'd been a minister, I didn't want anybody to know . . . He's an artist, so I thought he might understand, so I told him, and he said, 'I'm an atheist' or an agnostic, I forget what it was, and I said, 'I wish I could be' . . . At that stage I . . . would have liked to have been . . . I would have liked to have not had an experience, because then I could be like everybody else. But unfortunately I'd had an experience of God, which changed my life, and He's never left me, and I've never left Him. I left the church, it's a different thing altogether, I wouldn't put the two things at all together.

Life experience

The second theme focused on the way in which some church-leavers pointed to specific life experiences which had led them to question their faith and their religious beliefs. For a variety of different reasons some church-leavers felt that God had let them down. Sometimes belief in God had been challenged or damaged by the individual's own personal experience of suffering, and sometimes by the suffering they had witnessed in others. Sometimes church-leavers had become aware of alternative ways of thinking and alternative ways of life which had challenged their faith and their religious belief. Growing recognition of the role of religion in so many conflicts throughout the world also posed a challenge to faith. For example, Arron Coates, a post-graduate student in his twenties who had left a Roman Catholic church, pointed to life experience that had undermined his faith.

There were deaths in the family that have left people disorientated and disillusioned . . . [My cousin] got married a couple of years ago, and I was his best man . . . and he's the only one of the family that's had a church ceremony . . . and he's had a really hard time. He's had a really hard life, very difficult, and there's sort of a thing about fair-play, and what people deserve, and he's never got what he's deserved, and it's always really bugged me . . . It always seems that whatever can go wrong for him, does. And he's the least deserving because he's very kind-hearted, very sincere, he keeps up his faith, looks after my gran and family . . . And he got married to a very nice girl . . . and she was pregnant, and she had stillborn twins . . . The funeral, two unborn kids, was really disturbing, they were buried in a shoebox, they were given names, but like when my nanna died the year before, you can always say, 'they had a good life, and look at all the people that are here', and there's some sort of justification, and they've gone to a better place, and they had their time, and it's much easier to deal with. But when it's two kids that have never been born, and your faith dictates that they're going to go to heaven, it's really hard to get your head round, because nobody ever knew them, they never had any time, they never had any life, and yet they've got a name . . . And so I think that's what brought about my current spell of inactivity in the church.

Looking at a somewhat wider canvas, Russell Briggs, the middle-aged ex-minister, pointed to international events which had begun to undermine his faith.

You had the Christians, the Moslems, and the Jews, all fighting for one God and slaughtering each other, and the church is becoming more and more of an irrelevancy. The Christian Research Organisation [sic] says that over the next ten years, one million people will leave the church, because they're disillusioned with it, and I think that's a haemorrhaging that will happen.

Problems with belief

The third theme focused on problems that some church-leavers found with Christian doctrine and with Christian belief. Some church-leavers had come to the conclusion that many of the church's teachings were illogical or nonsensical. Some church-leavers had found that the church's teachings were difficult to reconcile with modern science. Some church-leavers had found it impossible to go on accepting the exclusive claims of Christianity to be the only true faith. For example, Alison Matthews, a young social worker who had left a Roman Catholic church, had been disturbed by the attitude of some Christians to people of other faiths.

> I noticed the attitudes of people, other people, in the Catholic Church in my own community, not all of them, but some of them, toward non-Christian religions, and toward my involvement with them. Some of their attitudes were very, very negative . . . and it was kind of, 'oh yes, well, we tolerate them, but basically they're not as good as us, they don't really know God, because they don't know Jesus', and I felt very, very angered by that, because, you know, I really felt that there was a lot that we could learn from them in terms of prayer and devotion to their religion and carrying out their religious beliefs in their everyday life. And living in a way that's very true to their belief, right through every part of their lives. And I started to look, I suppose then, at my Catholicism, and my Christianity, but especially my Catholicism, in a . . . more questioning way. Probably for the first time, I really questioned it, because it had always been so natural . . . in all my surroundings, most of the people I knew were Catholic, a lot of the people I mixed with were very actively Catholic until this point, and it just hadn't been something I'd ever questioned . . . And I started to look at . . . these issues of people's attitudes toward specifically non-Christian religions, and I didn't like what I saw there.

Responding to doubt

The fourth theme focused on the way in which church-leavers had felt unable to discuss their religious doubts and questions about faith within their church. Some church-leavers said that they felt nobody in the church would understand their doubts. Some felt that their church did not really allow people to discuss or to disagree with the teaching it provided. Some found that a questioning faith was just not acceptable to their church. This point was made clearly, for example, by Matthew Williams, a freelance graphic designer in his forties, who had left a New Church congregation.

> You didn't dare make your own decisions really, that's where it went wrong . . . After leaving . . . I got my mind back, I was just thinking again, and I just started thinking through loads and loads of things, and at the time I kind of felt like . . . I had this image that I was going down, in a bucket, down a well, and I was just going down, and down, and down, and [Jesus] said to me, 'see how far you can go, and see if I'm still there', and I'm still going down. It's pretty petrifying sometimes . . . I haven't stopped believing, and sometimes I'm willing to question everything, but I think, I kind of somehow kind of feel unless you're willing to question anything you haven't any faith anyway . . . Faith has to be tried, otherwise it's not faith.

Listening to the statistics

A set of questions in the survey set out to examine how much church-leavers cited these four themes concerned with matters of belief and unbelief as implicated in their own experience of leaving church. An overview of the findings is presented in Table 5, in the Appendix.

From these data it is clear that loss of faith was instrumental in the process of disaffiliation for only one church-leaver in every three. While 32% said that they had left church as a consequence of losing faith, 50% were clear that this was not the reason and the remaining 19% were less certain about the sequence of events.

The doubting of faith played a bigger part in church-leaving than the loss of faith. While 32% of church-leavers explained their exodus from church as a consequence of losing their faith, the proportion rose to 43% who explained their exodus from church as a consequence of doubting and questioning their faith. An even larger proportion of church-leavers (49%) traced their exodus from church to a growing awareness that church had lost its meaning for them.

The important part that doubting and questioning faith plays in church-leaving needs to be read alongside the number of church-leavers who felt that their local church neither welcomed nor wished to deal with people who doubted their faith. Thus, one in six church-leavers (16%) felt that nobody in their church would have understood their doubts. One in four church-leavers (25%) felt that their church did not allow people to discuss or disagree with its views. Between one in four and one in three church-leavers (29%) felt that a questioning faith did not seem acceptable to their church.

The number of people who left church as a consequence of feeling that God had let them down was relatively small. Such a view was expressed by one church-leaver in every ten (10%). The problem of suffering played a bigger part in church-leaving, but it was the suffering of others rather than the suffering of self which was the more significant. One in seven church-leavers said that they could not reconcile their own suffering with belief in God (14%), while two in seven said that they could not reconcile the suffering of others with belief in God (29%).

For half of the church-leavers (53%), the religious interpretation of life had become challenged by their growing awareness of alternative ways of thinking or living. For two-thirds of church-leavers (66%), the religious interpretation of life had become challenged by their growing awareness that so many people fight each other in the name of religion. Clearly life experiences challenge faith and for some lead to church-leaving.

Problems with Christian doctrine and with aspects of the church's teaching played a part in disaffiliation for between two-thirds and one-half of church-leavers. Thus, 40% of church-leavers reported that they found many of the church's teachings illogical or nonsensical. Slightly more focused their problem with Christian doctrine in terms of the conflict between science and religion: 42% said that the church's teachings were difficult to reconcile with modern science. Even more found the real stumbling block to faith to be posed by the exclusivity claims: 48% said that it was increasingly difficult to believe that Christianity is the only true faith.

Sex differences

Matters of belief and unbelief played a more important part in the process of disengagement from church among men than among women. Statistically significant differences were found in the responses of men and women to 5 of the 14 questions in this section. The differences were these.

Men were significantly more likely than women to attribute their church-leaving to a loss of faith: 38% of the men reported that they had lost their faith, compared with 28% of the women. For men more than for women, loss of faith was likely to be stimulated by intellectual problems with Christian teaching. Thus, 49% of the men found that the church's teachings were difficult to reconcile with modern science, compared with 37% of the women. Similarly, 55% of the men found it increasingly difficult to believe Christianity is the only true faith, compared with 44% of the women. For men more than for women, church-leaving was likely to be stimulated by a growing awareness of alternative ways of thinking or living. Such awareness was cited by 58% of the men compared with 50% of the women.

Not only were men more likely than women to question their faith, they were also more likely than women to feel that their church discouraged such questioning. One-third of the men (34%) said that a questioning faith did not seem acceptable to their church, compared with one-quarter of the women (26%).

Generational differences

There were no significant differences between the three generational groups with respect to the part played by matters of belief and unbelief in their decision to disaffiliate from their church. For example, 31% of those under the age of forty said that they had lost their faith, and so did 30% of those in their forties and fifties and 35% of those aged sixty or over.

Cohort differences

Matters of belief and unbelief played a more important part in the decision to disengage from church among those who decided to leave church over twenty years ago than among those who decided to leave church within the past twenty years. Statistically significant differences were found in the responses of the two groups to 8 of the 14 questions in this section.

Over one-third of those who left church over twenty years ago (36%) linked their church-leaving to the fact that they lost their faith. The proportion fell to 28% among those who left church during the past twenty years. Similarly, over half of those who left church over twenty years ago (55%) linked their church-leaving to the fact that church had lost its meaning for them. The proportion fell to 45% among those who left church during the past twenty years.

Intellectual problems with their faith were more important to those who left church over twenty years ago. Nearly half of those who left church over twenty years ago (48%) had found their church's teachings difficult to reconcile with modern science. The proportion fell to 37% among those who left church during the past twenty years. Similarly, 44% of those who left church over twenty years ago felt that many of their church's teachings were illogical or nonsensical, compared with 37% of those who left within the past twenty years. Over half of those who left church over twenty years ago (55%) found it increasingly difficult to believe Christianity is the only true faith, compared with 43% of those who left within the past twenty years.

Those who left church over twenty years ago were more likely to have been influenced by alternative philosophies and lifestyles. Three-fifths of those who left over twenty years ago (59%) had become aware of alternative ways of thinking or living, compared with 50% of those who left within the past twenty years.

The argument that religion is the cause of human conflict and wars was more influential in disaffiliation over twenty years ago than it is today. Thus, 73% of those who left church over twenty years ago cited as influencing their disaffiliation the consideration that so many people fight each other in the name of religion, compared with 60% of those who left church within the past twenty years.

Age at leaving

Matters of belief and unbelief are much more important in the disaffiliation process among those who left church at a younger age than among those who left church at an older age. Statistically significant differences were found in the responses to 7 of the 14 questions in this section between those who left before the age of twenty, those who left in their twenties or thirties, and those who left at the age of forty or over.

Religious doubt and loss of faith were particularly important for those who disaffiliated before the age of twenty. Thus, 49% of those who left church before the age of twenty said that they doubted or questioned their faith, compared with 43% of those who left in their twenties or thirties and 20% of those who left at the age of forty or over. Similarly, 37% of those who left church before the age of twenty said that they lost their faith, compared with 32% of those who left in their twenties or thirties and 20% of those who left at the age of forty or over.

Loss of meaning was particularly important for those who disaffiliated before the age of twenty. Almost three-fifths (57%) of those who left church before the age of twenty said that church had lost its meaning for them, compared with 48% of those who left in their twenties or thirties and 37% of those who left at the age of forty or over.

Growing awareness of alternative life-styles and philosophies was also particularly important to those who disaffiliated before the age of twenty. Two-thirds (65%) of those who left church before the age of twenty said that they became aware of alternative ways of thinking or living, compared with 51% of those who left in their twenties or thirties and 33% of those who left at the age of forty or over.

Intellectual problems with the faith were more important earlier in life. Half of those who left church before the age of twenty (50%) found many of their church's teachings illogical or nonsensical, compared with 36% of those who left in their twenties or thirties and 28% of those who left at the age of forty or over. Half of those who left church before the age of twenty (52%) found their church's teachings difficult to reconcile with modern science, compared with 38% of those who left in their twenties or thirties and 28% of those who left at the age of forty or over. Over half of those who left church before the age of twenty (56%) found it increasingly difficult to believe Christianity to be the only true faith, compared with 46% of those who left in their twenties or thirties and 35% of those who left at the age of forty or over.

Denomination

Comparison between church-leavers within the three denominational categories employed in the analysis revealed that matters of belief and unbelief played a more important part in disaffiliation from the Roman Catholic Church than from the Anglican Church or the Free Churches. Statistically significant differences were found in the responses of the three groups to 4 of the 14 questions in this section.

The church was more likely to have lost its meaning for Roman Catholics than for members of the Anglican Church or of the Free Churches. Three-fifths of the Roman Catholics (61%) reported that church had lost its meaning for them, compared with 47% of Anglicans and 49% of Free Church members. Half of the Roman Catholics (51%) complained that many of the church's teachings were illogical or nonsensical, compared with 39% of Anglicans and 36% of Free Church members.

The Roman Catholics were also much more likely than the other denominational groups to feel that their church was unwilling to listen to them or to discuss their problems with the faith. Almost half of the Roman Catholics (47%) felt that their church did not allow people to discuss or disagree with its view, compared with 23% of Anglicans and 17% of Free Church members. Similarly, 44% of Roman Catholics felt that a questioning faith did not seem acceptable to their church, compared with 27% of Anglicans and 23% of Free Church members.

Sudden or gradual leaving

Matters of belief and unbelief were more likely to lead to sudden disengagement than to gradual disengagement. Of the 14 questions included in this section of the survey, 9 revealed significant differences between those who gradually drifted away from church and those who left church suddenly.

Two-fifths of those who left church suddenly (39%) said that they lost their faith, compared with one-quarter (25%) of those who left church gradually. Half of those who left church suddenly (49%) said that they doubted or questioned their faith, compared with 38% of those who left gradually. Similarly, 54% of those who left church suddenly said that church had lost its meaning for them, compared with 45% of those who left gradually.

Doubts about Christian doctrine and teaching seem to lead more to sudden leaving than to gradual leaving. Thus, 46% of those who left church suddenly had come to the view that many of their church's teachings were illogical or nonsensical, compared with 35% of those who left gradually; 46% of those who left church suddenly found their church's teachings difficult to reconcile with modern science, compared with 38% of those who left gradually; 54% of those who left church suddenly found it increasingly difficult to believe Christianity is the only true faith, compared with 43% of those who left gradually.

The discovery of alternative philosophies or life-styles seems to lead more to sudden leaving than to gradual leaving. Three-fifths of those who left church suddenly (59%) had become aware of alternative ways of thinking or living, compared with half of those who left gradually (49%).

The experience that their church wished neither to listen to doubts nor to accept doubters was also associated more with sudden leaving. Thus, 18% of those who left church suddenly felt that nobody in the church would understand their doubts, compared with 13% of those who left gradually. One-third of those who left suddenly (33%) felt that a questioning faith did not seem acceptable to the church, compared with one-quarter of those who left gradually (25%).

Likelihood of returning

Church-leavers who had disengaged on grounds concerning matters of belief and unbelief were much less likely to regard themselves as potential returners than as permanent disaffiliates. Of the 14 questions included in this section of the survey, 11 revealed significant differences between potential returners and permanent disaffiliates.

Those who have doubted or lost their faith do not easily antici- pate rediscovering it. Among the permanent disaffiliates, 43%

said that they had lost their faith, compared with 15% of the potential returners. Among the permanent disaffiliates, 51% said that they had doubted or questioned their faith, compared with 32% of the potential returners. Among the permanent disaffiliates, 61% said that church had lost its meaning for them, compared with 28% of the potential returners.

Intellectual problems with Christian doctrine and belief were likely to keep people more permanently at a distance from the church. Three-fifths of the permanent disaffiliates (60%) found it difficult to believe Christianity is the only true faith, compared with one-quarter of the potential returners (25%). Among the permanent disaffiliates, 53% had judged their church's teachings to be illogical and nonsensical, compared with 24% of the potential returners. Among the permanent disaffiliates, 53% had found their church's teachings difficult to reconcile with modern science, compared with 22% of the potential returners.

The discovery of alternative philosophies and life-styles was likely to keep more people permanently at a distance from the church. Thus, 64% of the permanent disaffiliates said that they had become aware of alternative ways of thinking or living, compared with 38% of the potential returners.

Those whose faith had been challenged by the evidence of religious conflicts were more likely to maintain their distance from the church. Thus, 71% of the permanent disaffiliates pointed to the way so many people fight each other in the name of religion, compared with 49% of the potential returners.

Those whose faith had been challenged by the suffering of others were more likely to maintain their distance from the church. Thus, 36% of the permanent disaffiliates said that they could not reconcile others' suffering with their belief in God, compared with 17% of the potential returners.

The permanent disaffiliates were also more likely to feel that their church did not welcome debate about the faith. Thus, 35% of the permanent disaffiliates took the view that a questioning faith did not seem acceptable to their church, compared with 16% of the potential returners. Similarly, 29% of the permanent disaffiliates considered that their church did not allow people to discuss or disagree with its views, compared with 17% of the potential returners.

Pastoral implications

This section of the survey makes it clear that religious doubt and loss of faith play an important part in turning a significant number of church-goers into church-leavers. As many as one in three of our sample pointed to loss of faith as a key reason for leaving the church. Matters of belief and unbelief play a more important part in the disaffiliation of men than of women, of those who leave early rather than later in life, and of Roman Catholics rather than Anglicans or members of the Free Churches. There is also evidence that matters of belief and unbelief have played a less important part in disaffiliation during the past twenty years than may previously have been the case.

Those who disengage as a consequence of matters of belief and unbelief are likely to drop out of church life suddenly rather than gradually. In this sense they may not give much warning to their local church that they are about to leave. Having left church as a consequence of matters of belief and unbelief, such church-leavers are less likely to contemplate becoming church-returners.

From the perspective of pastoral practice, it is particularly important for churches to recognise how many of these church-leavers felt that they were unable to discuss their mounting problems with Christian teaching within their churches. Churches that close the door on a questioning faith may well find that the questioners make for the exit and close the door firmly and finally as they leave.

Within the Christian spectrum some churches clearly place a

higher premium on orthodoxy and on right belief than others. Those more liberal churches that welcome an open and questioning faith may well be able to fulfil an important ministry among individual church-goers who are feeling uncomfortable in congregations that discourage questioning the faith and that discourage testing the traditions of the church. Some churches may need to make their theological openness better known within the local neighbourhood, and could with advantage promote opportunities to discuss and debate faith issues in an open way. The challenge facing those more conservative churches is to decide whether it is preferable for their questioning members to fall into the hands of liberal congregations or to fall away from church attendance altogether.

6

Growing up and changing

Setting the scene

People change and grow, not only during the early years of life but throughout the life span. As children grow and mature through adolescence into adulthood they generally move progressively further away from the control and influence of their parents. Many who move away from the parental home and set clear physical distance between themselves and the location of their parents may, nevertheless, remain conscious of the psychological bonds for years to come. The language used to describe 'mother church' provides a clue as to how some people relate to the church in ways not dissimilar from the ways in which children relate to their parents. As we listened to our interviewees we became particularly conscious of the ways in which some church-leavers spoke of their relationship with the church, either consciously or unconsciously, in terms reminiscent of relationships (and sometimes struggles) with parent figures. The aim of the present chapter, therefore, is to examine the extent to which church-leavers themselves explain their distance from the church in terms of growing up and changing. Listening to our interviewees, three main themes emerged within the broad area of growing up and changing. We described these themes as: growing up, parents and children, and accepting responsibilities.

Growing up

The first theme spoke in terms of growing up and needing to break away from constraints that inhibited their natural process of growth. Some church-leavers spoke quite directly in terms like, 'I grew up and started making decisions on my own'. Others expressed the same kind of resentment in a more negative way, arguing, for example, 'The church was no longer helping me to grow'. The interesting observation is that sentiments of this nature were invoked not only to explain church-leaving during the teenage years, but later in life as well. For example, Justin Wyatt, a vicar's son who had left an Anglican church, told us that his church-leaving was part of his wider quest to find his own identity.

> When I did leave, it was quite hard to admit to other people in the village set-up, and to say, 'I don't believe in God', or whatever, because I was worried of the comeback on my parents. But now I've got to the stage where if people ask me, then I'll tell them quite openly. I don't have any problems with it anymore . . . I think I'd grown up and realised that I had, I had to lead my own life, and that was it.

Telling her story of church-leaving, Sarah Johnson, a homemaker in her thirties who had left an Anglican church, explained how the church was no longer helping her to grow.

> When we took our confirmation classes, the teaching we received then was excellent, so we knew that you could get the teaching, and stuff like that, but there just didn't seem, I don't know, we just didn't get out of it what we needed. We weren't growing, we were, as we see it now, we were being virtually starved . . . It was easy being there in a way because it was somewhere we could go along, quite comfortably, on a Sunday

morning, sing a few hymns, say a few prayers, take the children into Sunday school, come home, that's it, that's church, done, nice little package on a Sunday morning. We weren't really living out a Christian life while we were there because, I think, it was basically too easy, we weren't being stretched, we weren't being made to grow up.

Telling a very different story of church-leaving, Matthew Williams, a freelance graphic designer in his forties who had left a New Church congregation, also spoke of the church as an obstacle in his personal development.

I don't know whether this was a necessary part of growing up, and now leaving it is also another part of growing up, because what happened in the end was that, in the end, you didn't do anything, you didn't get anywhere, you didn't dare make your own decisions really, that's where it went wrong in a way.

Parents and children

The second theme linked disaffiliation much more directly with childhood experiences and with parental control. Some church-leavers said things like this: 'I associated church-going with my childhood and outgrew it.' Others spoke with a somewhat more critical voice: 'I was made to go to church by my parents and it put me off.' Once again the interesting observation is that sentiments of this nature were invoked not only to explain church-leaving during the teenage years, but later in life as well. This point was made clearly by Sharon Chapman, who had left a Methodist church. She told us that she still felt very strongly about the way her parents had forced Sunday school on her as a child.

I didn't know any different in that way, when I was younger . . . [Even when we went on holiday] we had to find all the local churches on a Sunday . . . and myself and my brother were packed off to all different Sunday schools where you didn't know anyone. I didn't enjoy it at all, I felt it was sort of forced on us, and we could never get away. And moving [house] a lot, as well, it was the same thing. We moved house quite a lot, and every time, it was first of all the church, and 'in you go', and I felt I was sort of pushed from pillar to post, so, yes. But that's how I grew up, so at the time, I suppose, really, although I didn't like it, I didn't think it was unusual . . . I think really it was when I moved away from home . . . when I was seventeen [that I left church]. And I think I'd had it rammed down my throat so much, that I thought now I'm going to live my own life now, and I really drew away from it. I couldn't get there anyway, because I didn't have enough transport-wise to get there, and I'd always felt that it was [my parents'] church and not mine. So I'd been forced to go, and although I'd made friends there it was because it was what they wanted and not what I wanted . . . Although I believe, and I will go back to church, and I want to, I feel it was their life, and it was something they pushed me into, and I wanted to do it under my own accord. So maybe that's one of the reasons I don't go, because I feel it's almost as though I'm going back, and saying 'OK, you were right', and I don't think the way they did it was . . . I don't think the church could have done more, it was very relaxed, I enjoyed it, it was the way I was brought up by a church-going family that turned me away . . . the actual church itself did not drive me away, it was my parents.

A similar story was told by another one of our interviewees in the following way.

If it was a case where maybe we weren't forced into going to church every Sunday, I'd probably up to this day, would still go, because I can remember just going to church on a Sunday, and not being able to go out like the rest of the kids, unless it was something to do with the church . . . Maybe because I was dragged to church every Sunday, you know, after a while you get fed up, you know, you want to do your own thing, you're getting older, when you go to school with your colleagues, they're going, you know, to the cinema, or they're going to the zoo, or whatever, we were always in church . . . Because it was like, school, church on Sunday, school, church on Sunday, school, church on Sunday, and because I had three older brothers, they were always going out. My mum wouldn't let me go with them anywhere, because they were boys and I was the only girl, and it took the reverend to come to the house and have a word with my dad, and he basically said, 'look, just, you know, you could let her go out, you know, spend an hour with her friends', you know, and then, I did and then [laughter], I just stopped going to church after that, I got a bit of freedom, and then I just didn't feel like going to church anymore, you know.

Accepting responsibilities

The third theme simply linked disengagement from church with a natural process of growth and change without recourse to blaming either 'mother church' or parental influences. Some church-leavers spoke quite disarmingly in ways like this: 'I changed – it wasn't the church's fault that I dropped off.' Others saw church-going as a habit into which some people drift and from which other people drift away. Some church-leavers explained their disaffiliation in ways like this: 'I got out of the habit of going to church.' For example, Alison Matthews, a young social worker who had left a Roman Catholic church, pointed to a particular moment when she suddenly saw her church-going as a habit she needed to break.

116

As I sat through Mass, suddenly the idea that I couldn't carry on going to church in this regular way, hit me so suddenly, and I realised that for months I'd been going to church just out of habit, and it hadn't been, the experience of going to Mass and of being involved in all these areas of the parish life, just hadn't been meaning the same thing to me as it had a few years ago, and I really had just been going out of habit. And just like a flash, it was, it's very difficult to explain, in a moment I knew I had to stop going. And I didn't know whether it would be for a while, while I sorted myself out, or whether it was for good, and the idea did seem very painful to me, but I knew that I would have to stop going to Mass.

A similar kind of account was given by Peter Kendall, a TV producer who had left a Methodist church. Peter, too, spoke of his church attendance as no more than a habit, and it was a habit he managed to break.

I was brought up in the church, or I grew up in the church, almost without having the environmental context to question certain things that I questioned later. And, so, I mean, for example, I would be so involved in what the church was doing, as if it were right. And that was a social thing, because it wasn't really a spiritual thing. Looking back I don't think I was really a spiritually committed Christian, I think I came into it out of habit . . . I don't really think I believed in God in a very in-depth sense. I believed in God as a habit, I believed in God as a sort of thing that you did, and I would pray, and I would go to church, and I would occasionally get emotional about it, but I don't think it registered that deeply with me, I just think it happened . . . when the understanding came to me that it was a sham, I mean, I don't mean that God was a sham, but my perception of God was a sham, I think that was the real point [when I decided to leave].

Listening to the statistics

A set of questions included in the survey set out to examine how much church-leavers cited these three themes concerned with growing up and changing as implicated in their own experience of leaving church. An overview of the findings is presented in Table 6, in the Appendix.

The data made it clear that the very process of growing up was implicated in disengagement from church for at least one church-leaver in every two. Thus, 54% of church-leavers said that they grew up and started making decisions on their own. While 54% of church-leavers saw their disengagement from church as part of the process of growing up, only half this number (29%) left because the church was no longer helping them to grow.

There is a real danger that church-going may be modelled as an activity of childhood which it is appropriate to leave behind as part of the maturing process. Two church-leavers out of every five (39%) said that they associated church-going with their childhood and then outgrew it. One out of every four church-leavers (25%) claimed that the fact that parents made them go to church as a child was a contributory factor for disengagement from church.

A major insight from this section of the survey is that the majority of church-leavers accept responsibility themselves for disengagement from the church and are not concerned to blame the church. Thus, 64% said that they changed and that it was not the church's fault that they dropped off. A slightly higher proportion (69%) put it more simply and said that they got out of the habit of going to church.

Sex differences

The process of growing up played a more important part in disengagement from church in the lives of men than in the lives of women. While 50% of the women said that disengagement from church was associated with the fact that they grew up and started making decisions on their own, the proportion rose significantly to 61% among the men. While 35% of the women said that they associated church-going with their childhood and outgrew it, the proportion rose significantly to 43% among the men. There were no significant differences, however, between the responses of men and women to the other questions in this section.

Generational differences

The notion that church is something you grow out of as you grow up is much more prevalent among younger church-leavers. Thus, 64% of church-leavers under the age of forty said that their church-leaving was associated with growing up and starting to make decisions on their own, compared with 53% of those in their forties or fifties and 48% of those aged sixty or over. Similarly, 48% of church-leavers under the age of forty associated church-going with their childhood and outgrew it, compared with 37% of those in their forties or fifties and 31% of those aged sixty or over.

The resentment of being made to go to church by their parents is also more prevalent among younger church-leavers. While just 18% of church-leavers aged sixty or over complained that they were made to go to church by their parents and that put them off going to church, the proportions rose to 26% among those in their forties or fifties and to 32% among those under the age of forty.

On the other hand, the argument that the church was no longer helping them to grow was made by similar proportions of all three age groups: 32% of those under the age of forty, 29% of those in their forties or fifties and 28% of those aged sixty or over. The notion that the church was not to blame for their disengagement was also supported by similar proportions of all three age groups. Thus, 66% of those under forty, 63% of those in their forties or fifties and 64% of those aged sixty or over said that they had changed and that it was not the church's fault that they dropped off.

Cohort differences

Those who left church over twenty years ago were much more likely to have been influenced by factors concerned with growing up and changing than was the case among those who decided to leave church within the past twenty years. Two-thirds of those who left over twenty years ago said that they grew up and started making decisions on their own, compared with 44% of those who left in the past twenty years. Over two-fifths (44%) of those who left over twenty years ago said that they associated church-going with their childhood and outgrew it, compared with 34% of those who left in the past twenty years.

Those who left church over twenty years ago were more likely to have felt alienated by the way in which their parents had sent them or had taken them to church. Thus, 29% of those who left over twenty years ago complained that they were made to go to church by their parents and that this had put them off, compared with 23% of those who left in the past twenty years.

On the other hand, the argument that the church was no longer helping them to grow was made by similar proportions of both groups: 33% of those who had left over twenty years ago and 27% of those who left in the past twenty years. The notion that the church was not to blame for their disengagement was also supported by similar proportions of both groups. Thus, 67% of those who left over twenty years ago and 62% of those who left in the past twenty years said that they had changed and that it was not the church's fault that they had dropped off.

Age at leaving

Factors associated with growing up and changing are much more likely to be important in influencing church-leaving before the age of twenty than later in life. Four out of every five people (79%) who had left church before the age of twenty explained that this disengagement was part of the process of growing up and making decisions on their own, compared with 45% of those who left in their twenties or thirties and 23% of those who left after their fortieth birthday. Three out of every five people (60%) who had left church before the age of twenty said that they associated church-going with their childhood and outgrew it, compared with 28% of those who left in their twenties or thirties and 15% of those who left after their fortieth birthday.

Individuals who left church under the age of twenty were also more likely to feel that church was not helping them to grow. This argument was made by 36% of those who left under the age of twenty, compared with 25% of those who left in their twenties or thirties and 23% of those who left after their fortieth birthday.

Individuals who left church aged forty or over were more likely to see the church sharing responsibility for their decision. While 65% of those who left under the age of twenty and 69% of those who left in their twenties or thirties said that they had changed and that it was not the church's fault that they had dropped off, the proportion fell to 53% among those who left after their fortieth birthday. While 71% of those who left under the age of twenty and 73% of those who left in their twenties or thirties said that they had simply got out of the habit of going to church, the proportion fell to 61% among those who left church after their fortieth birthday.

Denomination

The influence of parents in the process of church-leaving differs significantly from one denomination to another. It is Roman Catholics who are most likely to associate their disengagement from church with reaction to parental pressure, and Anglicans who are least likely to do so. Thus, 35% of Roman Catholics said that they were made to go to church by their parents and that this put them off, compared with 31% of Free Church members and 22% of Anglicans.

In a similar way, Roman Catholics are more likely to associate leaving church with the general growing-up process. While 34% of Anglicans said that they associated church-going with their childhood and outgrew it, the proportions rose to 44% among Free Church members and to 48% among Roman Catholics. While 51% of Anglicans said that they grew up and started making decisions on their own, the proportions rose to 59% among Free Church members and to 64% among Roman Catholics. The feeling that the church was no longer helping them to grow was voiced by 36% of Roman Catholics, 28% of Anglicans and 26% of Free Church members.

On the other hand, similar proportions of all three denominational groups accepted full responsibility for their own disengagement from church. Nearly two-thirds of all three groups (64% of Free Church members, 64% of Roman Catholics and 64% of Anglicans) agreed that they had changed and that it was not the church's fault that they had dropped off.

Sudden or gradual leaving

Overall, issues concerned with growing up and changing were no more likely to lead to sudden disengagement than to gradual disengagement. Of the six questions in this section, just two distinguished between sudden and gradual disengagement. On the one hand, the notion of outgrowing childhood-related matters tended to be associated with sudden leaving. Thus, 43% of those who left church suddenly said that they had associated church-going with their childhood and outgrew it, compared with 36% of those who had left gradually. On the other hand, the notion of getting out of the habit of church-going tended to be associated with gradual leaving. Thus, 74% of those who left church gradually said that they had got out of the habit of going to church, compared with 65% of those who left church suddenly.

Likelihood of returning

Church-leavers who had disengaged on grounds concerning growing up and changing were much less likely to regard themselves as potential returners than as permanent disaffiliates. Among the permanent disaffiliates, 68% associated their church-leaving with growing up and making decisions on their own, compared with 33% of the potential returners. Among the permanent disaffiliates, 48% associated their church-leaving with deciding that the church was no longer helping them to grow, compared with 20% of the potential returners.

Among the permanent disaffiliates, 48% said that they had associated church-going with their childhood and that they had outgrown it, compared with 20% of the potential returners. Among the permanent disaffiliates, 33% had been made to go to church by their parents and that had put them off, compared with 10% of the potential returners.

On the other hand, those who explain their church-leaving in terms of simply getting out of the habit were more likely to regard themselves as potential returners rather than as permanent disaffiliates. Thus, 78% of the potential returners explained their church-leaving in terms of getting out of the habit of church-going, compared with 63% of the permanent disaffiliates.

Pastoral implications

This section of the survey makes it clear that two out of every five church-leavers conceptualise their disengagement from church as part of the process of growing up and that one out of every four go so far as to say that being made to go to church as a child really served to put them off. This reason for leaving church is more prevalent among men than among women, is stronger among those under forty than over sixty, and is stronger among those who left church before the age of twenty. This reason for church-leaving is stronger among Roman Catholics than among Anglicans.

Those who disengage as a consequence of growing up and changing are likely to drop out of church suddenly rather than gradually. In this sense they may not give much warning to their local church that they are about to leave. Having left church as a consequence of growing up and changing, such church-leavers are less likely to contemplate becoming church-returners.

From the perspective of pastoral practice, it is particularly important for churches to recognise the long-term implications of the priority which they give (or fail to give) to ministry among children and young people. On the one hand, churches may be pleased to see parents bringing or sending their children to worship services or to Sunday school. On the other hand, unless the quality of pastoral care, the quality of faith formation, and the quality of worship experience are appropriate to engage and to develop the young person, it seems that bringing the child into the church can serve as an inoculation for life against future church attendance.

Churches could also consider running parenting programmes to offer support to those new to parenting or to those who are finding being a parent, especially of teenagers, challenging. This could, for instance, help prevent parents from being over zealous about encouraging their children to go to church, and help them recognise that children ultimately need to make their own choices, especially once they become adolescents. The Mothers' Union runs programmes to train people to lead and facilitate parenting groups (see http://www.themothersunion.org/parenting.aspx), as does the Family Caring Trust (see http://www.familycaring. co.uk/training.htm).

Effective ministry among children and young people requires high levels of resourcing and high levels of professional formation for the dedicated volunteer workers and ministers to whom such work is often committed. Churches and denominations that fail to recognise the opportunities and responsibilities in this area may be generating further problems for the future.

7

Life transitions and life changes

Setting the scene

For many regular church-goers their pattern of church attendance becomes part of a wider pattern or wider routine of life. In this sense church-going becomes an integral component of their way of life. When something happens to disturb or to disrupt their established way of life, their relationship with the church may be caught up in the wider process. Indeed, some previous research has suggested that at least one-third of church-leavers partly attributed their disengagement to 'life changes' and to 'contextual' reasons of this sort (Albrecht, Cornwall and Cunningham, 1988: 68). According to Bruce (1996: 90), change will tend to make for the disengagement especially of 'those whose commitment is too weak to survive the need for change'. The aim of the present chapter, therefore, is to examine the extent to which church-leavers themselves explain their distance from the church in terms of life transitions and life changes. Listening to interviewees, four main themes emerged within the broad area of life transitions and life changes. We described these themes as: going away from home, moving to a new area, growing family commitments, and changing status.

Going away from home

The first theme focused on the general experience of young people growing up and leaving the family nest of their childhood. Some church-leavers simply said that they had left the family home and had drifted away from church at the same time. Others said that they had moved away from the family home to go to college or to university and that they had drifted away from the church as part of that major life transition. For example, leaving the home was at the heart of Siobhan's reason for leaving church, as a young Roman Catholic from Northern Ireland.

> Once people get out of their own homes, they just want to do things certain ways, you know, just differently. So, I think, at least for a while, people stop going, just to get used to something different, because it's not expected of them, they have the right to do whatever they want, whenever they feel. But I think it's just more or less half and half, I know a lot of people who have gone to university, and haven't continued to like believe the way they have when they were at home. But at the same time there's a good amount that still go . . . some people just stop going, at least for a while, and they will return to it. But at the same time, I think, once you get a taste for not going, it just feels strange to actually go back to that again.

Moving to a new area

The second theme focused on moving home somewhat later in life. A number of our interviewees explained their church-leaving by saying simply 'I moved house'. The disruption of the move itself was enough to disturb and to terminate their pattern of church-going. Indeed, it never occurred to some of them to try to find a new church in their new area. Others, however, when they moved to a new area tried to settle into a new church, but failed to find a church that they liked or where they felt at home. One

127

perspective on the impact of moving home was given by Alison Matthews, a young woman in her twenties who had left a Roman Catholic church.

It was quite a shock to me, to the system really, moving back up to N [after finishing college], and I started going back to the parish that I'd been going to as a child and a teenager, and basically it was a shock not sort of living very, very close to my place of worship and being able to pop in any time, day or evening, that I wanted to, and so I wasn't, you know, just for practical reasons, I wasn't going as often as I used to.

Another of our interviewees, Justine Sullivan, a young teacher who had left an Anglican church, talked about the difficulties that a mobile young person faces in settling into local church life.

I think moving around didn't help, we'd done so much moving around that each time we had to get to know a new congregation, or find the right church for you, or where you're sort of meant to be, it kind of, you lose the continuity that's important in relationships.

Kate White, a computer analyst, told us about her experience of failing to be welcomed into membership of a new church after moving house.

We decided we wanted to find a church in the area, so we looked around a bit. We were driving past this [Baptist] church on a Sunday afternoon and it was like people coming in and out, and lots of activity, and we thought, 'that seems like a good place to go in', and we went there once and we thought, 'that's where God's telling us to go', so we went back the next week and said, 'we want to become members'. And we filled in a form and did all that stuff, and then three months later we said to the minister that we wanted to become members, and he said, 'well, how can you? You don't know anyone, you've not been here very long.' We said, 'well, we think God wants us to be here'. But he said, 'oh, no, I don't think so'. It was like we were just sort of, we were unsuitable.

Growing family commitments

The third theme focused on the ways in which growing family commitments may interfere with allegiance to church. Some of our interviewees spoke in fairly general terms about how their church-leaving was prompted by what they described as 'growing family commitments'. A major commitment comes, for example, with the role of carer. At one end of life, parents are experiencing all sorts of demands from their children growing up in a mobile society. Some parents said simply, 'my children needed me to provide transport on Sunday.' At the other end of life, the middle-aged are experiencing the need to give time to their own ageing parents, who often may live at some distance. Some of our interviewees said, 'I needed to visit my (or my spouse's) parents on Sundays.' This perception of the impact of family commitments on church attendance was well expressed by John Ingram, one of the Anglican vicars whom we interviewed to find out their perceptions of church-leaving.

There are more and more things that you can do on a Sunday these days, other than go to church. And people who are a little bit on the edge of things don't really need a tremendous excuse not to come to church. And if they have to visit, or if they have to decorate, or if they have to shop, then they will do that . . . Certainly around here, there is tremendous pressure on Sundays, because if people are working, then they are working all the time, and Sunday is frequently the only day they have to do anything, other than work. And I think that is a very serious problem. And as the children grow up, there's opportunities for the kids to go and play football, or gymnastics, or dancing, or horse riding, all of which happens on a Sunday . . . For example, we have a number of young families on the fringe of church membership. We might only see them once every six weeks or so, but they are recognisably members of the congregation. And what happens in fact is one Sunday they visit his parents, and the following Sunday they visit her parents, and then the third Sunday they might well come to church. But if they've got two young children, one of the children might be ill, so they don't come on that Sunday, and then the next Sunday they visit his parents again, and then they visit her parents, and then they might then come to church.

Another view on the pressures placed on Sunday by family commitments was voiced by Gareth Wilkinson, a businessman in his forties who had left a Methodist church.

My children are all active in their own interests, and, you know, unfortunately a lot of those interests are available on a Sunday, and only available on a Sunday, you know, like the boys playing cricket, that is Sunday morning . . . The pressure on the time is particularly acute, you know, if you have children. I will often go Sunday evening to a Friday evening and not see my children. I'll be sleeping in the same house as them, but I will often get back from work after they have gone to sleep, and leave before, always leave before, they wake up. I mean, in that I'm not unusual . . . but what it means for me, and for many others, is that the hours that are available at the weekend are the subject of lots of pressure and lots of contention.

Changing status

The fourth theme focused on what can best be described as the changing status of the individual himself or herself along life's journey. For some their church-leaving was associated with marriage break-up. For some their church-leaving was associated with the onset of illness. For some their church-leaving was associated with bereavement, especially with the loss of a spouse and the need to adjust to a different life-style after bereavement. A teenager interviewed at the MAYC annual national event provided a helpful insight into how illness had disrupted his grandmother's attendance at church.

[My Gran] couldn't really get there, she wasn't very mobile, and she'd just had a stroke as well. She hasn't recovered. I think she misses [church] a lot. She tries but I don't think she can really get there.

Sarah Johnson, who had left an Anglican church, pointed to the death of her mother as pivotal to her church-leaving.

I always felt that there should be more to church than I was getting, and when, I think the start, the realisation of it all came when my Mum died, and because she'd been there always at the church, had worked at the Sunday school for as long as I could remember, and when she died I thought, you know, my world fell apart, but I thought at least I'll get the support of the church, the church will be there for me, the church will uphold my family through this, and we didn't get what we wanted, we didn't get the support, we didn't get help that we needed, and that came like an extra, like a double blow at that time, and that's when, I think, we came to the realisation that this really wasn't right.

Matthew Williams, a freelance graphic designer in his forties who had left a New Church congregation, pointed to the death of his father as somehow bound up with his church-leaving.

I suddenly realised how incredibly angry I was, and I was telling people who had left this story [of receiving incompetent counselling], I suddenly realised that I couldn't carry on in the church with this history, which had made me so unhappy for so long, and I just became incredibly unhappy, what with trying to deal with the grief of my father dying, it was all kind of bound up, and that's how I kind of left.

Listening to the statistics

A set of questions included in the survey set out to examine how much church-leavers cited these four themes concerned with life transitions and life changes as implicated in their own experience of leaving church. An overview of the findings is presented in Table 7, in the Appendix.

From these data it is clear that moving to a new area is implicated in disengagement from church for one in every three church-leavers. Thus, 33% said that a factor involved in their church-leaving was moving to a new area. For 27% of church-leavers the impetus came at the time when they left home, and for 16% this was specifically associated with moving into higher education. One of the real problems about moving into a new area is settling into a new church which feels right and appropriate at the time. One in six church-leavers (16%) specifically said that they moved home and that they failed to find a church they liked in their new area.

Increased family commitments ranked alongside moving home as an equally powerful factor leading to disengagement from church. One in three church-leavers (33%) said that a factor involved in their church-leaving was that they had increased family commitments. For some, such family commitments included caring for children, while for others they included caring for elderly parents. Thus, 7% said that their children needed them to provide transport on Sundays, while 11% said that they needed to visit their (or their spouse's) parents on Sunday.

Another kind of major change in life that can impact church-going and church-leaving concerns changing personal status. For 10% of church-leavers the experience of bereavement had been implicated in the process, for 8% the change of status involved divorce and for 7% the change of status involved illness.

Sex differences

Life transitions and changes played a somewhat more important part in the path to disengagement from church among women than among men. Statistically significant differences were found in the responses of men and women to three of the issues explored in this section. The differences were these.

First, while men and women were equally likely to say that moving to a new area, leaving home or going away to higher education played a part in their disengagement from church, women were significantly more likely than men to have experienced problems in finding a church that they liked in their new area. Thus, 20% of the women said that they moved and did not find a church that they liked in their new area.

Second, women were significantly more likely than men to cite increased family commitments as being implicated in their disengagement from church. This reason was cited by 40% of the women, compared with 23% of the men. In particular, women were more likely than men to be distracted from church-going by the demands made by children. While just 4% of the men said that their children needed them to provide transport on Sundays, the proportion doubled to 9% among the women.

Third, women were significantly more likely than men to cite bereavement as a factor interrupting their pattern of church-going. Twice as many women as men (12% compared with 6%) noted bereavement as a factor in their disengagement from

133

church. This finding is consistent with the fact that the life expectancy for women is significantly longer than for men.

Generational differences

Moving to a new area and then not finding a new church has played a steady role in contributing to church-leaving across the three generational groups analysed in this study. Thus, 33% of those under the age of forty traced their disengagement from church to moving to a new area, and so did 33% of those in their forties or fifties and 34% of those aged sixty or over. What really changes, however, is the role of higher education in this process of disruption. Among those aged sixty or over, just 6% associated their church-leaving with moving away to higher education, but the proportions rose to 16% among those in their forties or fifties, and to 27% among those under the age of forty. In other words, the expansion of higher education opportunities over the past decades has carried new implications for the churches.

The role played by increased family commitments in church-leaving is understandably higher later in life. While 23% of those under the age of forty identified the part played by increased family commitments in their disengagement from church, the proportions rose to 38% among those in their forties or fifties, and to 36% among those aged sixty or over.

The significance of illness and bereavement in church-leaving also increased with age. While just 3% of those aged under forty associated illness with their disengagement from church, the proportions rose to 7% among those in their forties or fifties and to 12% among those aged sixty or over. While just 5% of those aged under forty associated bereavement with their disengagement from church, the proportions rose to 9% among those in their forties or fifties and to 15% among those aged sixty or over.

Cohort differences

Life transitions and changes, overall, played similar roles in church-leaving among those who decided to leave church over twenty years ago and among those who decided to leave church within the past twenty years. For example, moving to a new area was implicated in disengagement from church for 34% of those who left within the past twenty years, and for 32% of those who left over twenty years ago. Marriage break-up was implicated in disengagement from church for 10% of those who left within the past twenty years, and for 7% of those who left over twenty years ago.

Age at leaving

Life transitions and life changes are implicated in different ways according to the age at which church-leaving takes place. Going away from home and entering higher education has its greatest effect on church-leaving before the age of twenty. Thus, 22% of those who left church before their twentieth birthday cited going to higher education as a significant factor in their disengagement from church, compared with 15% of those who left church in their twenties or thirties and 6% of those who left church aged forty or over.

Moving to a new area has its greatest effect on church-leaving during the twenties and thirties. Thus, 42% of those who left church in their twenties or thirties associated leaving church with moving house, compared with 27% of those who left before their twentieth birthday and 31% who left after their fortieth birthday. Similarly, 24% of those who left church in their twenties or thirties said that they moved home and did not find a church that they liked in their new area, compared with 9% of those who left before their twentieth birthday and 15% of those who left after their fortieth birthday.

135

Growing family commitments also has its greatest effect on church-leaving during the twenties and thirties. Thus, 43% of those who left church in their twenties or thirties associated leaving church with increased family commitments, compared with 23% of those who left before their twentieth birthday and 37% of those who left after their fortieth birthday.

Changing status has its greatest effect on church-leaving after the fortieth birthday. Thus, 14% of those who left church after their fortieth birthday associated leaving church with marriage break-up, compared with 9% of those who left in their twenties or thirties and 5% of those who left before their twentieth birthday. Similarly, 17% of those who left church after their fortieth birthday associated leaving church with illness, compared with 7% of those who left in their twenties or thirties and 3% of those who left before their twentieth birthday. Following the same trend, 17% of those who left church after their fortieth birthday associated leaving church with bereavement, compared with 11% of those who left in their twenties or thirties and 6% of those who left before their twentieth birthday.

Denomination

Moving to a new area was less disruptive of church-going for Roman Catholics than for Anglicans or members of the Free Churches. While 36% of Anglicans and 32% of Free Church members associated their church-leaving with moving to a new area, the proportion dropped to 26% among Roman Catholics. While 18% of Anglicans and 16% of Free Church members said that they moved home and did not find a church that they liked, the proportion fell to 7% among Roman Catholics. This denominational difference may be consistent with Catholic teaching on the objective importance of receiving the sacrament at Mass and the consequent lowering of emphasis on the subjective identity with a specific congregation.

Growing family commitments were also less likely to be associated with disruption of church-going for Roman Catholics than for Anglicans or members of the Free Churches. While 37% of Anglicans and 33% of Free Church members associated their church-leaving with increased family commitments, the proportion fell to 21% among Roman Catholics. This denominational difference may be consistent with the view that attending Mass is part of those family commitments. On the other hand, there were no significant differences in the impact of changing status on disengagement from church among the three denominational groups. Marriage break-up, illness and bereavement accounted for similar levels of church-leaving among Roman Catholics, Anglicans and Free Church members.

Sudden or gradual leaving

Some life transitions and life changes were more likely to lead to sudden leaving rather than to gradual leaving. In particular, there were higher proportions among the sudden leavers of those who associated their church-leaving with going away from home or going away to higher education. Thus, 31% of those who left church suddenly associated their disengagement from church with leaving home, compared with 21% of those who had left gradually. Similarly, 19% of those who left church suddenly associated their disengagement from church with going away to higher education, compared with 13% of those who had left gradually.

Other life transitions and life changes were more likely to lead to gradual leaving rather than to sudden leaving. In particular, there were higher proportions among the gradual leavers of those who associated their church-leaving with growing family commitments. Thus, 39% of those who left church gradually associated their disengagement from church with increased family commitments, compared with 28% of those who had left

137

suddenly. Similarly, 9% of those who left church gradually associated their disengagement from church with their children needing transport on Sundays, compared with 5% of those who had left suddenly.

Likelihood of returning

Overall, church-leavers who had disengaged on grounds concerning life transitions and life changes were more likely to regard themselves as potential returners rather than as permanent disaffiliates. Of the ten questions included in this section of the survey, five revealed significant differences between potential returners and permanent disaffiliates. Individuals who had left church through moving to a new area, through growing family commitments or through illness were likely to be among the potential returners.

Among the potential returners, 53% had left church on moving to a new area, compared with 28% among the permanent disaffiliates. Among the potential returners, 38% said that they had moved home and did not find a church they liked in their new area, compared with 11% among the permanent disaffiliates.

Among the potential returners, 41% had left church on facing increased family commitments, compared with 26% among the permanent disaffiliates. Among the potential returners, 9% had left church on responding to the transport needs of their children, compared with 4% among the permanent disaffiliates.

Among the potential returners, 14% had left church through illness, compared with 6% among the permanent disaffiliates.

Pastoral implications

This section makes it clear that one in every three church-leavers found that moving to a new area was significantly implicated in their disengagement from church. A number of these church-leavers had tried to find a church in their new area, but had failed to settle down in the new congregation. For such people church-leaving had tended to be sudden.

In many ways such people have become church-leavers almost by accident rather than by active decision. From the perspective of pastoral practice, there are two key lessons that can be learned. First, there is a lesson for those congregations aware of members moving to a new area. More care could be taken to make commendation to churches in the area to which they are moving. This may be particularly important in respect of young members who are moving away from home for the first time, say into higher education. Second, churches need to think carefully about ways of welcoming newcomers to the area (wherever this still remains possible). Human contact within the early days of arriving within a new community may determine whether or not newcomers explore (and feel welcome within) the churches in their new neighbourhood.

This section also makes it clear that one in every three church-leavers found that growing family commitments were significantly implicated in their disengagement from church. Such commitments can take a number of forms, including the demands of growing children and the demands of ageing parents. For such people church-leaving had tended to be gradual. This reason for church-leaving was more prominent among women, and less prominent among Roman Catholics. Such people may have become church-leavers more by accident than by active choice. From the perspective of pastoral practice, unobtrusive observation of the gradual process of disengagement could be very helpful. There may be alternative strategies that could help meet the growing family commitments rather than such radical disengagement from church life. There may be ways in which the local church can signal its recognition of the need for partial disengagement and find ways of helping such individuals continue to stay in touch with the congregation more easily than they had imagined.

Finally, this section demonstrates how church-leavers who disengage for reasons concerning life transitions and life changes are among those who are more likely to become church-returners. Here are people who may well welcome opportunities like 'Back to Church Sunday' as a way of re-establishing a pattern of life that they probably never consciously decided to abandon in the first place.

'Back to Church Sunday', pioneered by the Anglican Diocese of Manchester, has already shown some success in providing opportunities for potential church-returners to explore re-engagement with local church life.

8

Alternative lives and alternative meanings

Setting the scene

The majority of church-goers clearly have lives outside the church as well as inside the church, and the constraints, pressures and demands of those 'alternative lives' are also subject to change and to fluctuation. For example, the study reported by Gallup (1988: 45) drew attention to the fact that one in eight church-leavers in the United States of America claimed that their 'work schedule' was a factor in their disengagement from church. Other studies point more specifically to Sunday working as a factor underlying church-leaving. Work, however, is only one of the 'alternative lives' which may interfere with church attendance. The aim of the present chapter, therefore, is to examine the extent to which church-leavers themselves explain their distance from the church in terms of alternative lives and alternative meanings. Listening to our interviewees, three main themes emerged within the broad area of alternative lives and alternative meanings. We describe these themes as: tensions with work, tensions with relationships, and tensions with time.

Tensions with work

The first theme focused on tensions that are generated between commitment to church and the realm of work. Some of our interviewees said that their work schedule interfered with attendance at church. Others said simply that they could not get to church services because they had to work on Sundays. An interesting account of how the work schedule of someone working for an international company can affect commitment to church was provided by Gareth Wilkinson, a businessman in his forties and a lapsed Methodist.

I work [for an American Corporation], so I typically go to the States, once or twice a month, that's where I report to, New York, and I often travel on weekends. The company I work for is Jewish, so it has a particular disrespect for Sundays, so I often spend Sundays on aeroplanes to New York, and for the same reason I often spend Friday night on the way back, so of course they defend Saturday, not Sunday.

The Revd Adrian Dickinson, a Methodist minister, asked for his perceptions of why people leave church, pointed to Sunday employment as a major reason among students.

Having been a chaplain for ten years, you see . . . students depending on the loans, but also increasingly seeking part-time work to finance their way through college. And I suspect that with the growth of opportunities for Sunday work, a lot of the students will have taken that.

A Methodist teenager, interviewed at a MAYC national event, told us how he drifted from church after getting a Sunday job.

I started working on a Sunday morning, so I sort of drifted away, and I haven't really been back since . . . I want to get involved again. I mean, it was basically because I got a job on a Sunday morning. But I do want to get back in.

Tensions with relationships

The second theme focused on tensions that are generated between commitment to church and the realm of personal relationships. For some church-leavers the close personal relationship simply takes a higher priority than church attendance. Thinking back as to what triggered their departure from church, some of our interviewees recognised that, since their partner was not attending church, they too lost touch with church-going. Others found that their church-going became a cause for tension with their partner, and leaving church became a way of resolving that tension. For example, Dorothy King, a lapsed Anglican in her seventies, pointed to her marriage at a young age as the decisive factor in leaving church.

> I got married, out in the country actually it was. It was wartime and it was a little village church, which was very nice. But my husband was not a church-goer, you know. He was in the RAF, and I think, like a lot of them, he used to go to parade and that sort of thing, but he always said he was an atheist. I started my children saying prayers, my first one, you know, but then I got self-conscious about it, I think, because he didn't believe in it, and then I'm afraid I sort of stopped in the end . . . I had drifted away from [going to church] a little bit beforehand . . . and then when I met Bert, well, I just, it gradually dropped off altogether, I'm afraid. I was only eighteen when I met him, and I had my first child when I was twenty . . . I suppose I was very young, and, you know, I just followed him really.

The Revd Elsie Brooks, a Methodist minister, with a large block of retirement housing near her church, pointed to the influence of non-church-going partners on the church attendance of their spouses.

143

A lot of the people who have come into the retirement flats, a lot of them are lapsed something or other, you know they used to be involved with churches when they were younger, and they were brought up, but then when they got married and had a family, or whatever, and they moved away, and their husband wasn't particularly interested, their church-going lapsed.

Tensions with time

The third theme focused on tensions that are generated between commitment to church and other demands that are made on time. Some of our interviewees said that they were influenced by their friends and by how their friends spent leisure time; and they found that most of their friends were not church-goers. Some of our interviewees said that they had found other interests and activities. A common cry made by some in today's world is that they had simply become far too busy to find time for church. Some felt that going to church had just become too unfashionable to take seriously. Suzanne, a student, told us how Sunday became the only day when she could have time to herself in a busy life.

Sunday was my wee day off. I used to work, like, every Monday to Friday at school, Saturday I had to go to music, I was up at half eight on Saturday mornings. So suddenly I was able to lie in. I . . . think a lot of it is that little thing of having to go on Sunday, it is not something which is totally important to the faith. OK, I know it would be nice for church numbers, and the fact that the church won't close down, if we don't all suddenly decide not to go when we become sixteen. But I like to make it more individual than thinking I had to turn up, and also often to turn up for the choir all the time, I was working for exams, and I couldn't afford to go every Wednesday and Friday to choir practice.

Reflecting later in life, Peter Kendall, a TV producer in his forties who had left a Methodist church, also pointed to the mid-teen years as the point when life began to fill up with things beyond the local church.

It was [when I was] fifteen, and being a teenager, and becoming interested in things outside of the church, one being girls, obviously. And I remember once, when we were at the youth club, we had a ballroom dancing class. And, it was only a one-off, but I thought it was great, and went and got formal classes, and I started going dancing. And that took me into a social circle, if you like, that was outside. But more importantly, at fifteen, it was the General Election, and I got involved locally with the Labour Party and I became secretary of the Young Socialists, and got very active, and that gave me another social focal point, outside of the church. And also an ideological point outside of the church. The church really had given me my only ideology, up until that point. And at fifteen I began, therefore, to compare and contrast.

Justin Wyatt, a student who had left an Anglican church, told us how he had found other more interesting things to do on Sundays.

Every Sunday I would wake up and think, 'oh, I've got to go to church again', and I could always think of a lot better things to do with my time. I now coach five-a-side football on a Sunday, and would have liked to have got involved in that a lot earlier. Or, you know, go out for a walk, or listen to music. I didn't get any benefits from going to church, or I didn't feel any benefits, whereas if I got to spend time with people, or go for a walk, I found it much more productive.

145

Listening to the statistics

A set of questions included in the survey set out to examine how much church-leavers cited these three themes concerned with alternative lives and alternative meanings as implicated in their own experience of leaving church. An overview of the findings is presented in Table 8, in the Appendix.

From these data it is clear that alternative lives and alternative meanings have played a very important part in disengagement from church. Three out of every five church-leavers (59%) said simply that they had found other interests and activities. One out of every two church-leavers (52%) put the matter quite simply by saying that they were just too busy.

Other interests and other activities often generate a new circle of friends and companions, and such networks may not be supportive of church-going. Nearly one out of every two church-leavers (46%) pointed to the power of the peer group and associated their disengagement from church with the fact that most of their friends were not church-goers. A much smaller number, however, chose to express their disengagement from church in terms of fashionability. Just 14% of church-leavers said that they felt church-going was unfashionable.

While friends have a clear influence on patterns of church-going, partners may be highly significant as well. One in three church-leavers (32%) associated their disengagement from church with the fact that their partner was not attending church. A very much smaller proportion, however, considered that their church-going was actually causing tensions with their partner (5%).

The conflict between work and church attendance was cited by around one in every four church-leavers as implicated in their disengagement from church. Thus, 28% said that their work schedule interfered with attendance at church, while 25% said more specifically that they had to work on Sundays.

Sex differences

In many ways alternative lives and alternative meanings played a similar role on the path to disengagement from church among men and among women. First, there were no statistically significant differences in the proportions of men and women who considered that tensions with work were associated with their disengagement from church. Thus, 26% of the men said that their work schedule interfered with attendance at church, and so did 27% of the women. Second, there were no statistically significant differences in the proportions of men and women who considered that tensions with time were associated with their disengagement from church. Three out of every five men (61%) had found other interests and so had three out of every five women (57%).

On the other hand, tensions with relationships played a more significant role in church-leaving among women than among men. Twice as many women as men associated their disengagement from church with the fact that their partner was not attending church (40% compared with 21%). Twice as many women as men went further to say that their church-going was causing tension with their partner (7% compared with 3%).

While tensions with relationships played a more significant role in church-leaving among women than among men, tensions with fashionableness played a more significant role among men than among women. Thus, 17% of the men had felt that church-going was unfashionable, compared with 10% of the women. This finding is consistent with the general view that church congregations comprise a considerably higher proportion of women than of men and that as a consequence men may tend to feel somewhat 'out of place' and somewhat 'less at home'.

Generational differences

Tensions with work and tensions with relationships have played a steady role in contributing to church-leaving across the three generational groups analysed in this study. For example, in terms of tensions with work, 26% of those under the age of forty linked their disengagement from church with having to work on Sundays, and so did 23% of those in their forties or fifties and 24% of those aged sixty or over. In terms of tensions with relationships, 30% of those under the age of forty linked their disengagement from church with the fact that their partners were not attending church, and so did 35% of those in their forties or fifties and 31% of those aged sixty or over.

Tensions with time, however, were significantly more likely to be cited by the youngest age group. While 43% of those aged sixty or over said simply that they were too busy to attend church, the proportions rose to 53% of those in their forties or fifties and to 58% of those under the age of forty. While 50% of those aged sixty or over had found other interests or activities, the proportions rose to 60% among those in their forties or fifties and to 65% of those under the age of forty.

The importance of fashionableness also played a more prominent role in church-leaving among the youngest age group. While 8% of those aged sixty or over had felt that church-going was unfashionable, the proportions rose to 14% among those in their forties and fifties, and to 19% among those under the age of forty.

Cohort differences

Alternative lives and alternative meanings, overall, played similar roles in church-leaving among those who decided to leave church over twenty years ago and among those who decided to leave church within the past twenty years, except in respect of one important difference. The pressures generated by work have increased in significance over the past twenty years. While one in every four church-leavers (24%) who left over twenty years ago had found that their work schedule interfered with attendance at church, the proportion rose to one in every three church-leavers (31%) who left within the past twenty years.

Age at leaving

Alternative lives and alternative meanings are implicated in different ways according to the age at which church-leaving takes place.

Tensions with work were least likely to be cited by those who left church before the age of twenty. One in every five people who left church before their twentieth birthday (21%) complained that their work schedule interfered with attendance at church, compared with 33% of those who left church in their twenties or thirties and 30% of those who left church aged forty or over.

Tensions with relationships were most likely to be cited by those who left church in their twenties or thirties. Nearly two out of every five people who left church in their twenties or thirties (38%) complained that their partner was not attending church, compared with 28% of those who left church before their twentieth birthday and 30% of those who left church aged forty or over.

Tensions with time were least likely to be cited by those who left church aged forty or over. While 40% of those who had left church aged forty or over complained that they were too busy, the proportions rose to 56% among those who left in their twenties or thirties, and to 53% of those who left before their twentieth birthday. While 36% of those who had left church aged forty or over complained that most of their friends were not church-goers, the proportions rose to 49% of those who left in their twenties or thirties, and to 50% of those who left before their twentieth birthday.

149

Denomination

Tensions with work and tensions with relationships have similar impact on disengagement from church across all three denominational groups. In terms of tensions with work, 27% of Free Church members, 26% of Roman Catholics and 23% of Anglicans associated their church-leaving with having to work on Sundays. In terms of tensions with relationships, 33% of Free Church members, 31% of Roman Catholics and 32% of Anglicans associated their church-leaving with the fact that their partner was not attending church.

On the other hand, tensions with time were significantly less likely to be cited by Roman Catholic church-leavers. While 62% of Free Church members and 59% of Anglicans said that they found other interests and activities, the proportion fell to 47% of Roman Catholics. While 45% of Free Church members and 56% of Anglicans said that they were too busy, the proportion fell to 38% among Roman Catholics. While 51% of Free Church members and 49% of Anglicans said that most of their friends were not church-goers, the proportion fell to 31% among Roman Catholics. Such significant differences point to distinctiveness in the culture and commitment within the Roman Catholic Church.

Sudden or gradual leaving

Alternative lives and alternative meanings were equally likely to be cited by those whose disengagement from church was sudden and by those whose disengagement from church was gradual.

Likelihood of returning

Those individuals who associated their church-leaving with either tensions with relationships or tensions with time were neither more nor less likely than average to consider returning to church. However, those who associated their church-leaving with tensions with work were much more likely than average to count themselves among the potential returners. Among the potential returners, 44% had left church consequent to their work schedule interfering with their pattern of church-going, compared with 20% among the permanent disaffiliates. Among the potential returners, 33% had left church consequent to having to work on Sundays, compared with 20% of the permanent disaffiliates.

Pastoral implications

Tensions with work in general and Sunday working in particular is a factor involved in disengagement from church for one in every four church-leavers. It is a factor of equal significance among men and among women, across the age groups, and across the denominations. It is a factor that has increased in importance over the past twenty years. Those who left church because of pressures of work are more likely to be attracted back to church than to remain permanently disengaged from church. Good pastoral practice needs to be alert to the changing work-related pressures experienced by church members and to offer appropriate support to those who are experiencing such pressures. Given the importance of work in people's lives, churches may wish to enable members to lower their level of commitment when work-related pressures increase, without feeling pressured to maintain a level of practice for which they no longer have time, or feeling guilt for allowing their pattern of church attendance to decline.

For busy people there may be different ways of keeping in touch with their local congregation, say by e-mail contact or by special monthly services for the time-starved. An increasing number of churches are nowadays offering the chance to worship on weekdays, as well as Sundays. These include shoppers' services, office-workers' lunchtime services, early-morning services to drop into on the way to work, and evening services, sometimes with a 'fresh expressions' flavour. Often additional services like these are shorter than conventional Sunday worship and can be attractive to those with very limited free time.

Tensions with relationships is a factor involved in disengagement from church for one in every three church-leavers. It is a factor of greater significance among women than among men. Those who left church because of pressures from relationships are as likely to remain permanently disengaged from church as they are to return. Good pastoral practice needs to be particularly aware of the implication of the general gender imbalance in church congregations where there are usually two women for every one man. A significant proportion of female church-goers may be leaving a non-church-going male partner at home. The danger is that the social networks generated for the female church-goer may exclude or isolate the non-church-going male partner. There is a strong case, therefore, for churches to generate social network opportunities within which the non-church-going partner can feel equally at home. Such opportunities would be designed not to evangelise the non-church-going partner, but to support the church-going partner.

Tensions with time is a factor involved in disengagement from church for three in every five church-leavers. It is a factor of particular significance for church-leavers under the age of forty. It is a factor that affects Roman Catholics less than members of other denominations. Those who left church because of pressures from time are as likely to remain permanently disengaged from church as they are to return. Good pastoral practice may speculate about the distinctive strengths of the Roman Catholic Church, which seems to hold the capability of lessening the pull of other interests and activities away from church-going. Perhaps the Roman Catholic Church may enable some busy members to participate by Mass attendance at a convenient time (including Saturday evening) without expecting more intimate engagement.

9

Incompatible life-styles

Setting the scene

Several commentators have drawn attention to ways in which life-style issues may encourage some church-goers to disengage from church membership (Richter and Francis, 1998). It has been suggested that some church-goers may feel that their life-style makes them unacceptable to the local congregation. It has also been suggested that some church-goers may lose patience with the teachings of their church if these teachings stand in opposition to their life-style choices. The aim of the present chapter, therefore, is to examine the extent to which church-leavers themselves explain their distance from the church in terms of incompatible life-styles. Listening to our interviewees, four main themes emerged within the broad area of incompatible life-styles. We described these themes as: growing self-awareness, clash of values, clash of teaching, and specific life-style issues.

Growing self-awareness

The first theme focused on a growing self-awareness of the tension between the person our interviewees thought they really were and the public image associated with church attendance. Some church-leavers said that their church-going had become hypocritical. Some said that they were going to church for the wrong reasons. Some said that they could not keep going to church and at the same time be true to themselves. For some leaving church was a positive attempt to assert their personal identity: 'I wanted to stop pretending to be someone I was not.' One of the fullest accounts of the growing sense of hypocrisy as a reason for leaving church was given by Samuel Hartley, a young Roman Catholic church- leaver.

> I couldn't square my views on [sex] with the church's views. I thought, 'well, I don't want to be hypocritical about this . . . obviously they think that thing, and I think this, [so] we should, we'd better, go our own ways' . . . I'd suddenly decided that I probably was going to, you know, have sort of homo-sexual feelings which were quite frightening, but I couldn't, I couldn't feel sort of bad in myself . . . I couldn't believe God didn't like the things I was feeling. But the church didn't, there didn't seem to be any room in the church, for people like me . . . I just didn't feel able to share this part of my life . . . There's no way that it could be squared with how my friends believed, what they thought living as a Catholic meant . . . I had this sense, probably quite wrongly, that people couldn't cope with the fact that I was, I was a homosexual Catholic, that under-neath I was living this double life. So, I made a conscious deci-sion to stop going to these prayer meetings which were held once a week, and distance myself from my Catholic friends, and in so doing left the church. It was just my own sense of hypocrisy.

Alison Matthews, a young social worker who had left a Roman Catholic church, also spoke about a growing sense of hypocrisy.

> I sometimes question whether it would be easier just to forget all my problems and questionings and just get on with going to Mass. And, I suppose I could do that, but I wouldn't feel that it was something that was totally, totally genuine. It wouldn't be

completely from the heart, and for me that's not good enough, it's not good enough for God.

Clash of values

The second theme focused on the sense of a clash of values. Some of our interviewees said that they felt their life-style was not compatible with participation in the church. Some said that they felt their values were not compatible with participation in the church. Others said simply that the church did not give them room to be themselves. A good illustration of what was meant by a clash of life-styles was provided by Nicholas White, a freelance producer who had left an independent Baptist church. He told us that he and his wife found that they were never really accepted by the church.

> I think the difficulty we had with them as well was that we were considered to be very cosmopolitan, compared to, I suppose, most of the people there. We'd lived abroad, we'd travelled, I was in the Arts and it just didn't, none of that really settled well. That was kind of, like, 'oh right, so you don't have a proper job, and your wife earns lots of money'. And nobody would actually go, 'isn't that wrong?', but they, you know, it was there, it was all kind of there . . . we didn't rest easy.

Matthew Williams, a freelance graphic designer, speaking of when he left an Anglican church in his teens, told us how he felt growing conflict between participation in church activities and his life at art school.

> I was at art school . . . and then it got more and more difficult, because I suddenly found I either had to be a Christian or an artist, or somehow there was a contradiction between being an artist and a Christian . . . Eventually within a year I moved [in

155

with] some other people at college . . . and they lived a totally Bohemian kind of life-style . . . That was about 1977 and I got involved in punk and had a very good time actually. I went quite wild, you know . . . and I was able to fully paint without conscience . . . I remember when I was at college I used to run away when I saw Christians coming down the corridor . . . because there was this tremendous guilt at the same time.

Later, Matthew Williams joined up with a New Church, which he also left. He told us that once again he experienced a conflict of values between church life and being an artist.

I was into this extreme problem about being an artist, and this constant thing all the time about pursuing something which I was really passionate about. And sometimes in the church context I got very strong support, and sometimes it's just been awful really. And there was one very strong thing within the evangelical church – that this world is passing, you're just here for a while really, and things in this world aren't very important. Although people always seemed to end up getting into making money, and I can't work out how that was compatible! But there's always this kind of element of well, 'why get involved in painting', I mean, 'you're no good if you're a painter . . . what's the point, you know'.

Clash of teaching

The third theme focused on a real clash with aspects of the church's teaching. Some of our interviewees said that they disagreed with the church's theological teachings. Others said that they disagreed with the church's stance on key moral issues. Richard Elliott, a man in his sixties who had left an Anglican church, provided a very good example of how someone can disagree with the teachings of their local church and of the national church.

I objected to teaching, which seemed to me to deny the authority of Scripture. And the particular issue which forced me really to leave was the one of the church's attitudes to homosexuality, to divorce and to fornication, in general, to immorality, of one sort or another. So I left the church really on scriptural grounds . . . The real reason for leaving was that I couldn't add up what was being said with what the Scriptures were saying. And when I resigned, it was because the [General] Synod at that time had fudged the issue of homosexuality, and it seemed to me that there was a lack of clear moral teaching, a failure to tell the nation (because they have the ears of the nation, archbishops, and bishops, etc.), a failure to tell the nation that the Bible says that homosexuality, homosexual activities, are sinful.

Arron Coates, a postgraduate student who had left a Roman Catholic church, cited his disappointment with the church's attitudes to contraception.

I haven't really got clear views, but I think sometimes the church is too stuck in its views, and really what it does is, by refusing to have any sort of leeway or any form of discussion on the issues, especially when it comes to young people, firstly it's driving people away, and secondly it's getting people into trouble, because they're getting into situations that they're not educated to handle. And I think the church has a responsibility to educate young people particularly in these things. And also, and what it's doing is, it's also reinforcing what I think are old-fashioned views with parents and grandparents and things, because the church is sticking to its old, old values and things.

Specific life-style issues

The fourth theme focused on specific life-style issues. Some of our interviewees said that they had left the church because of conflict over sexual ethics. Some had grown to feel uncomfortable in church because they were having sex outside marriage. Some had grown to feel uncomfortable in church because they were practising same-sex relationships. Others said that they had left church because of conflict over substances: they were taking illegal drugs. This theme of specific life-style issues was emphasised by Tom Mosley, an Anglican clergyman interviewed about his perceptions of why people leave church.

> I assume that they feel unsupported, or unwelcome in some way. I don't know why that is, I don't know why they feel unsupported because we do try. But I can see why they feel the church isn't the place for them anymore, because I think they feel they've broken the rules, and people see church as a place where they try to keep people together . . . When I talk to non-church people, people have said to me, 'I'm not good enough to go to church', and I find that is their understanding. And I never feel that my own congregation [is] in any sense, holier than thou, or giving that impression, but clearly somehow that's conveyed.

Arron Coates told us how having sex outside marriage drove a wedge between him and the Roman Catholic Church.

> I think the church is making it impossible for people to keep the faith, because it's still expecting people to be perfect or Christ-like, and it seems you've either got to be Christ-like or you've got to repent. And I feel guilty when I go to confession and I say . . . 'bless me Father, for I have sinned and I've had sex with my girlfriend that I love very much', and, [he replies] 'oh, well, that's a dreadful thing, you know, and the church's teaching', and blah de blah de blah . . . and you listen to them and you think, 'oh, God'. Because I am sorry that I'm doing anything that offends the church, because I want to be part of the church, but I don't want to be a part where I've to continually

apologise for something that I don't really feel that bad about
. . . In my heart I don't think it's a bad thing, because I'm not
doing anything reckless, I'm doing something . . . in a loving
relationship. I find that hard to match up as being sinful, or
something that I should be dreadfully sorry about.

Listening to the statistics

A set of questions included in the survey set out to examine how
much church-leavers cited these four themes concerned with
incompatible life-styles as implicated in their own experience of
leaving church. An overview of the findings is presented in Table
9, in the Appendix.

From these data it is clear that incompatible life-style issues
were implicated in the process of disengagement from church for
as many as two in every five church-leavers. Thus, 39% of church-
leavers said that they felt their life-style was not compatible with
participation in the church. For one in three church-leavers
(33%) the point was clarified further by making the statement
that they felt their values were not compatible with participation
in the church.

The recognition of incompatibility of life-style and continued
church attendance could often be associated with growing self-
awareness. In this sense, 31% of church-leavers had come to the
conclusion that they were going to church for the wrong reasons;
and 29% said that they could not keep going to church and be
true to themselves. One in four church-leavers (25%) expressed
their growing self-awareness through the conclusion that their
church-going was hypocritical. One in five church-leavers (19%)
wanted to stop pretending to be someone they were not. One in
five church-leavers (19%) expressed a similar feeling in a somewhat different way by saying that the church did not give them
room to be themselves.

159

The issue of incompatible life-styles could also be expressed through clashes with the church's teaching. In this case the clash was more likely to be over moral issues rather than theological issues. Nearly one in three church-leavers (30%) considered that their disengagement from church was associated with disagreement with the church's stance on key moral issues. The proportion dropped to one in five church-leavers (20%) who considered that their disengagement from church was associated with disagreement with the church's theological teachings. In terms of specific life-style issues, 13% of church-leavers associated their disengagement from church with having sex outside marriage, 2% with being practising homosexuals or lesbians and 3% with taking illegal drugs.

Sex differences

Incompatible life-style issues played a larger role in the disengagement of men from church life than in the disengagement of women from church life, and this applied across all four themes explored in this section.

First, men were more likely than women to associate their church-leaving with growing self-awareness. Thus, 34% of the men said that they could not keep going to church and be true to themselves, compared with 26% of the women. Similarly, 38% of the men said that they were going to church for the wrong reasons, compared with 27% of the women.

Second, men were more likely than women to associate their church-leaving with a fundamental clash of values. This point is illustrated by the way in which 40% of the men had felt that their values were not compatible with participation in church life, compared with 29% of the women.

Third, men were more likely than women to associate their church-leaving with a fundamental clash of teaching over theology and morality, but especially over theology. Thus, 28% of the men had disagreed with the church's theological teaching, compared with 15% of the women. One in three men (35%) had disagreed with the church's stance on key moral issues, compared with 28% of women.

Fourth, men were more likely than women to associate their church-leaving with specific life-style issues. For example, 3% of the men distanced themselves from church in light of their sexual orientation, compared with 1% of women; and 5% of the men distanced themselves from church in light of taking illegal drugs, compared with 2% of women. Similar proportions of men and women, however, distanced themselves from church in light of having sex outside marriage: 11% of the men and 14% of the women.

Generational differences

Incompatible life-style issues played a significantly more important role in the disengagement from church among the youngest group of church-leavers, and this applied across all four themes explored in this section.

First, growing self-awareness was referred to much more frequently by the youngest group of church-leavers. While 18% of those aged sixty or over considered that their church-going was hypocritical, the proportions rose to 25% among those in their forties and fifties, and to 33% among those under the age of forty. While 25% of those aged sixty or over said that they had been going to church for the wrong reasons, the proportions rose to 30% among those in their forties and fifties, and to 41% among those under the age of forty.

Second, the clash of values was referred to much more frequently by the youngest group of church-leavers. While 26% of those aged sixty or over had felt their life-style was not compatible with participation in the church, the proportions rose to 40% among those in their forties and fifties, and to 54% among those under the age of forty. While 28% of those aged sixty or over had felt their values were not compatible with participation in the church, the proportions rose to 32% among those in their forties and fifties, and to 42% among those under the age of forty.

Third, the clash with the church's moral teaching was referred to much more frequently by the youngest group of church-leavers. While 28% of those aged sixty or over and 26% of those in their forties and fifties had disagreed with the church's stance on key moral issues, the proportion rose to 41% among those under the age of forty. No similar age trend was found, however, in respect of the church's theological teaching.

Fourth, specific life-style issues were referred to more frequently by the youngest group of church-leavers, especially the matter of sex outside marriage. While 6% of those aged sixty or over and 9% of those in their forties and fifties cited having sex before marriage as associated with their disengagement from church, the proportion rose to 26% among those under the age of forty. While 2% of those aged sixty or over and 2% of those in their forties and fifties cited taking illegal drugs as associated with their disengagement from church, the proportion increased threefold to 6% among those under the age of forty. No similar age trend was found, however, in respect of sexual orientation.

Cohort differences

The two themes of growing self-awareness and clash of values played similar roles in church-leaving among those who decided to leave church over twenty years ago and among those who decided to leave church within the past twenty years. The two other themes in this section, however, showed significant cohort differences. The clearest differences concerned specific life-style issues. As society generally becomes more liberal and more permissive, so the potential expands for growing disparity between life-style choices and the perceived expectations of the church. While 8% of those who left church over twenty years ago associated their disengagement from church with the fact that they were having sex outside marriage, the proportion rose to 17% among those who left church within the past twenty years. While 2% of those who left church over twenty years ago associated their disengagement from church with the fact that they were taking illegal drugs, the proportion doubled to 4% among those who had left church within the past twenty years. No similar cohort differences were found, however, in respect of sexual orientation.

In terms of clash of teachings, theological issues have become less prominent and moral issues have become more prominent. Among those who left church over twenty years ago, 23% cited disagreement with the church's theological teaching. Then the proportion dropped to 17% among those who left church in the past twenty years. Among those who left church over twenty years ago, 27% cited disagreement with the church's stance on key moral issues. Then the proportion rose to 34% among those who left during the past twenty years.

Age at leaving

Incompatible life-style issues played a larger role in disengagement from church during the earlier stages of life, and this applied across all four themes explored in this section.

First, growing self-awareness was referred to much more frequently by those who left church under the age of twenty. For example, 42% of those who left church before their twentieth birthday said that they had been going to church for the wrong reasons, compared with 27% of those who left church in their twenties or thirties and 18% of those who left church after their fortieth birthday. Over one-third of those who left church before their twentieth birthday (36%) said that they could not keep going to church and be true to themselves, compared with 26% of those who left church in their twenties or thirties and 20% of those who left church after their fortieth birthday.

Second, the clash of values was referred to much more frequently by those who left church under the age of twenty. For example, 44% of those who left church before their twentieth birthday had felt that their values were not compatible with participation in the church, compared with 30% of those who left church in their twenties or thirties and 18% of those who left church after their fortieth birthday. Nearly half of those who left church before their twentieth birthday (48%) had felt that their life-style was not compatible with participation in the church, compared with 40% of those who left church in their twenties or thirties and 20% of those who left church after their fortieth birthday.

Third, the clash of teaching was referred to much more frequently by those who left church under the age of twenty. For example, 27% of those who left church before their twentieth birthday had disagreed with the church's theological teachings, compared with 16% of those who had left church in their twenties or thirties and 10% of those who had left church after their fortieth birthday. One-third of those who had left church before their twentieth birthday (34%) had disagreed with the church's stance on key moral issues, compared with 30% of those who left church in their twenties or thirties and 24% of those who left church after their fortieth birthday.

Fourth, specific life-style issues were referred to more frequently by those who left church under the age of twenty, especially the matter of sex outside marriage. One in every six of those who left church before their twentieth birthday (17%) associated their disengagement from church with having sex outside marriage, compared with 12% of those who left church in their twenties or thirties and 5% of those who left church after their fortieth birthday. No similar statistically significant differences were found, however, between the three groups in terms of reference to sexual orientation or to illegal drugs.

Denomination

Incompatible life-style issues generally played a larger role in disengagement from church for Roman Catholics than for Anglicans or for Free Church members, and this applied across all four themes explored in this section.

First, Roman Catholics were more likely to associate their church-leaving with growing self-awareness. Thus, 41% of Roman Catholics argued that their church-going was hypocritical, compared with 21% of Anglicans and 24% of Free Church members. Two out of every five Roman Catholics (42%) considered that they were going to church for the wrong reasons, compared with 28% of Anglicans and 32% of Free Church members. Two out of every five Roman Catholics (39%) considered that they could not keep going to church and be true to themselves, compared with 25% of Anglicans and 33% of Free Church members.

Second, Roman Catholics were more likely to associate their church-leaving with a clash of values. Thus, 41% of Roman Catholics had felt that their values were not compatible with participation in the church, compared with 30% of Anglicans and 39% of Free Church members. Similarly, 28% of Roman Catholics argued that the church did not give them room to be themselves, compared with 18% of Anglicans and 16% of Free Church members.

Third, Roman Catholics were more likely to associate their church-leaving with a clash of teaching, and especially over moral issues. Thus, 31% of Roman Catholics had disagreed with the church's theological teaching, compared with 18% of Anglicans and 18% of Free Church members. One in every two Roman Catholics (48%) had disagreed with the church's stance on key moral issues, compared with 29% of Anglicans and 22% of Free Church members.

Fourth, Roman Catholics were more likely to associate their church-leaving with specific life-style issues, and especially with matters of sex. One in three Roman Catholics said that their disengagement from church was related to having sex outside marriage, compared with 9% of Anglicans and 10% of Free Church members. Illegal drugs also held a higher profile among Roman Catholics: 8% of Roman Catholics said that their disengagement from church was related to taking illegal drugs, compared with 2% of Anglicans and 2% of Free Church members. No similar statistically significant differences were found, however, between the three denominational groups in terms of sexual orientation.

Sudden or gradual leaving

Some incompatible life-style issues are more likely to lead to sudden leaving than to gradual leaving within three of the four themes explored in this section. In terms of growing self-awareness, 29% of those who left church suddenly associated their disengagement from church with the recognition that their church-going was hypocritical, compared with 21% of those who had left gradually. In terms of clash of values, 43% of those who had left church suddenly associated their disengagement from church with the recognition that their life-style was not compatible with participation in the church, compared with 36% of those who had left gradually. In terms of clash of teaching, 25% of those who had left church suddenly associated their disengagement from church with disagreement with the church's theological teaching, compared with 15% of those who had left gradually. On the other hand, illegal drugs, sexual orientation and sex outside marriage did not distinguish between sudden and gradual leaving.

Likelihood of returning

Overall, church-leavers who had disengaged on grounds concerning incompatible life-styles were more likely to regard themselves as permanent disaffiliates than as potential returners. Of the 12 questions included in this section of the survey, 9 revealed significant differences between permanent disaffiliates and potential returners.

In terms of growing self-awareness, among the potential returners just 16% had left church on the recognition that they could not keep going to church and be true to themselves, compared with 40% among the permanent disaffiliates. Among the potential returners just 17% had left church on the recognition that they had been going to church for the wrong reasons, compared with 43% among the permanent disaffiliates.

In terms of clash of values, among the potential returners just 12% had left church on the recognition that their values were not compatible with participation in the church, compared with 45% of the permanent disaffiliates. Among the potential returners just 9% had left church on the recognition that the church did not give them room to be themselves, compared with 24% of the permanent disaffiliates.

In terms of clash of teaching, among the potential returners just 5% had left church following disagreement with the church's theological teaching, compared with 30% of the permanent disaffiliates. Among the potential returners just 16% had left church following disagreement with the church's stance on key moral issues, compared with 38% of the permanent disaffiliates.

On the other hand, illegal drugs, sexual orientation and sex outside marriage did not predispose church-leavers to remain as permanent disaffiliates rather than to become potential returners.

Pastoral implications

This section makes it clear that two in every five church-leavers found that incompatible life-style issues were significantly implicated in their disengagement from church. Moreover, such reasons for church-leaving tend to be associated with permanent disaffiliation rather than with potential returning. Overall, such issues are more likely to be significant for men, for those under the age of forty, and for Roman Catholics. There is a tendency for these issues to lead to sudden leaving rather than to gradual leaving. These data raise three particular questions for pastoral practice.

The first question concerns ways in which the churches can engage more effectively with men. It is well recognised that men are outnumbered by women in most church congregations in a ratio of two women for every one man. Listening to church-leavers it becomes clear that men tend to leave church because of life-style issues. Indeed, part of male emancipation seems to be associated with breaking away from the feminised environment of the church. Good pastoral practice needs, therefore, to take more seriously ways of engaging with men on their own terms, and ways of proclaiming the gospel that are compatible with a masculine outlook on the world. One resource that sets out to help churches create an environment where men can flourish in every aspect of the church's life is the website Church for Men. It claims that 'instead of creating a little outpost of masculinity called "men's ministry", we help churches unleash the masculine spirit throughout the organization' (http://www.churchformen.com/ourmission.php). One of the most influential thinkers in this field has been Fr Richard Rohr (see, for instance, his book, *From Wild Man to Wise Man: reflections on male spirituality* (Rohr, 2005)).

The second question concerns reflecting on the ways in which life-style issues impact the denominations so differently. The conflict between life-style choices and church-going is expressed so much more strongly by Roman Catholics than by Anglicans or by Free Church members. Given the fact that there remains so much healthy debate between denominations and within denominations on life-style issues, denominational switching could, perhaps, sometimes be seen as healthier than complete disaffiliation from church life.

The third question concerns reflecting on the church's attitude toward sex outside marriage. Among reasons for church-leaving this issue has become much more significant for those who have left the church within the past twenty years and for church-leavers under the age of forty. It is also a particularly pertinent reason among Roman Catholic church-leavers. Different theological positions will respond to this issue in different ways. The debate, however, may need to recognise the current practical significance of the issue for those who are now placing themselves outside the church's pastoral networks as a consequence of feeling that their life-style choice creates an intolerable tension with the church's expectations.

10

Not belonging and not fitting in

Setting the scene

In an early study of church-leaving, Warren J. Hartman (1976: 40) discovered that the most frequently given reason by those who had dropped out of church was 'their failure to feel that they were accepted, loved or wanted'. These were individuals who, according to Hartman, 'felt that they did not belong and that others in the church . . . did not demonstrate any real love and concern for them'. Churches are, after all, social institutions and there may be numerous reasons why different individuals find it difficult to feel accepted or find it difficult to fit in well with the social group. Indeed, the very characteristics of the social group that enable one individual to feel at home may make another individual feel a total outsider. The aim of the present chapter, therefore, is to examine the extent to which church-leavers themselves explain their distance from the church in terms of not belonging and not fitting in. Listening to our interviewees, four main themes emerged within the broad area of not belonging and not fitting in. We described these themes as: social exclusion, personal marginalisation, personal visibility, and tensions and conflicts.

Social exclusion

The first theme focused on the feeling of social exclusion. Some church-leavers said simply that they did not feel part of the church. Others pointed more specifically to cliques or 'in groups' from which they felt excluded, either deliberately or accidentally. Some church-leavers felt that they had contributions to make to the local church that were simply not valued and so they felt themselves squeezed out. Others put it more starkly and said that they were not allowed to play an active part in the church. This feeling of social exclusion was well expressed by Arron Coates, a postgraduate student and Roman Catholic church-leaver, who tried to explain why his grandmother, a devout Catholic, left church.

My nan and grandad divorced, and my nan never set foot in church again after being divorced, because she felt it was a shameful state to be in. Apart from going at Christmas, she didn't go back in until she died, in a box. And because she was Irish and she'd come from a very Catholic, very Irish background, she used to go to church every night of the week. She got divorced, she didn't ever marry again, but she felt she was in a shameful state, that the church looked down upon her, that she was too ashamed to go back to church. And I didn't even realise until she died, I didn't realise that was why she didn't go to church until she died, and it wasn't until we were sat round with the priest and he was trying to work out what he was going to say about her, that my aunties and my dad were saying, 'oh, yes, she used to go to church'. She used to take people in off the street and look after them. She was a brilliant Catholic, Christian person, and yet was sort of forced into a state of shame by the church's teaching.

Another example of social exclusion was related by Josephine and Charles Mason, who had both left Anglican churches, and who were in their early forties. Josephine explained her feelings in the following way.

We did this Alpha-course, and that was a big turning point, because it's a Christian basics course. We went along every week, we met very interesting sincere people, we did our bit, you know, we expressed our views, and our feelings about various things, but we missed the residential weekend that they had at the end of the course, we just couldn't go. And when the group reconvened the following week, and we went along, it was a bit like being strangers at a party really because everybody had sort of moved on in this huge way, they'd all bonded together spiritually, and had all sorts of amazing charismatic experiences, and we just sort of felt, 'well, is this the same sort of Alpha-group?' And I think that was the beginning of the end really.

Charles picked up the conversation at this point.

I can remember it being quite difficult, because of the strange feeling that people we had got to know in our group and the leaders of our group, would be superficially polite, but they weren't really terribly interested in us, because we obviously weren't part of their particular little club any longer, and so the reasons for attending got less and less and less.

Personal marginalisation

The second theme focused on the feeling of personal marginalisation, where individuals felt on the edge of local church life. Some church-leavers were marginalised by the sense of powerlessness. For one church-leaver this was expressed by saying that she felt powerless to bring about change within the church. For another church-leaver this was expressed by saying that the church did not listen to him. One church-leaver had felt marginalised by being pressured to join the church before she was ready. Another church-leaver felt marginalised by being spiritually out of his depth in the local church. Nicholas and Kate White, a couple in their forties who had both left an independent Baptist church, felt powerless to make their voice heard in the local church. Kate drew attention to one specific example.

> The minister had this peculiar thing . . . if you were singing a chorus fast, that was praise, and if you were singing a chorus slowly, that was worship. So occasionally they'd have these things where, like, someone could, like sort of, let the spirit move, so that we can start singing something. If someone started singing something slowly before we'd had lots of fast ones, he'd stop them and say, 'no, no, no, we're not ready to worship yet, we're still praising'.

Nicholas continued the story as follows.

> Which to us was a little bizarre, to say the least. We were just kind of going, 'oh, I see, the Holy Spirit is about tempo, that's fine, OK, it's fine, no problem' [laughter]. But of course you weren't allowed to say things like that, because then you were criticising the minister.

Adrian, a Methodist teenager, interviewed at a MAYC national event, reflected perceptively on the experience of one of his friends.

> Yes, I brought one of my best friends along once, and she came for a few weeks, but then she decided it wasn't her scene, so she left . . . When people start going to church, they feel that they've got to fit in with everybody else, and I know a lot of people at my church were really deep Christians already, and she was like a beginner, and we were, and she felt that she had to rush into it, and she just couldn't do that.

Personal visibility

The third theme focused on issues concerned with personal visibility. Some of our interviewees explained that there were not enough people of their own age in the congregation. As a consequence they could feel isolated and exposed. Others were put off by the fact that there were just not enough people of any age in the congregation. It is not possible to retain invisibility in a small group. Some of our interviewees felt uncomfortable about the expectations placed on them in the services and complained that they were expected to do embarrassing things in the worship service. For others the problem of visibility was expressed in a very different way. For them the problem was that there were too many people in the congregation and they remained invisible in the crowd. Matthew Williams, a freelance graphic designer in his forties, left a New Church congregation where he felt over-whelmed by the young people. He summed up his feelings like this.

I felt so ill-at-ease that I just left, and that's the last time I've been. I just left, I just couldn't handle it anymore, it was just too much to me, and I just couldn't handle all these young happy people . . . The majority of people are a lot younger than our age really . . . I couldn't stand all this. I've never been able to sing a chorus since I've been there, since leaving, and I just thought I can't stick this, so I left and that was the last time I went to church.

The problem for Sarah Johnson, a homemaker in her thirties, was that there had been an absence of younger people in her church.

We were the youngest couple. The next married couple to us were in their forties, but they were old forties, do you know what I mean [laughter]? I mean, they were only like ten years

174

older than us, but it seemed like a big gap, so there wasn't any-body our age.

Tensions and conflicts

The fourth theme focused on the experience of tensions and conflicts within the church. Some church-leavers spoke of their personal tension with a church leader. Other church-leavers spoke of their personal tension with a church member. Some said that they had experienced a clash of principles with the leadership of the church. Others spoke in terms of wider and more general relationship problems within their church: 'Relationships within the church had become soured', they said. Nicholas White, a man in his forties who had left an independent Baptist church, spoke eloquently about his problems with the minister.

> [The minister] just had this complete obsession that we were kind of trying to manipulate, and we just said 'no, it's not the case at all'. And eventually, I mean, it just escalated. There was all sorts of instances, basically nothing. This man just considered we were unsuitable . . . I won't go into it, unless you really need us to, but it was just unbelievable. I mean, he'd preached against me from the pulpit, and it culminated in his wife slapping me round the face in public, just because I was arguing with her husband. Then him persuading the elders that we should be dis-fellowshipped.

Real fear of the minister was expressed by Matthew Williams, a freelance graphic designer in his forties who had left a New Church congregation.

> I was so afraid of [the minister], I actually said to him, 'look, I've been having bad thoughts about you'. What I meant was I was having fantasy arguments with him in my head, but I was

so afraid of actually expressing that in the words that I was having fantasy arguments with him in my head, I actually said 'I've been having bad thoughts about you'. He didn't question me about this, but he immediately went onto this homosexual thing, and anyone with any sense would have said, 'well, what do you mean?' .... He said, 'I won't tell anyone, and don't you tell anyone', so I didn't tell anyone for two years, but in fact he told the elders straight away at the next elders meeting, and what happened was the elders would gossip throughout the whole church.

Listening to the statistics

A set of questions included in the survey set out to examine how much church-leavers cited these four themes concerned with not belonging and not fitting in as implicated in their own experience of leaving church. An overview of the findings is presented in Table 10, in the Appendix.

From these data, it is clear that social exclusion plays a significant part in the process of disengagement from church for nearly one in every two church-leavers. Thus, 45% made the point that they did not feel a part of the church. One in four church-leavers (25%) put things more strongly and complained that there were cliques or 'in groups' within their church from which they felt excluded. For a small number of church-leavers this feeling of social exclusion extended to the view that their particular gifts and presence were just not welcomed by the church. In this sense, 7% said that the church did not value what they had to offer and 6% said that they were not allowed to play an active part in church life.

The sense of marginalisation and powerlessness within the local church was quite widespread among church-leavers. One in every four church-leavers (25%) had felt powerless to bring about change within the church. Some had clearly tried, but 13% came to the conclusion that the church did not listen to them.

Personal marginalisation also took a second form. While some felt marginalised by being ignored, others felt marginalised by being pressured to commit or to conform in one way or another. Thus, 13% said that they felt pressured to join the church before they were ready. A similar proportion (14%) had found themselves spiritually out of their depth in their local church.

The issue of personal visibility was important to a number of church-leavers. In particular, the lack of peer support was a crucial factor. More than one in five church-leavers (22%) associated their disengagement from church with the fact that there were not enough people of their own age in the congregation. For others the problem was more general and they found the whole church just too small for their taste or comfort. As many as 15% of church-leavers associated their disengagement from church with feeling that there were not enough people in the congregation. By way of contrast, just 2% of church-leavers associated their disengagement from church with feeling that there were too many people in the congregation.

Another way of feeling too visible in the local church is by being invited to participate in ways with which some individuals may feel uncomfortable. One in ten church-leavers (9%) associated their disengagement from church with being expected to do embarrassing things in the worship service.

Conflicts and tensions in the local church can also lead to some individuals feeling that they are not really belonging, not really fitting in. A small number of church-leavers associated such conflicts and tensions with their disengagement from church. For 6% relationships within the church had become soured. For 5% the problem had been a clash of principles with the leadership of the church. For 3% there was tension with a church member. For another 3% there was tension with a church leader. In light of such tension and conflict some individuals just preferred to leave.

Sex differences

In most respects issues related to not belonging and not fitting in functioned at similar levels in the path to disengagement from church among women and among men. Two of the 16 items in this section, however, recorded statistically significant differences between the responses of men and women which reveal some clues concerning the ways in which their experiences of church differ. On the one hand, women tended to be more conscious of the effect of cliques to sour church life: 29% of the women had experienced cliques or 'in groups' from which they had felt excluded, compared with 19% of the men. On the other hand, men tended to be more conscious of the effect of power issues to sour church life: 28% of the men had felt powerless to bring about change within the church, compared with 22% of the women.

Generational differences

In most respects issues related to not belonging and not fitting in functioned at similar levels in the path to disengagement from church among all three generational groups. Two of the 16 items in this section, however, recorded statistically significant differences between the responses of the three age groups which reveal some clues concerning the ways in which their experiences of church differ. On the one hand, it is the younger church-goers who are most likely to feel that they stand out in the church congregation as too visible and as too different. Thus, 29% of those under the age of forty and 25% of those in their forties or fifties trace their disengagement from church to feeling that there were not enough people of their own age there, compared with 12% of those aged sixty or over. On the other hand, it is the older church-goers who are most likely to feel that they are in some senses left behind by developments in the church. Thus, 22% of those aged sixty or over trace their disengagement from church to feeling

178

that they were spiritually out of their depth, compared with 10% of those in their forties or fifties and 12% of those under the age of forty.

Cohort differences

In most respects issues related to not belonging and not fitting in played similar roles in the church-leaving process of those who left over twenty years ago and those who left in the past twenty years. Three of the 16 items in this section, however, drew attention to issues which played a larger part in church-leaving during the past twenty years than had been the case previously. The first issue concerned the growing visibility of those who belonged to an age group not well-represented in the congregation, and this generally meant younger people. Over the past twenty years the proportion of people who traced their disengagement from church to the fact that there were not enough people of their own age in the congregation increased from 17% to 25%. The second issue concerned the detrimental effect of cliques on church life. Over the past twenty years the proportion of people who traced their disengagement from church to cliques or 'in groups' from which they felt excluded increased from 21% to 29%. The third issue concerned the detrimental effect of poor relationships within the church. Over the past twenty years the proportion of people who traced their disengagement from church to the way in which relationships within the church had become soured increased from 3% to 8%.

Age at leaving

In most respects issues related to not belonging and not fitting in functioned at similar levels in the path to disengagement among those who left under the age of twenty, those who left in their twenties or thirties, and those who left after their fortieth birthday. Three of the 16 items in this section, however, recorded statistically significant differences which highlighted ways in which some factors are more important in prompting disengagement from church at different stages in life. First, the detrimental impact of cliques increases across the age range. While 17% of those who left church before their twentieth birthday associated their leaving with feeling excluded by cliques or 'in groups', the proportions increased to 29% among those who left in their twenties or thirties and to 35% among those who left after their fortieth birthday. Second, the detrimental impact of being pressured to join the church was greatest during the first twenty years of life. Nearly one in five of those who left church before their twentieth birthday (18%) did so feeling pressured to join the church before they were ready, compared with 9% of those who left in their twenties or thirties and 8% of those who left after their fortieth birthday. Third, large congregations began to play a more important role in church-leaving among those who left church later in life. Thus, 6% of those who left church after their fortieth birthday had felt that there were too many people in the congregation, compared with just 1% of those who left church earlier in life.

Denomination

In most respects issues related to not belonging and not fitting in played a similar part in disengagement from church among Anglicans, Free Church members and Roman Catholics. Four of the 16 items in this section, however, recorded statistically significant differences which help to profile the distinctive experiences of the three denominational groups.

One of the four items draws attention to the distinctive experience of the Anglican Church. A higher proportion of Anglicans associated their disengagement from church with a sense of uncomfortable visibility in the congregation. One in ten Anglicans (11%) complained that they were expected to do embarrassing things in the worship service, compared with 3% of Roman Catholics and 3% of Free Church members. For Anglicans these 'embarrassing things' may range from extravagant actions accompanying choruses in the family service to exchanging the peace in a contemplative early-morning Communion service.

The other three items draw attention to the distinctive experiences of the Roman Catholic Church. On the positive side, fewer people disengaged from a Roman Catholic church because they found the congregation to be too small. Just 8% of Roman Catholics complained that there were not enough people in the congregation, compared with 16% of Anglicans and 19% of Free Church members. On the negative side, more people disengaged from a Roman Catholic church because they found that they were not listened to or because of tensions with the leadership. One in five Roman Catholic church-leavers (20%) complained that the church did not listen to them, compared with 13% of Anglicans and 6% of Free Church members. One in eleven Roman Catholic church-leavers (9%) had experienced a clash of principles with the leadership of the church, compared with 6% of Anglicans and 2% of Free Church members.

Sudden or gradual leaving

Generally issues related to not belonging and not fitting in held equal weight among those whose church-leaving was gradual and those whose church-leaving was sudden. The main exception to this pattern, however, concerned those whose disengagement involved the feeling that there were not enough people of their own age in the church. For such people, disengagement tended to be gradual. Thus, the complaint that there were not enough people of their age in the congregation was voiced by 26% of those whose leaving was gradual, compared with 17% of those whose leaving was sudden.

Likelihood of returning

Generally issues related to not belonging and not fitting in did not help to distinguish between those who saw themselves as permanent disaffiliates and those who saw themselves as potential returners. Three items in this section, however, provide interesting exceptions to the general rule. On the one hand, one item helped to predict greater openness to returning. Those who had left church feeling that there were not enough people of their own age in the congregation were nearly twice as likely to place themselves among the potential returners than among the permanent disaffiliates (28% compared with 17%).

On the other hand, two items helped to predict greater reluctance to returning. First, those who had left with the view that they did not feel a part of the church were much more prominent among the permanent disaffiliates than among the potential returners (56% compared with 33%). Second, those who had left with the view that they felt pressured to join the church before they were ready were three times as likely to place themselves among the permanent disaffiliates than among the potential returners (17% compared with 5%).

Pastoral implications

Although theologically conceived as a divine institution, from an empirical perspective the church seems to be vulnerable to many of the conditions familiar among other social organisations. The church, after all, comprises fallen human beings who are subject to normal human weaknesses and shortcomings. This section makes it clear that common sociological factors concerned with social exclusion, personal marginalisation, personal visibility, and tensions and conflicts are implicated in the process of disengagement from church for around half of those who leave church. Moreover, this section also makes it clear that such factors are generally of equal weight among men and women, across the age groups, and across the denominations.

Many of the issues raised by the themes of social exclusion, personal marginalisation, personal visibility and tensions and conflicts are issues to which well-trained pastors should be sensitive, and problems that can and should be creatively managed by church-leaders. The difficulties caused by cliques and 'in groups' within the church provide a good example of the kind of problem that needs to be properly managed, especially in light of the way in which this specific problem has grown in importance over the past twenty years. On the one hand, it is very easy for a group of people who work, pray and worship together to project (unintentionally) the feeling of being inward looking and exclusive rather than inclusive. Only the kind of ministry leadership that is able to transcend the local worshipping community and take an objective view (as if from outside) is capable of identifying the strengths and dangers within such groups. Ironically, it may sometimes be the local ministry team (which should ideally facilitate such objectivity) that projects the impenetrable characteristics of the most insidious church-related clique.

Church leaders require a deep and properly informed understanding of group and social dynamics in order to spot the dangers and to promote appropriate and sensitive intervention strategies. There may also be a role for the roving consultant making periodic health checks on the social inclusivity of the local church.

Some people may find it more conducive to belong to a virtual church on the internet, such as St Pixel's, which describes itself as 'an experiment in online Christian community, sponsored by the Methodist Church of Great Britain and supported by an international and ecumenical group of Christians' (http://www.stpixels. com/view_releases.cgi). People can belong to an online church on their own terms, participating as much or as little as they choose, and revealing as much or as little of their actual identity as they wish. They can interact with people literally anywhere in the world and at any time. Indeed, sometimes they may decide to meet face-to-face in what St Pixel's calls 'real-life meets'. People can belong to a conventional church as well as to St Pixel's. If the online church offers a richer sense of belonging, then it can sometimes make up for deficiencies in the real-life church and help some individuals to keep real-life contact with the Christian community.

11

Costs and benefits

Setting the scene

Several commentators have begun to apply a form of economic theory to modelling and to interpreting aspects of 'religious markets' (see, for example, Iannaccone, 1992, 1994). This way of thinking offers a fresh set of insights into understanding how church-going and how church-leaving may function for some individuals. For some, their church-going may entail high costs, say, in terms of time-commitment, in terms of personal conflicts, or in terms of financial contributions, but such high costs may be offset by high returns, say, in terms of personal support, in terms of social engagement, or in terms of spiritual fulfilment. However, a time may come when the cost-benefit analysis ceases to balance the account. For others, their church-going may entail few costs and offer few benefits. The aim of the present chapter, therefore, is to examine the extent to which church-leavers themselves explain their distance from the church in terms of costs and benefits. Listening to our interviewees, three main themes emerged within the broad area of costs and benefits. We described these themes as: not meeting my needs, not helping my spiritual growth, and too many demands, too little return.

Not meeting my needs

The first theme focused on how the church was just not meeting the individual church-leaver's needs. For some church-leavers

185

the problem was that the church did not meet their personal needs. Others found that the church did not meet their children's needs. Some said quite simply that 'there was nothing in it for me'. Others expressed the cost-benefit analysis in somewhat more calculated terms by comparing their own situation with that of their non-church-going friends. As these church-leavers saw things, their non-church-going friends did not seem to miss out on anything. This set of ideas was expressed in a succinct way by Jennie, one of the Methodist teenagers interviewed at a MAYC national event.

> In [our church] there's nothing . . . A couple of friends my age left, and really they just don't feel the church has anything relevant to them, and anything to offer them . . . They don't really think there's anything in it for them, and they don't really enjoy it that much.

Not helping my spiritual growth

The second theme discussed the costs and benefits of church membership in terms of the church's failure to contribute to the individual church-leaver's spiritual growth. Some church-leavers said that the church was not helping them to find meaning and purpose in their life. Others said that the church was not meeting their spiritual needs. Some complained that the church was not providing them with enough teaching and guidance. Others complained that it was all too easy to drift in and out of their church because their church did not expect enough by way of commitment. Sarah Johnson, an Anglican church-leaver in her thirties, found her investment in the local church was not rewarded by adequate and appropriate teaching.

> I did O-level and A-level RE at school and actually learnt an awful lot more about the Bible and the Christian faith at school

than I learnt at church, and to me that said a lot. That there wasn't the time given over to the teachings that we wanted . . . As an example, I think in the Church of England, and especially where we were, Satan was pushed under the carpet because he wasn't a very nice man to talk about, and such, and certain aspects are explored more than others, rather than the whole Bible . . . We didn't receive teaching on a lot of issues and a lot of things that I would have preferred to.

Deborah Clarke, an Anglican church-leaver in her forties, felt that her style of spirituality had now moved away from being resourced by the local church.

I think that the picture which most attracts me [nowadays] is that of a slightly hermit-like existence, and so . . . what I'm imagining is, sort of living my spiritual life at a distance, able to draw strength from the spiritual charge of the church without necessarily being a member of a worshipping community, and meeting fellow travellers on the way, that way I think. I suppose I have moved from wanting to intellectually understand to being much more drawn into silence and wondering at the symbols and the metaphysical and all that sort of thing. I can't see myself in a conventional parish situation, sort of sitting on a pew week-by-week and being fed by the regular liturgy. It's a shame.

Karl Osborne, an Anglican clergyman interviewed about his perceptions of church-leaving, recognised that, in a consumer-oriented society, individuals may well invest in the church in order to meet a specific need, but once that need has been met, they move on again.

The Church of England [is] something that people think they can just dip into when they want to, and tennis is sometimes more important. Because the Church of England hasn't had this strong sense of who is and who isn't a member, people do come into the church during times in their lives when they feel they need extra support, through difficult pastoral situations, and I suppose if they receive that support, and they're helped through that particularly bad patch in life then when they feel strong enough again to pick up the reins and to go on, they may drift out for the same reasons that they drifted in.

Too many demands, too little return

The third theme discussed the costs and benefits of church membership in terms of too many demands outweighing too little return. Some church-leavers spoke in general terms that their participation in church had become a chore, with too little enjoyment compensating for the effort. Others were much more specific in their criticism and complained that the church was making increasing demands on their time, or making increasing demands on their money. It was the financial demands made by his church that helped to push Arron Coates, a postgraduate student, into leaving a Roman Catholic church. He made his point like this.

I have real difficulty with going to church every week and having a different collection plate shoved under your nose. I have a real problem when you go expecting to hear a homily and instead you get something about refugees or missionaries or something, which I accept is part of the gospel and spreading the word, but sometimes I feel that you kind of get into the church if you've got a wallet big enough to give things away . . . Sometimes I feel that going to church can get very expensive, and so that grates me because the Pope's quite a wealthy chap really . . . It seems to contradict everything that's in the Bible, that the church should be so wealthy, and so that is a real problem for me. Because I feel obliged to give and I shouldn't.

For Gareth Wilkinson, a businessman in his forties who had left a Methodist church, the cost was experienced in terms of the demands on his parents.

The church was a very big part of [my parents'] lives . . . and I can recall spending an awful lot of time at the church premises in my early years . . . [I think my leaving church was a reaction against] the way the church was imposed on me and forced on me, together with a wish to be able to go to church without it having to become my life . . . I never was in a position where I was able to opt into the church. And I think as a result I opted out as soon as I could, as a rebellious teenager, and I've probably opted out ever since, for those reasons.

A similar story was told by Sharon Chapman, an ex-Methodist in her thirties, who felt that the commitment made by her parents to church life had significantly disadvantaged her educational opportunities.

[My parents] moved to X purely because of the fact that they felt they wanted to be nearer the church, and the petrol side was costing a lot of money. No exaggeration, they moved because of the church, they wanted to be nearer the church, and not have to drive there every Sunday, and to evening meetings during the week, etc. So they moved in my fourth year [at school], and for the first term in the fifth year I tried to manage, but it was like three trains and a bus, and I just couldn't do it. I was leaving for school at seven and getting home at about half six, seven o'clock, and then three hours' homework in your O-level year, so I changed schools. And I think that was the final straw, I thought, 'no, the reason we've moved is because of the church'. So that's what made me, OK, I got my O-levels, I got nine of them, and I carried on for a little while doing A-levels, but I thought, 'no, I'm going to leave'. So I think there's a lot of resentment there, that the church maybe stopped me doing what I wanted to do, but that's why I left the church. Basically I felt that had been a decider there in my career for the future, and they put that first.

Listening to the statistics

A set of questions included in the survey set out to examine how much church-leavers cited these three themes concerned with costs and benefits as implicated in their own experience of leaving church. An overview of the findings is presented in Table 11, in the Appendix.

From these data it is clear that two out of every five church-leavers associated their disengagement from church with the impression that they were not getting good value from the commitment that they had invested. All three themes explored in this chapter lead to a similar conclusion.

First, two out of every five church-leavers (40%) said quite directly that the church did not meet their needs. Comparing their own situation with that of their friends, 36% of church-leavers had come to the conclusion that their non-church-going friends did not seem to miss out on anything. Expressing a similar realisation, 29% of church-leavers said that there was nothing in it for them. While some church-leavers spoke in terms of the church failing to meet their own personal needs, others reflected more on how the church was, or was not, meeting the needs of their family. In this context, 11% associated their disengagement from church with the church's failure to meet their children's needs.

Second, two out of every five church-leavers (38%) said quite directly that the church was not helping them to find meaning and purpose in their life. For 36% of church-leavers, the church was not meeting their spiritual needs. While some church-leavers spoke in terms of the church not helping in their spiritual growth, others commented on the failure of the church's teaching to foster their personal commitment. Thus, 16% of church-leavers said that their church was not providing them with enough teaching and guidance. For 32% the problem was that it proved too easy to drift in and to drift out of their church, because that church did not expect strong commitment.

Third, two out of every five church-leavers (41%) recognised that their participation in church had become a chore, with little enjoyment. However, while the benefits of church membership seemed low, for the majority of church-leavers the costs also seemed low. Only 5% complained that the church had been making increasing demands on their money. Only 6% complained that the church had been making increasing demands on their time.

Sex differences

Generally the cost-benefit analysis of church-going and of church-leaving was applied in similar ways by men and by women. However, men were more inclined than women to endorse 2 of the 11 items in this section. Men were more inclined than women to come out with the direct complaint that the church did not meet their needs (46% compared with 36%). Men were also more inclined than women to make the direct complaint that there was nothing in it for them (34% compared with 26%).

Generational differences

Generally the cost-benefit analysis of church-going and of church-leaving was applied in similar ways across the three generational groups: those under the age of forty, those in their forties or fifties, and those aged sixty or over. There were, however, two (partly predictable) ways in which age differences were profiled within this section. The first difference concerns the part played by children in the lives of church-goers and the role that children play in their disengagement from church. Thus, 13% of those in their forties and fifties and 15% of those aged sixty or over associated their disengagement from church with the complaint that the church was not meeting their children's needs. The proportion dropped to 6% among those under the age of forty. The second difference concerns the drop in disposable income that accompanies retirement. Thus, 9% of those aged sixty or over associated their disengagement from church with the complaint that the church was making increasing demands on their money. The proportion dropped to 5% among those in their forties or fifties and to 2% among those under the age of forty.

Cohort differences

Some aspects of this way of looking at church attendance through a form of cost-benefit analysis were significantly more important among those who left church more than twenty years ago than among those who left church within the past twenty years. The complaint that the church did not meet their needs was voiced by 46% of those who left church over twenty years ago, compared with 36% of those who left within the past twenty years. The complaint that 'there was nothing in it for me' was voiced by 34% of those who left church over twenty years ago, compared with 24% of those who left within the past twenty years. The comparison with non-church-going friends was also more frequently cited by those who left church over twenty years ago. Thus, 42% of those who left church over twenty years ago observed that their non-church-going friends did not seem to miss out on anything, compared with 32% of those who left within the past twenty years. In similar vein, 43% of those who left church over twenty years ago said that the church was not helping them to find meaning and purpose in their life, compared with 34% of those who had left church within the past twenty years. However, the remaining seven items in this section did not reveal any statistically significant differences between the two cohorts of leavers.

Age at leaving

Some aspects of this way of looking at church attendance through a form of cost-benefit analysis were significantly more important for those who left under the age of twenty than for those who left later in life. This trend is evident throughout all three themes described in this section. In terms of the theme 'not meeting my needs', 48% of those who left before their twentieth birthday said simply that the church did not meet their needs, compared with 35% of those who left in their twenties or thirties and 35% of those who left after their fortieth birthday. Similarly, 40% of those who left before their twentieth birthday said that there was nothing in it for them, compared with 23% of those who left in their twenties or thirties and 19% of those who left after their fortieth birthday.

In terms of the theme 'not helping my spiritual growth', 47% of those who left before their twentieth birthday said that the church was not helping them to find meaning and purpose in their life, compared with 34% of those who left in their twenties or thirties, and 30% of those who left after their fortieth birthday. In terms of the theme 'too many demands, too little return', 51% of those who left before their twentieth birthday complained that their participation in church had become a chore, with little enjoyment, compared with 35% of those who left in their twenties or thirties and 33% of those who left after their fortieth birthday.

There was, however, one aspect of the cost-benefit analysis that weighted toward the later stages of life. One in ten of those who left church after their fortieth birthday (10%) complained that the church was making increasing demands on their money, compared with 6% of those who left in their twenties or thirties and 3% of those who left before their twentieth birthday.

Denomination

In many ways the cost-benefit analysis worked in similar ways across the three denominational groupings: the Roman Catholics, the Anglicans, and the Free Church members. Two of the items in this section, however, drew attention to the ways in which the Roman Catholic experience differed significantly from that of the other two groups. While around one in three Anglicans (35%) and one in three Free Church members (32%) considered that their church did not expect strong commitment with the consequence that it was easy to drift in and out, the proportion dropped to one in six Roman Catholics (16%) who shared this view. While the Roman Catholic Church demanded a higher level of commitment, it seemed also to be offering a lower level of reward. Nearly half of the Roman Catholics (47%) complained that the church was not meeting their spiritual needs, compared with 36% of Anglicans and 31% of Free Church members.

Sudden or gradual leaving

Some of the themes explored in this section on costs and benefits tended to lead to sudden withdrawal from the church rather than to gradual withdrawal. For example, 46% of those who had left suddenly associated their disengagement from church with the view that the church did not meet their needs, compared with 36% of those who had left gradually. Similarly, 36% of those who had left suddenly had come to the view that there was nothing in it for them, compared with 22% of those who had left gradually. Two in every five church-leavers who had left suddenly (42%)

had found that the church was not meeting their spiritual needs, compared with 32% of those who had left gradually. Two in every five church-leavers who had left suddenly (43%) had concluded that the church was not helping them find meaning and purpose in their life, compared with 35% of those who had left gradually. On the other hand, the other seven items in this section failed to distinguish between sudden and gradual leavers.

Likelihood of returning

Overall, church-leavers who had disengaged on grounds concerning costs and benefits were more likely to regard themselves as permanent disaffiliates than as potential returners. This pattern persisted across all three themes discussed within this section.

First, church-leavers who associated their disengagement from church with not having had their needs met were less likely to place themselves among the potential returners. While 53% of the permanent disaffiliates complained that the church did not meet their needs, the proportion fell to 26% among the potential returners. While 40% of the permanent disaffiliates complained that there was nothing in church-going for them, the proportion fell to 10% among the potential returners. While 41% of the permanent disaffiliates considered that their non-church-going friends did not seem to miss out on anything, the proportion fell to 24% among the potential returners.

Second, church-leavers who associated their disengagement from church with not being helped in their spiritual growth were less likely to place themselves among the potential returners. While 48% of the permanent disaffiliates considered that the church was not helping them to find meaning and purpose in their life, the proportion fell to 24% among the potential returners. While 44% of the permanent disaffiliates complained that the church was not meeting their spiritual needs, the proportion fell to 23% among the potential returners.

195

Third, church-leavers who associated their disengagement from church with too many demands and too little return were less likely to place themselves among the potential returners. While 47% of the permanent disaffiliates felt that church had become a chore, with little enjoyment, the proportion fell to 30% among potential returners.

Pastoral implications

This section makes it clear that two out of every five church-leavers associated their disengagement from church with the general impression that their church-going had not been giving good returns on the commitment that they had invested. This way of looking at things influenced church-leavers of both sexes, across the age range, and throughout the various denominations. Church-leavers who took this view of things tended to leave church suddenly rather than gradually and then tended to see themselves as remaining outside the church rather than becoming potential returners.

Good pastoral practice needs to recognise that it is neither uncommon nor unnatural for some church-goers to come to the point where they feel that the church is not giving a good return on their investment. It is important for church leaders to be aware of what is going on, but at the same time to be cautious about taking responsibility or blame for such disengagement.

There is, however, one issue raised in this section concerning which pastoral sensitivity may be more important. Overall, 5% of church-leavers felt that the church was making increasing demands on their money, and this proportion rose to 10% among those who disengaged later in life. Ageing church members living on pensions and reduced incomes may sometimes begin to feel hard pressed in meeting all their previous financial commitments. It would be a great shame if lack of pastoral insight allowed such ageing church members to marginalise themselves from church life, at a time in life when they have so much to offer the church and at the same time so much to receive from the church.

12

Disillusionment with the church

Setting the scene

From a sociological perspective, the church functions on a number of levels in ways highly similar to other voluntary associational organisations. On this account, reasons for disengagement from church may also be highly similar to reasons offered for disengagement from other voluntary bodies. In their perceptive study of volunteering, Thomas and Finch (1990) offered insights into the motivations and experiences of individuals engaging with a range of voluntary bodies. Their analysis suggested that one of the key reasons people leave voluntary organisations in general is because they have become disenchanted or disillusioned with the organisation. If this is so in voluntary organisations in general, disenchantment and disillusionment may be even more prominent among those who leave religious organisations, where idealism and high expectations are often assumed to be central to the gospel proclamation. The aim of the present chapter, therefore, is to examine the extent to which church-leavers themselves explain their distance from the church in terms of disillusionment with the church. Listening to our interviewees, four main themes emerged within the broad area of disillusionment with the church. We described these themes as: the fragmented vision, the local church, issues of justice and power, and issues of sex and sexuality.

The fragmented vision

The first theme focused on what can be described as the fragmented vision, or as the discontinuity between the ideal and the reality in the life of the church. Some church-leavers said quite simply that they were disillusioned by the church's failure to live up to its ideals. Others felt that the church, as they experienced it, lacked a sense of purpose and vision. Some pointed to 'the splits between the denominations' as a cause for disillusionment. Others found that the church was much too preoccupied with maintaining buildings rather than concentrating on core gospel matters. Disillusion caused by the church's failure to live up to its ideals was well expressed by Justin Wyatt, a student in his twenties who had left an Anglican church.

> What the church stands for is a great idea, I mean, I'm a socialist, and obviously Jesus was, well, this character was the greatest socialist there ever was, if you take it as being all true. Yet, the church seems to have lost its direction on that, and it's become such a money-making organisation, you know, gambling its money on the stock exchange, and it claims to have lost all these millions of pounds, but it shouldn't have done anything to lose them anyway. And it shouldn't have had all this surplus money in the first place . . . I mean the congregation that comes over here to church, from the village, is very right wing, yet they'll come to church and spout about giving to others, and whatever . . . yet they'll go home and they'll not do any of it, and it just seems a bit hypocritical, really.

For Richard Elliot, a man in his sixties who had left an Anglican church, disillusionment came about when the General Synod failed to articulate what he understood as being a clear biblical condemnation of homosexuality.

I'd always accepted that lots of things were being said by various bishops and various members of the clergy, who could have been a minority of the whole. But, then, when the church together came to discuss it finally, and they fudged the whole issue, and they refrained from saying that it was immoral, I can't remember the exact wording of it, but what it meant was that they fudged the issue, they wouldn't say yes, and they wouldn't say no, and they wouldn't condemn it, and they didn't take the biblical attitude, which disgusted me. Because I thought that here was a thing, the whole church is here in the [General] Synod, and now is their opportunity to speak out, and to say, 'well, the word of God says that this is a sin, and you know, it's unfortunate that people will persist in this sort of activity, but the Bible says that it's a sin, and it will be judged by God', but they don't get down to ever saying that. They try to say something different . . . That's my basic opposition, or the reason I left the church was because of that.

The local church

The second theme focused on ways in which the local church could be a cause of disillusionment for some of its members. Some church-leavers said that they were disillusioned by local factions within the church. Some church-leavers argued that they disliked the hypocrisy they saw in other church-goers. Other church-leavers said that they felt some fellow church-goers were not authentic Christians. Disillusionment with the hypocrisy of fellow church-goers was cited by Arron Coates, a postgraduate student in his twenties, as fuelling his decision to leave a Roman Catholic church.

We had a real Catholic ethos, we were young people, teenagers, sort of sixteen, seventeen, eighteen, that would go to church, would enjoy going to church, and would go together as friends, you know, and would do things for the church, and play an active part in the Catholic school, but they are all disillusioned, because I don't think the church means anything to them anymore. And it makes me, it does make me really sad, because it's a faith that I was proud of, and still have tinges of pride, because there are people doing a lot of good, just because people, I think, need God, really . . . [If I go to church] I think, 'God, you people just aren't here for the right reason'. They're here . . . because it's Sunday and they're Catholics, they've got to go to church, so they sit at the back, they mumble through a few things, they give money whenever a basket's passed under their nose, and as soon as he says, 'go in the name of God', they're out, and I just feel really uncomfortable because that's not what I want to be a part of. So that's partly why I don't go.

Disillusionment caused by hypocrisy was cited by Gareth Wilkinson, a businessman in his forties, as fuelling his decision to leave a Methodist church.

I began, began to be aware of some real hypocrisy. Some of the characters in the church who were in the position, to me, of being really strong, correct people, role models, examples, you know, actually in my experience turned out to be not that. And so there was also that growing disillusionment. There was also this, also a lot of very big egos. And I was left with the impression, and this still happens to me, that many of the people who were lay people, but were in positions of great power and influence in the church, had a correspondingly low power and influence at their place of work. It was almost as if they were exercising their power in the church rather than during the week. Now, I'm not being critical of them for that, but what I did observe, very acutely when I was a child, was that we had some real little Hitlers, who were perhaps ill-equipped to be in those positions of responsibility and authority and sort of leadership.

201

Issues of justice and power

The third theme focused on ways in which the church's attitude toward issues of justice and power could be a cause of disillusionment for some of its members. Some church-leavers said that they were disillusioned by the church's materialism. Others were disillusioned by the church's abuse of power. For another group the church's lack of response to social injustice was the major ground for disillusionment. Other church-leavers were disillusioned by church-goers' racism. Disillusion hit Arron Coates, a postgraduate student who had left a Roman Catholic church, when he discovered a stalwart member of the church shouting racial abuse at a football match.

> You get particular families who are really prominent in each parish . . . and the woman is there in the door selling the *Roman Catholic News*, or whatever it's called, and all the sons are altar boys, and dad is doing the readings and the collecting, and they organise whatever charity group is going on, or whatever's going on, if there's a bingo on, he's calling the numbers, that's your parish family. Well, there was one in my church . . . And once, I was at a football match, and there was a black player playing, and there were people shouting, 'get back on your banana boat, you black so-and-so', and I mean, it was them, it was the dad and the ten-year-old boy shouting out really racist abuse. That was on the Saturday, and then on the Sunday they're in church, and my church is dominantly white, and their chests out, looking like great Catholics, and everyone saying, 'oh, it's great to see you here, you're doing such a fine job', you know, and I was thinking that I don't really want to be part of this congregation, and that I really don't want to be part of the church there, you know.

Alison Matthews, a young social worker who had left a Roman

Catholic church, had found the church's materialism and abuse of power offensive.

> I look at some churches, like the Salvation Army, you know, that really see, as the main focus of their religion and their witness to their belief, caring for the poor and needy like Jesus did, and I look at the Catholic Church . . . sure there are great people within the Catholic Church who do wonderful things for the poor and needy, but I look at the main focal power base of the Catholic Church, which is the Vatican, and there's gold, and there's wealth, and there's wonderful works of art there, and that angers me, that really angers me. And I looked at that again, because I was in the process of questioning my belonging to the church . . . and realised that that was something that I found very, very, very difficult to come to terms with. And I questioned whether in belonging to the church, I was condoning something which I felt deep inside me to be morally wrong, and that was that religion is used to create power for certain individuals. I believe it is.

Issues of sex and sexuality

The fourth theme focused on ways in which the church's attitude toward issues of sex and sexuality could be a cause of disillusionment for some of its members. Some church-leavers said that they had been disillusioned by church-goers' attitudes to women. Some had been disillusioned by church-goers' attitudes to homosexuals. Others had been disillusioned by church-goers' attitudes to lesbians. For Alison Matthews, a young social worker who had left a Roman Catholic church, a decisive issue was to do with the Catholic Church's attitude toward women.

> Basically the whole power hierarchy, is exclusively male, you know, we're sort of led to believe that just because women can

203

go up on the altar and do readings, and even girls can be altar servers now. And isn't that great? And what are we moaning about? Whereas, the whole power hierarchy of the priesthood, and therefore priests, bishops, cardinals, whatever, and eventually the Pope, it's exclusively male and probably always will be, and especially, you know, now the Anglican Church is allowing female ordination, and the Catholic Church is welcoming people from the Anglican Church, who are joining the Catholic Church specifically because of that issue, and that angered me a lot, because I thought, you know, there's surely a whole lot more that the Catholic Church is about than this one issue. I mean, there's the whole issue of transubstantiation and stuff like that, where we differ from the Anglican Church, and I think that's where it's important, that's about belief, that's about God, and your relationship with God, and when you take the bread and wine, what it is that's actually happening there, and to me that's a very important issue. And the fact that people were being allowed to become Catholics just because they didn't think women should be allowed to be priests, which is something I totally very strongly disagree with anyway, that angered me very much.

Listening to the statistics

A set of questions included in the survey set out to examine how much church-leavers cited the four themes concerned with disillusionment with the church as implicated in their own experience of leaving church. An overview of the findings is presented in Table 12, in the Appendix.

From these data it is clear that a number of church-leavers had become disillusioned with the church in a variety of ways. It is the local church which stands in the front line for much of this criticism. Nearly half of the church-leavers (47%) associated their disengagement from church with dislike for the hypocrisy that they saw in other church-goers. In similar vein, 31% of church-leavers felt that other church-goers were not authentic Christians. One in five church-leavers (21%) said that they were disillusioned by local factions within the church.

Taking a somewhat wider view than that of the local church, one in three church-leavers (32%) associated their disengagement from church with what they saw as the church's failure to live up to its ideals. One in four church-leavers (25%) felt that the church lacked a sense of purpose and vision. More specifically, both the denominational structures and the concern with maintaining buildings came in for significant criticism. Thus, 31% of church-leavers were disillusioned by splits between church denominations, and 17% considered that the church was much too preoccupied with maintaining buildings.

Issues of justice and power figured quite prominently in the disillusionment about the church experienced by church-leavers. Well over one-quarter of church-leavers said that they were disillusioned by the church's materialism (31%), disillusioned by the church's lack of response to social injustice (29%), or disillusioned by the church's abuse of power (28%). One in every five church-leavers (21%) said that they were disillusioned by church-goers' racism.

Issues of sex and sexuality also figured quite prominently in the disillusionment about church experienced by church-leavers. One-quarter of church-leavers said that they were disillusioned by church-goers' attitudes to women (24%), disillusioned by church-goers' attitudes to homosexuals (24%), or disillusioned by church-goers' attitudes to lesbians (24%).

Sex differences

Generally disillusionment with the church played a very similar role in the disengagement of both men and women from the church, across all four themes explored in this section. The only item in this section that received a statistically significant level of difference in response between men and women concerned the issue of power. While 25% of the women were disillusioned by the church's abuse of power, the proportion rose to 34% among the men.

Generational differences

In terms of the fragmented vision and in terms of issues of sex and sexuality there were significant differences between the youngest age group (under forty) and the oldest age group (sixty or over). The fragmented vision held a higher profile in the disillusionment of the older group, while issues of sex and sexuality held a higher profile in the disillusionment of the younger group.

In terms of the fragmented vision, disillusionment caused by the church's failure to live up to its ideals was expressed by 28% of those under the age of forty and by 28% of those in their forties or fifties, but the proportion rose to 41% among those aged sixty or over. Disillusionment caused by splits between church denominations was expressed by 26% of those under the age of forty and by 29% of those in their forties or fifties, but the proportion rose to 38% among those aged sixty or over.

In terms of issues of sex and sexuality, 30% of those under the age of forty were disillusioned by church-goers' attitudes to women, compared with 23% of those in their forties or fifties and 19% of those aged sixty or over. One-third of those under the age of forty (33%) were disillusioned by church-goers' attitudes to homosexuals, compared with 18% of those in their forties or fifties and 23% of those aged sixty or over. One-third of those under the age of forty (34%) were disillusioned by church-goers' attitudes to lesbians, compared with 18% of those in their forties or fifties and 23% of those aged sixty or over.

Cohort differences

Disillusionment with the church, overall, played similar roles in church-leaving among those who decided to leave the church over twenty years ago and among those who decided to leave the church within the past twenty years. Just one item in this section recorded a statistically significant difference between the two groups, and this item concerned denominationalism. Disillusionment caused by splits between church denominations played a more important role in church-leaving over twenty years ago than within the past twenty years. This concern was voiced by 27% of those who disengaged from church within the past twenty years, compared with 34% of those who disengaged over twenty years ago.

Age at leaving

Issues of sex and sexuality play a more important role in church-leaving during the younger years of life. Thus, 29% of those who left church before their twentieth birthday said that they were disillusioned by church-goers' attitudes to women, compared with 22% of those who left church in their twenties or thirties and 15% of those who left church after their fortieth birthday. Over one-quarter of those who left church before their twentieth birthday (28%) said that they were disillusioned by church-goers' attitudes to homosexuals or lesbians, compared with 22% of those who left church in their twenties or thirties and 16% of those who left church after their fortieth birthday.

Dislike of hypocrisy also plays a more important role in church-leaving during the younger years of life. Half of those who left church before their twentieth birthday (49%) or who left church in their twenties or thirties (48%) voiced their dislike for the hypocrisy they saw in other church-goers, compared with 37% of those who left after their fortieth birthday. In other respects, however, disillusionment with the church played a

207

similar role in disengagement from church at the three stages of life (under twenty, twenties or thirties, and forty or over).

Denomination

Disillusionment with the church played a higher profile role in the decision to leave church among Roman Catholics than among members of other denominations. For example, in terms of the fragmented vision, 31% of Roman Catholics associated their church-leaving with the criticism that the church lacked a sense of purpose and vision, compared with 25% of Anglicans and 17% of Free Church members.

In terms of issues of justice and power, 42% of Roman Catholics had been disillusioned by the church's materialism, compared with 31% of Anglicans and 23% of Free Church members. Similarly, 45% of Roman Catholics had been disillusioned by the church's lack of response to social injustice, compared with 26% of Anglicans and 28% of Free Church members. Half of the Roman Catholics (48%) had been disillusioned by the church's abuse of power, compared with 25% of Anglicans and 22% of Free Church members.

In terms of issues of sex and sexuality, 35% of Roman Catholics had been disillusioned by church-goers' attitudes to homosexuals, compared with 21% of Anglicans and 21% of Free Church members. One-third of Roman Catholics (34%) had been disillusioned by church-goers' attitudes to lesbians, compared with 20% of Anglicans and 22% of Free Church members. A similar, although not statistically significant trend was found in respect of attitudes to women: 29% of Roman Catholics had been disillusioned by church-goers' attitudes to women, compared with 24% of Anglicans and 19% of Free Church members.

Only in terms of disillusionment with the local church were the levels expressed by Roman Catholics consistent with those expressed by the other denominational groups.

Sudden or gradual leaving

Similar levels of disillusionment with the church were often shared by those whose leaving had been gradual and by those whose leaving had been sudden. Four aspects of disillusionment with the church were, however, associated more often with sudden leaving. For example, 37% of the sudden leavers had been disillusioned by the church's failure to live up to its ideals, compared with 27% of the gradual leavers. One-third of the sudden leavers (33%) had been disillusioned by the church's abuse of power, compared with 25% of the gradual leavers. Similarly, 35% of the sudden leavers had been disillusioned by the church's lack of response to social injustice, compared with 25% of the gradual leavers. Over one-quarter of the sudden leavers (27%) had been disillusioned by church-goers' attitudes to women, compared with 21% of gradual leavers.

Likelihood of returning

Church-leavers who had disengaged on grounds of disillusionment with the church were more likely to regard themselves as permanent disaffiliates than as potential returners. Of the 14 questions in this section, 13 revealed significant differences between potential returners and permanent disaffiliates, suggesting that disillusionment builds real and lasting barriers between former church-goers and the church today.

In terms of the fragmented vision, 29% of the permanent disaffiliates complained that the church lacked a sense of purpose and vision, compared with 18% of the potential returners. Two out of every five permanent disaffiliates (41%) had been disillusioned by the church's failure to live up to its ideals, compared with 20% of the potential returners. One out of every three permanent disaffiliates (34%) had been disillusioned by splits between the denominations, compared with 18% of the potential returners. One in every five of the permanent disaffiliates (20%) had been disillusioned by the church's preoccupation with maintaining buildings, compared with 12% of the potential returners.

In terms of the local church, 56% of the permanent disaffiliates had disliked the hypocrisy they saw in other church-goers, compared with 33% of the potential returners. While 37% of permanent disaffiliates had felt that other church-goers were not authentic Christians, the proportion fell to 23% among potential returners.

In terms of issues of justice and power, there were much higher levels of disillusionment among the permanent disaffiliates than among the potential returners concerning the church's materialism (37% compared with 20%), the church's abuse of power (37% compared with 12%), the church's lack of response to social injustice (37% compared with 8%), and church-goers' racism (28% compared with 10%).

In terms of issues of sex and sexuality, there were much higher levels of disillusionment among the permanent disaffiliates than among the potential returners concerning church-goers' attitudes to women (31% compared with 14%), church-goers' attitudes to homosexuals (31% compared with 17%) and church-goers' attitudes to lesbians (31% compared with 16%).

Pastoral implications

This section makes it clear that disillusionment with the church has a significant part to play in turning large numbers of church-goers into church-leavers. It is also clear that church-leavers had become disillusioned in a variety of ways, and that particular issues are of greater significance to some clearly defined sectors of church-leavers. The church's abuse of power is of particular salience among men. Church-goers' attitudes toward women, homosexuals and lesbians are of particular salience among

210

younger people and among those who leave church before their twentieth birthday. Disillusionment is a particularly salient factor among Roman Catholic church-leavers. Moreover, church-leavers who leave disillusioned with the church are among those likely to remain disaffiliated from the church.

At one level, disillusionment with the church is almost unavoidable. Theologically, the church recognises that it is not a perfect institution and that church-goers are not perfect human beings. The church is continually being shaped and perfected by its Lord. Church-goers are continually being formed and perfected by their Lord. In the meanwhile, the church and church-goers offer an imperfect vision of what they are called, by the grace of God, to become.

Such a theology, however, provides no excuses for the damage done to the gospel by such imperfect witness. One of our key findings from *Gone but not Forgotten* was the vital importance of following up those who had left churches and the need to take the trouble to listen to why people had decided to leave. British churches tend to be over-diffident about approaching leavers and afraid of being seen as too intrusive. But church-leavers can all too easily interpret this diffidence as lack of interest and abandonment by their former church. Listening to the arguments voiced by church-leavers should continually challenge the church to assess its priorities, to evaluate its commitments and to review its public face. The command not to place stumbling blocks in the paths of others needs to be heard and heeded with all seriousness (Leviticus 19.14). Listening to church-leavers has demonstrated that the stumbling block of denominational divisions has become less prominent during the past twenty years. Here is some good evidence that stumbling blocks can be removed from the path to faith and some good evidence of the progress that has been (and is being) made by the ecumenical processes.

On the other hand, while problems caused by denominational divisions appear to be receding a little, the younger generation of church-leavers are experiencing greater difficulties with the church's attitude toward women and toward same-sex relationships. The ways in which the church handles materialism, power, social injustice and racism continue to matter to church-goers, to church-leavers, and to the world as a whole.

13

Being let down by the church

Setting the scene

Every so often a high profile case hits the media demonstrating how an individual church or church-leader has seriously let down a number of people. Roland Howard's (1996) description of the rise and fall of the 'Nine O'clock Service' provided a powerful account of one such case. He argued that the Nine O'clock Service developed into a cult which enabled abusive leadership to flourish. Far from being the more open, democratic, non-sexist, alternative community it claimed to be, this group was characterised by fear, a guilt-inducing culture, extreme hierarchy, dependency, manipulation, sexism, and excessive secrecy. Howard (1996: 41) went on to suggest that similar experiences may be reproduced in a less high-profile way in other churches. The aim of the present chapter, therefore, is to examine the extent to which church-leavers themselves explain their distance from the church in terms of being let down by the church, either in dramatic or less dramatic ways. Listening to our interviewees, three main themes emerged within the broad area of profoundly disappointing experiences with the church or its leaders. We described these themes as: lack of care and support, lack of professionalism, and abuse of power.

Lack of care and support

The first theme focused on ways in which the local church has been perceived by some church-leavers as showing a lack of care and support when people needed it. Some church-leavers said quite simply that the church had failed them in some way. Others said that they had felt let down by the church at a time when they needed its support. Some church-leavers said that they did not find the church to be caring and supportive. Others placed the blame more squarely on the clergy, claiming that the clergy did not provide sufficient care for them. The story told by Sarah Johnson, a homemaker in her thirties who had left an Anglican church, illustrates how the feeling of being let down by the local church can really hurt.

> When the children were born there was only, there was only the children's godparent who would come to see us, especially when [my daughter] was born, because by then my Mum had died, so basically I was on my own. My husband was here but I felt more on my own, and there was only one of the children's godparents from the old church who bothered to visit, and at the time I was feeling very low . . . What made me cross was when Mum died that my Dad, even though we lived [further away], my Dad was only just round the corner, and yet my Dad never got a visit from the fellowship either, so that spoke a lot to me. I think he had one or two visits in the whole time, by a couple of people. That spoke a lot, because I'd made excuses for them, I just kept saying to myself 'they're not coming because we live so far away', because I don't think you want to feel that hurt . . . and you make excuses, and I made those excuses, but Dad never got any support, Dad never got the fellowship. I think he could be a cantankerous old person at times [laughter], I'm not saying he's the easiest person, but yes, I think he felt let down as well.

The way in which some church-leavers had felt let down by the clergy was well known to John Ingram, a vicar whom we interviewed to find out his perceptions of why people leave church. He told about how he meets disappointed people.

> I meet some very disappointed people . . . I guess, if it's a case of well . . . 'the vicar never came to visit me when I was in trouble', well, they'll never ever trust another vicar, and so that's sort of a bit of, well, like any broken relationship . . . it's very difficult to sew it together again.

Lack of professionalism

The second theme focused on ways in which the local church has been perceived by some church-leavers as showing a lack of professionalism. Some church-leavers had felt misdirected by the church when they needed its support. Some church-leavers complained that the church's pastoral care was unprofessional to them as individuals. Other church-leavers complained that the church's pastoral care was unprofessional to others whom they knew. An example of how unprofessional practice in the area of child protection had finally pushed a church-goer into becoming a church-leaver was provided by Nicholas White, a freelance producer who had left an independent Baptist church. He told us of the church's unprofessional pastoral care which had reinforced his previous decision to leave.

> There was a young lad in that church who had been abused when he was . . . a boy, he was about eleven, in a children's home by a member of staff who was a member of that church . . . and this young lad knew us and knew we were foster parents, and came to us one night, told us what had happened. He'd gone to the minister a couple of years before and told him what had happened and wanted help, and the minister just

said, 'well, we'll pray with you' and that was it, just basically 'if you forgive and forget now' and left it. And so we said, 'right, what do you want to do?', and he said 'I want to go into the police', because he found other children basically had been abused by the same person. Now this person wasn't any longer a member of the church, but certainly everyone knew him . . . So we said, 'OK', and then we asked him. He basically he was leaving a situation that wasn't very good, and so we said, 'look, we haven't got [foster] children at the moment, stay with us while you go through this, because it's going to be pretty awful'. So we had to ring up the [minister] and . . . we basically said 'this is the situation, and it's a problem obviously because we've fallen out with you, but we want this young man to be able to carry on going to the youth group, because that's his environment and his safety, and it's wrong to kind of drag him out of that just because he's living with us, so we don't want any problems between us and you, and we want everyone to kind of be adult about this.' And their initial response was quite definitely 'kindly persuade him not to go to the police', and we just said, 'forget it', you know, 'we're foster parents, our train-ing says that, yes, there are other things at stake here far way and beyond your feelings or what you think is going to be wrong.'

Abuse of power

The third theme focused on ways in which the local church had been perceived by some church-leavers as showing an abuse of power. Some church-leavers complained that the church's pastoral care had been psychologically abusive to them. Others complained that the church's pastoral care had been sexually abusive to them. Some even complained that they had been threatened with physical violence by a church leader. In this con-text Matthew Williams, a freelance graphic designer in his forties who had left a New Church congregation, told us about his experience of being subject to abusive counselling.

> I had some very extremely horrific counselling . . . [The minister] accused me of being a homosexual or being in love with him, and I believed him [laughter], and I kind of, and he said 'you mustn't tell your wife, because your wife will be very upset' . . . I said 'well, surely I'm not a homosexual, to have sex is related to desire, and if I was a homosexual I should, surely there should be some sexual fantasies, or something', and I told him of various dreams I'd had about my father, and he interpreted these dreams to mean that I was homosexual. The only thing I think now, is that he actually had strong homosexual leanings himself and wasn't willing to face up to it. So the way he kind of worked within the church was [with] . . . this group, there were about five men, all young men, all of us quite handsome really, and he was kind of trying to help us and so on, and then when the church fell apart he pushed us right away and suddenly became very cold, and horrific really in a way. And I think I had some kind of psychological problems relating to my father when I think about it, and he kind of used those, and he abused it really. And everyone in the church was never encouraged to go outside the church for counselling, everyone was always counselled in the church, and the counselling was absolutely horrific, it was really abusive.

Listening to the statistics

A set of questions included in the survey set out to examine how much church-leavers cited these three themes concerned with being let down by the church as implicated in their own experience of leaving church. An overview of the findings is presented in Table 13, in the Appendix.

From these data it is clear that there is a significant number of church-leavers who disengage from church feeling that they have been let down by the church. For some being let down by the church involved what they saw to have been a lack of care and support. One in every five church-leavers (20%) had not found the church to be caring and supportive. Looking at more specific issues, 14% said that the clergy had not provided sufficient care for them; 14% said that they had felt let down by the church at a time when they needed its support; and 14% said that the church had failed them in some way.

For some being let down by the church involved what they saw to have been a lack of professionalism. As many as one in ten church-leavers (10%) had felt misdirected by the church when they needed its support. This note of criticism was sharpened when 4% felt that the church's pastoral care to them had been unprofessional and when 5% felt that the church's pastoral care of others had been unprofessional.

For some being let down by the church involved what they saw to have been an abuse of power. Although the number of church-leavers who felt that they had been the victim of direct abuse of power is small, the fact that such cases exist at all may be a proper matter of concern. The evidence shows that 4% of church-leavers had felt that the church's pastoral care had been psychologically abusive to them; 1% had felt that the church's pastoral care had been sexually abusive to them; and 1% reported that they had been threatened with physical violence by a church leader.

Sex differences

Being let down by the church is a factor that had a similar level of influence in the disengagement of both men and women from the church. The one item within this set of ten items that recorded a statistically significant difference between the responses of men and women concerned the care provided by the clergy. This issue was felt more acutely by the women than by the men. Thus, 17% of the women complained that the clergy did not provide sufficient care for them, compared with 10% of the men.

Generational differences

Being let down by the church is a factor that had a similar level of influence in the disengagement from church among all three generational groups analysed in this study (those under the age of forty, those in their forties or fifties, and those aged sixty or over). The one item within this set of ten items that recorded a statistically significant difference between the responses of the three age groups concerned the sense of having been failed by the church. This issue was felt more acutely by the oldest age group. Thus, 19% of those aged sixty or over said that the church had failed them in some way, compared with 13% of those in their forties or fifties and 11% of those under the age of forty.

Cohort differences

Being let down by the church is a factor that had a similar level of influence in the disengagement from church of those who left over twenty years ago and of those who left in the past twenty years. The one item within this set of ten items that recorded a statistically significant difference between the responses of the two cohorts concerned the care provided by the clergy. This issue was felt more acutely by the more recent cohort. Thus, 17% of those who left church within the past twenty years complained that the clergy did not provide sufficient care for them, compared with 11% of those who left church over twenty years ago.

Age at leaving

Being let down by the church is a factor that had an increasingly important influence in the disengagement from church at later stages in life. This is seen most clearly in connection with perceived lack of care and support. One in 11 of those who left church before their twentieth birthday (9%) felt that the church had failed them in some way, but the proportions increased to 17% among those who left in their twenties or thirties and to 17% among those who left after their fortieth birthday. One in 11 of those who left church before their twentieth birthday (9%) had felt let down by the church at a time when they needed its support, but the proportions increased to 15% among those who left in their twenties or thirties and to 21% among those who left after their fortieth birthday.

While 9% of those who left before their twentieth birthday criticised the clergy for not providing sufficient care for them, the proportions rose to 15% among those who left in their twenties or thirties, and to 23% among those who left after their fortieth birthday. While 17% of those who left before their twentieth birthday had not found the church to be caring and supportive, the proportions rose to 19% among those who left in their twenties or thirties and to 30% among those who left after their fortieth birthday.

A similar age-related pattern occurred in respect of criticising the church as lacking in professionalism. While 3% of those who left before their twentieth birthday criticised the church's pastoral care to them as unprofessional, the proportions rose to 4% among those who left in their twenties or thirties and to 9% among those who left after their fortieth birthday.

The remaining five items in this section did not reveal significant differences between the three groups.

Denomination

Being let down by the church has been discussed in this chapter in terms of three main themes. Two of the themes (lack of care and support and lack of professionalism) had a similar level of influence in the disengagement from church of Anglicans, Free Church members and Roman Catholics. The third theme discussed in this chapter (abuse of power), however, recorded statistically significant differences between the responses of the three denominational groups. The abuse of power had been felt most acutely by Roman Catholic church-leavers. Thus, 11% of Roman Catholics complained that the church's pastoral care was psychologically abusive to them, compared with 3% of Anglicans and 0% of Free Church members. Roman Catholics also were more likely to mention physical violence: 3% of Roman Catholics complained that they had been threatened with physical violence by a church leader, compared with less than 1% of the other two denominational groups. Although not statistically significant, 3% of Roman Catholics complained that the church's pastoral care had been sexually abusive to them, compared with 1% of Anglicans and 1% of Free Church members.

Sudden or gradual leaving

Being let down by the church is a factor which is almost as likely to lead to gradual leaving as to sudden leaving. For example, 15% of those who left suddenly had felt that the church had failed them in some way, and so had 14% of those who left gradually. On the other hand, there were three issues explored in this section that were more likely to lead to sudden leaving. Thus, 17% of the sudden leavers had felt let down by the church at a time when they needed its support, compared with 12% of the gradual leavers. Those who directly accused the church of unprofessionalism were twice as likely to be found among the sudden leavers. Thus,

6% of the sudden leavers complained that the church's pastoral care to them was unprofessional, compared with 3% of the gradual leavers; and 6% of the sudden leavers complained that the church's pastoral care to others was unprofessional, compared with 3% of the gradual leavers.

Likelihood of returning

Church-leavers who had disengaged feeling that they had been let down by the church are to be found in equal percentages among those who regard themselves as permanent disaffiliates and those who regard themselves as potential returners. For example, in terms of lack of care and support, 16% of the potential returners felt that the clergy had not provided sufficient care for them, and so had 16% of the permanent disaffiliates.

Pastoral implications

This section makes it clear that a significant number of church-leavers went feeling let down by the church in one way or another. Several pastoral implications follow from the different themes explored in this chapter.

The first implication follows from the recognition that 14% of church-leavers felt that the church had failed them, or that they had been let down by the church at a time when they needed its support (and this proportion rises to 21% among those who leave church after the age of forty). Here are people who feel hurt by the church. Whether they have a right to feel hurt or not is in many senses immaterial. Where there is hurt, the church holds a mandate to hold out the hand of reconciliation and the hand of healing.

The second implication follows from the recognition that 14% of church-leavers left blaming the clergy for not providing sufficient care for them. The proportion is significantly higher among female church-leavers and among those who left after the age of forty. Moreover, the culture of placing blame on the clergy has been more prevalent within the past twenty years. In this context, pastoral care needs to be extended not only to the church-leaver who goes away blaming the clergy, but also to the clergy who carry the weight of blame and the potential consequent guilt. Often the expectations that others place on the clergy are too high. Often the expectations that clergy place on themselves are too high. Mechanisms are clearly needed to help clergy deal with their own emotions when church-leavers let them know (sometimes very clearly) that they are blaming the clergy for their disengagement from church life.

The third implication follows from the recognition that between four and five church-leavers in every hundred go away feeling that the church's pastoral care has been unprofessional. The proportion is significantly higher among those who leave after the age of forty. Whether the accusation is fairly grounded or not, it clearly reminds church leaders of the proper expectations placed on pastoral practice in contemporary society. For professionally trained, ordained and lay licensed ministers within the various denominations the need is more than keeping in touch with professional standards through continuing professional development programmes. The need is for the regular, disciplined review of their individual practice as demanded by so many other 'caring professions'. It is also important to recognise how seriously pressure of work can begin to erode professional judgements.

At the same time, an increasing amount of the church's programme of pastoral care is being devolved onto volunteer lay people. The theology is correct that the whole baptised people of God are called to share in the vocation of ministry and mission. Yet baptism alone does not equip the people of God with the professional skills needed to exercise the ministry of pastoral care.

The churches that are properly committed to developing the ministry of the whole people of God need to be equally committed to providing the professional education and training that underpins such ministry.

The fourth implication follows from the accusations regarding abuse of power in the pastoral relationship. Four church-leavers in every hundred go away feeling psychologically abused, with one in every hundred going away feeling sexually abused. According to these church-leavers, some denominations are more open to the abuse of power than others. Given the seriousness of such accusations, a heavy responsibility continues to remain with those who take responsibility for selecting, training and ordaining church leaders and then providing them with a licence to practice. Some would maintain that routine psychological assessment of candidates for ministry could prove really useful in identifying those most susceptible to abusing the power placed into their hands by the church.

Overall, the kind of issues discussed in this chapter reflect badly on the ways in which churches tend to handle matters of pastoral breakdown. Churches need to become better at listening to, identifying and responding to the reasons underpinning such experiences.

14

Problems with relevance

Setting the scene

In their study of the 'drift from the churches' among children and young people in the United Kingdom, Kay and Francis (1996) drew attention to the importance of the notion of 'relevance' as a key to holding the membership of young people, and also to the importance of the opposite complaint of 'irrelevance' as a key to understanding the drift of young people from the churches. The complaint that 'the church seems irrelevant for life today' stood at the heart of Kay and Francis' (1996) analysis of the declining attitude toward Christianity during the teenage years. Views on what shapes an appreciation of the relevance of the church and what shapes dismissal of the church as irrelevant are, of course, likely to vary from individual to individual. The aim of the present chapter, therefore, is to examine the extent to which church-leavers themselves explain their distance from the church in terms of problems with relevance. Listening to our interviewees, three main themes emerged within the broad area of problems with relevance. We described these themes as: irrelevance, another planet, and de-institutionalised faith.

Irrelevance

The first theme focused on ways in which some church-leavers had come to regard the church as simply irrelevant to their life and to their experiences. In particular some church-leavers said that sermons were irrelevant to their everyday life. Others took a broader view and complained that the church's teaching was irrelevant to their everyday life. For some church-leavers irrelevance was voiced in terms of the church being anachronistic. Some said that the church was stuck in its views. Others complained that the church was too old-fashioned. It was one of the teenagers, Geoff, who was interviewed at the MAYC annual event, who expressed this theme of irrelevance as seen through the eyes of young people.

> A couple of, like, friends my age left, that I know, and really they just don't feel the church has anything relevant to them, and anything to offer them. And, you know, people are just becoming really disillusioned with the church, because everybody thinks it's dying . . . I think that there's a, like, a big generation gap thing as well. And also, the problem that, like, society thinks differently now, so what the church is trying to teach doesn't seem accepted, people feel that's alienating.

Another perspective on the apparent irrelevance of church teaching was given by Arron Coates, a postgraduate in his twenties, who had left a Roman Catholic church. He expressed his view like this.

> I think the church will run itself into the ground by not being receptive to the modern world and so on, and changing attitudes. I mean, OK, that's my own educated view of it. And I think there are issues like contraception that really need to be addressed. You know, I went to a Catholic school, I didn't get any education on contraception all the time I was there, and that is just irresponsible, you know, and I think it's arrogant of the church to think that because people have a Catholic education that they're somehow immune to the social problems and

some of the health risks of the world. My school had quite a high abortion rate, you know with teenage pregnancy rate, and I can only attribute that to the fact that people weren't being educated.

Another planet

The second theme focused on ways in which some church-leavers had come to feel that the church was really on 'another planet'. Some church-leavers actually expressed their discontent with the church as directly as this: to them the church felt like another planet. Some said that the church failed to connect with the rest of their life. Some said that they were not interested in the activities the church had on offer. Others summed up their feelings by saying that they were bored. This feeling that the church really belongs to another planet was well expressed by Kate White, a computer analyst who had left an independent Baptist church. She stated her case like this.

I wouldn't go back to a church because I don't think it's relevant. It's like there's no other aspect of life where you'd go on sitting in a room and do these strange actions, these standing up and sitting down, and singing along with the children, doing the actions in the choruses, and listening to someone who doesn't really know what they're talking about, talking at you for twenty minutes. So why do you have to do that for religion? It's not something that makes sense . . . I can no longer see why any intelligent person would go in and put themselves through a church service.

David, a member of a Methodist youth group, told us that he had stopped attending church because he was bored by it all.

I can't see any real point in going. It's just, I don't find it very interesting. Some old person standing up in front of one, waffling on about the Bible and God, it just doesn't interest me, really . . . I just got bored with it, and I didn't want to go, and I just didn't go.

Another teenager, Tracey, interviewed at the MAYC annual national event, also pointed to boredom.

It was boring. I didn't enjoy it. And it was old-fashioned . . . I was only young anyway, but, you know, it was very boring . . . It was just all boring. The minister was like really old and miserable.

Clergy also came in for criticism from Siobhan, a lapsed Roman Catholic teenager from Northern Ireland.

A lot of the priests are out of touch, you know, they're quite old, and it's just, you know, they don't really hold your concentration. You know, they talk more or less at the same level the whole time, and you know, you just get a bit bored and restless. I would prefer if there was something that kind of breaks the ice, and holds your attention more.

De-institutionalised faith

The third theme focused on ways in which some church-leavers had developed their faith in a de-institutionalised way outside the churches. Some church-leavers said that they had come to the view that you do not need to go to church to be a Christian. Others expressed their theology of de-institutionalised Christianity by saying that churches are not really necessary because people have God within them. Some church-leavers wanted to follow their own spiritual quest without the involvement of religious institutions. Others took the view that they distrusted most institutions and included the church in that overall attitude of distrust. It was Peter Kendall, a television producer in his forties who had left a Methodist church, who associated his church-leaving with a more general distrust of institutions.

> I tend not to like institutions that much. I don't mean that I don't like them in any sort of glib way, I just think institutions tend to always have alternative agendas . . . People argue that institutions [that] have a purpose, whether it's God or whether it's to achieve a social end, often get those purposes diverted because they create other agendas, because the people in them are in competition for power and whatever, and, you know, and there's sexual agendas, and all sorts of things that get in the way . . . Certainly the Methodist church was the first time that I began to formulate my opposition to institutions, and my first move away from the church was not to reject Christianity, but to reject what I call Churchianity. So there was Churchianity and Christianity, and Churchianity was the institutional form of the idea.

Alison Matthews, a social worker in her twenties who had left a Roman Catholic church, saw God as actively developing her faith by leading her away from church.

> I feel that God led me away from the church, in his mysterious wisdom, in order for me to discover more about my faith, and more about myself, and more about my relationship with God. And God will lead me somewhere, and I don't think it's right to question too much where God will lead me, because if I start rationalising about that, then I won't really be following my heart and following God, which is really what the whole reason for my leaving was about . . . I don't know right now if I'm looking to find another church that I feel completely comfortable with, because I don't know if there is such a church. I think it's not a problem for me right now to be worshipping on my

own, to be praying alone, in fact I've found that quite a positive experience, to be alone with God in a sense, without being guided by the human elements within the church, just to follow my instinct and my heart, and what I see to be God's will for me.

Listening to the statistics

A set of questions included in the survey set out to examine how much church-leavers cited these three themes concerned with problems with relevance as implicated in their own experience of leaving church. An overview of the findings is presented in Table 14, in the Appendix.

From these data it is clear that a high proportion of church-leavers had experienced problems with the relevance of the church to their lives in the contemporary world. This case is made consistently across the three themes explored in the present chapter.

First, nearly half of the church-leavers complained about the disconnection between the church and the rest of their lives. Thus, 46% of church-leavers said quite simply that the church had failed to connect with any other aspect of what they did or considered important. For 43% the truth of the matter was that they were simply not interested in the activities on offer at their local church. For 39% the situation could be summed up in the devastating dismissal of the church: they were bored. This perceived disconnection between church and the rest of life was summed up by 23% of church-leavers who said that, for them, the church felt like 'another planet'.

Second, at least one-third of church-leavers complained about the irrelevance of so much of the church's teaching. Thus, 33% of church-leavers considered that the church's teaching was irrelevant to their everyday life, and a somewhat higher proportion

(38%) considered that sermons were irrelevant to their everyday life. For some this problem with relevance was associated with the view that the church's teaching failed to keep in step with the modern world. One in every three church-leavers (33%) considered that the church was stuck in its views, and one in every four (26%) thought that the church was too old-fashioned.

Third, three-quarters of church-leavers had clearly disconnected the Christian faith from church attendance. In this sense, church attendance itself had become a matter of irrelevance, since for them, a de-institutionalised faith was taking over from institutionalised religion. Thus, 75% of church-leavers had taken the view that they did not need to go to church to be a Christian. Two out of every five church-leavers (40%) took the view that people have God within them and that, as a consequence, churches are not really necessary. One out of every three church-leavers (36%) explained that they wanted to follow their own spiritual quest, without religious institutions. For many church-leavers the distrust of the institutional church was part of a wider distrust of institutions. One in every four church-leavers (27%) said that they distrusted most institutions, including the church.

Sex differences

Problems with relevance is a factor that had a highly similar level of influence in the disengagement of both men and women from the church, and this applied across all three themes explored in this section. The one item within this set of 12 items that recorded statistically significant differences between the responses of men and women concerned the internalisation of de-institutionalised faith: 43% of the women claimed that people have God within them, so churches are not really necessary, compared with 35% of the men.

Generational differences

Problems with relevance were significantly more prominent in the minds of younger church-leavers, particularly when irrelevance was associated with a previous age or an outdated worldview. Thus, 37% of those under the age of forty associated their disengagement from church with the view that the church was too old-fashioned, compared with 24% of those in their forties or fifties and 18% of those aged sixty or over. Two out of every five church-leavers under the age of forty (41%) complained that the church was stuck in its views, compared with 32% of those in their forties or fifties and 27% of those aged sixty or over. Boredom played a significantly more prominent part in the disengagement from church among the younger generation of church-leavers. Half of the church-leavers under the age of forty (51%) said that they were bored with and by the church, compared with 39% of those in their forties or fifties and 28% of those aged sixty or over. For 27% of church-leavers under the age of forty the church had felt like 'another planet', compared with 25% of those in their forties or fifties and 16% of those aged sixty or over. Views concerning a move toward a de-institutionalised faith, however, did not vary significantly between the three age groups analysed in the present study.

Cohort differences

In many ways problems with relevance is a factor that had a similar level of influence in the disengagement from church of those who left over twenty years ago and of those who left in the past twenty years. Three of the 12 items within this section, however, revealed statistically significant differences between the responses of those who left over twenty years ago and those who left within the past twenty years. These items identify interesting shifts in perspective. While 33% of those who left over twenty years ago had distrusted most institutions, including the church, the proportion fell to 22% among those who left within the past twenty years. While 44% of those who left over twenty years ago considered sermons irrelevant to their everyday life, the proportion fell to 28% among those who left within the past twenty years. While 40% of those who left over twenty years ago had found the church's teaching irrelevant to their everyday life, the proportion fell to 28% among those who left in the past twenty years.

Age at leaving

Problems with relevance is a factor that played a significantly more important role in disengagement from church during the earlier stages of life. This trend is seen clearly throughout all three themes explored in the present chapter.

First, the simple complaint of irrelevance is voiced most clearly by those who left church before their twentieth birthday. Thus, 46% of those who left before their twentieth birthday complained that the church's teaching was irrelevant to their everyday life, compared with 27% of those who left in their twenties or thirties and 21% of those who left after their fortieth birthday. A similar trend applied to sermons: 47% of those who left before their twentieth birthday complained that sermons were irrelevant to their everyday life, compared with 33% of those who left in their twenties or thirties and 30% of those who left after their fortieth birthday. The complaint that the church was too old-fashioned was voiced by 36% of those who left before their twentieth birthday, by 22% of those who left in their twenties or thirties and by 13% of those who left after their fortieth birthday. The complaint that the church was stuck in its views was voiced by 40% of those who left before their twentieth birthday, by 32% of those who left in their twenties or thirties and by 21% of those who left after their fortieth birthday.

233

Second, the complaint that the church was on another planet was voiced most clearly by those who left church before their twentieth birthday. For 56% of those who left before their twentieth birthday, the church had failed to connect with the rest of their life, compared with 43% of those who left in their twenties or thirties and 33% of those who left after their fortieth birthday. The complaint that they were not interested in the activities on offer was voiced by 49%, 41% and 36% of the three groups. Over half of those who went before their twentieth birthday (55%) had left feeling bored with and by the church, compared with 33% of those who left in their twenties or thirties and 23% of those who left after their fortieth birthday. The church was dismissed as being on another planet by 33% of those who left before their twentieth birthday, compared with 18% of those who left in their twenties or thirties and 16% of those who left after their fortieth birthday.

Third, the distrust of institutions was strongest among those who left church before their twentieth birthday. One in every three church-leavers who left before their twentieth birthday (34%) said that they distrusted most institutions, including the church, compared with 24% of those who left in their twenties or thirties and 19% of those who left after their fortieth birthday.

Denomination

In a number of ways problems with relevance are voiced most strongly by Roman Catholic church-leavers. In terms of the first theme, 46% of Roman Catholics associated their disengagement from church with the complaint that the church was stuck in its views, compared with 31% of Anglicans and 25% of Free Church members. Sermons had been judged as irrelevant to their everyday life by 47% of Roman Catholics, compared with 36% of Anglicans and 35% of Free Church members.

In terms of the second theme, 57% of Roman Catholics associ-

234

ated their disengagement from church with the complaint that the church failed to connect with the rest of their life, compared with 44% of Anglicans and 47% of Free Church members. Half of the Roman Catholics (52%) said that they were just not interested in the activities on offer, compared with 44% of Anglicans and 32% of Free Church members.

The third theme did not, however, record statistically significant differences between the three denominational groups except in respect of one item. The Anglicans were most likely to believe that you do not have to go to church to be a Christian. This view was endorsed by 78% of Anglicans, compared with 70% of Roman Catholics and by 67% of Free Church members.

Sudden or gradual leaving

Generally problems with relevance is a factor which is almost as likely to lead to gradual leaving as to sudden leaving. However, there were four issues explored in this section which were more likely to lead to sudden leaving. Thus, 39% of the sudden leavers had found the church's teaching irrelevant to their everyday life, compared with 28% of the gradual leavers. Two-fifths of the sudden leavers (42%) judged sermons as irrelevant to their everyday life, compared with 34% of the gradual leavers. Nearly half of the sudden leavers (48%) had not been interested in the activities on offer, compared with 40% of the gradual leavers. One-third of the sudden leavers (32%) had distrusted most institutions, including the church, compared with 23% of the gradual leavers.

Likelihood of returning

Church-leavers who had disengaged following problems with relevance were much more likely to place themselves among the permanent disaffiliates rather than among the potential returners. Having left the church feeling that it was irrelevant to their lives, such church-leavers were reluctant to give the church another chance. For example, just 12% of the potential returners had dismissed the church's teaching as irrelevant to their everyday life, compared with 42% of the permanent disaffiliates. Just 17% of the potential returners had dismissed the church as too old-fashioned, compared with 31% of the permanent disaffiliates.

While just 7% of the potential returners had felt the church to be like 'another planet', the proportion rose to 29% among the permanent disaffiliates. While just 17% of the potential returners had been bored with and by the church, the proportion rose to 48% among the permanent disaffiliates. While 29% of the potential returners considered that the church had failed to connect with the rest of their life, the proportion rose to 54% among the permanent disaffiliates.

Church-leavers who had disengaged following problems with the relevance of institutionalised faith were much more likely to be found among the permanent disaffiliates. Thus, 43% of the permanent disaffiliates said that they had wanted to follow their own spiritual quest, without religious institutions, compared with 25% of the potential returners. Nearly two-fifths of the permanent disaffiliates (37%) said that they distrusted most institutions, including the church, compared with 14% of the potential returners. Over two-fifths of the permanent disaffiliates (42%) believed that people have God within them, so churches are not really necessary, compared with 24% of the potential returners.

Pastoral implications

This section makes it clear that a high proportion of church-leavers left feeling simply that the church was irrelevant to their lives. Around two-fifths of them had found sermons irrelevant, had been bored, lost interest in what the church had on offer, and had simply found that the church failed to connect with the rest of their lives. Three-quarters of them had taken the view that you do not need to go to church to be a Christian. Problems with relevance were of particular significance to church-leavers under the age of forty and to those who left before their twentieth birthday. Problems of relevance were of particular importance to Roman Catholic church-leavers. Moreover, those who left church having lost confidence in the relevance of the church were significantly less likely to want to try again by becoming church-returners. There are important pastoral implications that follow from such an analysis, but the path is neither simple nor straightforward.

First, the problem of irrelevance to the contemporary world and to contemporary lives is a perennial one facing the churches. On the one hand, there is the need to connect with contemporary culture, with contemporary life-styles and with contemporary issues. On the other hand, there is the need to remain faithful to the tradition. While the traditional way of being church continues to serve well many of those whose world-view has been shaped by that tradition, clearly for many the traditional way of being church remains an insuperable stumbling block. It is for this reason that contemporary experiments with 'fresh expressions' of church may be so important. Such experiments, however, need to be well-informed and carefully researched. There are plenty of good examples on the Fresh Expressions website (http://www.freshexpressions.org.uk/section.asp?id=256). The Fresh Expressions organisation is a five-year initiative set up by the Archbishops of Canterbury and York, together with the Methodist Council, building on the 2004 report, *Mission-shaped Church* (Archbishops' Council, 2004).

Second, the high proportions of church-leavers who complain of boredom in church need to be taken seriously. The privileges and responsibilities entrusted to those who conduct public worship are enormous. The presentation of liturgy, the provision of music, and the preaching of sermons are all highly skilled professional activities which can and need to be conducted to high standards. Time and resources invested in initial and continuing professional development in such areas is crucial both for ordained leaders and for lay volunteers. While the responsibility for personal boredom may rest heavily with some church-leavers, the churches themselves should not ignore the challenge posed by such an accusation.

Third, the fact that three out of every four church-leavers take the view that you do not need to go to church to be a Christian provides a salutary reminder that empty pews do not necessarily proclaim the death of Christian Britain. The 2001 national census for England and Wales recorded 72% of the adult population as Christian, the vast majority of whom must also share the view that you do not need to go to church to be a Christian. While a sectarian view of the church might wish to dismiss such people as deluded or as plainly wrong and misinformed, a more inclusive view of the church might recognise the Holy Spirit being active among such people and calling them to experiment with new expressions of church or to reconnect with traditional expressions of church on occasions like 'Back to Church Sunday', the major Christian festivals, or significant family events like weddings, baptisms and funerals.

15

Problems with change

Setting the scene

The management of change often emerges as one of the major difficulties facing churches at local, national and international levels. On the one hand, there is the strong pull from the tradition to protect the status quo and to hand on to the next generation the unchanged values and structures of the past. On the other hand, there is the strong pull from the social context to proclaim afresh the works of the Lord in a new language and in a new way to the next generation. The Roman Catholic Church still seems to be struggling with the conflict between continuity and discontinuity generated by the Second Vatican Council (see Louden and Francis, 2003). The Church of England still seems to be struggling with the debate initiated by a new generation of services consolidated by the publication of the *Alternative Service Book 1980*, continued in *Common Worship*, and strenuously opposed by the Prayer Book Society (Francis, Robbins and Astley, 2005). The aim of the present chapter, therefore, is to examine the extent to which church-leavers themselves explain their distance from the church in terms of problems with change. Listening to our interviewees, three main themes emerged within the broad area of problems with change. We described these themes as: the global direction, worship and liturgy, and local church.

The global direction

The first theme focused on broad and global dissatisfaction with the direction in which the church was going. Some church-leavers said simply that they did not like the direction in which the church was going. Others said that they did not like the changes that had happened in the church. Tim Harvey, a Church of Ireland clergyman interviewed to find out his perceptions of church-leaving, pointed very clearly to the way in which even subtle changes can have a devastating impact on some church-goers. He related the following experience.

There are all sorts of little things, that in our [Northern Ireland] context, create counter-reactions. To give you an example, shortly after I came to this parish I had a baptism, and it had been my practice in my [previous] parish to give a baptismal candle, and I did so at the first baptism, and I think most people didn't notice it, but the second baptism they did, and several people walked out. [It was] deemed Romanist. And it was something that candles were just not associated with in the Church of Ireland. The fact that I actually copied the practice from a Methodist minister friend, was neither here nor there.

Matthew Williams, a freelance graphic designer in his forties who had left a New Church congregation, described the way in which a new minister had made a significant change to church policy and upset established church members on the way.

Another [minister] took over. [Up to that point] we were really into outreach, [but the new minister] led us into inreach, and he decided we were really into inreach, and we moved out of X, [although] the general thing in the church was that we'd been called to [this] area ... and all the, kind of, the poor areas ... So a lot of people fought against this, but that's what happened

240

... and we moved out from this radical, sort of, outward looking Christianity, to kind of, what became quite a middle-class kind of Christianity which was all about socialising.

Worship and liturgy

The second theme focused specifically on the changes that had taken place in worship and liturgy. Some church-leavers did not like the new hymns. Some did not like the new service book. Some did not like the new translations of the Bible. Such discontent with liturgy and worship was well expressed by one of our interviewees, Richard Elliott, a man in his sixties who had left an Anglican church.

I didn't like the discarding of the Book of Common Prayer, which they discarded at this church, because they said the books were a bit musty, so they got rid of them. It was a good excuse to get rid of them and never use the Book of Common Prayer again, and instead of a sort of uniformity in worship, which the prayer book was designed to provide ... you have a sort of miscellaneous collection of services, in different parishes. You have different services, depending on the idiosyncrasies of the vicar. And when a new vicar comes it changes ... The new vicar came, this chap changed it all, and now has cards with prayers and things on, and so that's something that I don't like, the continuing changing, according to the actual vicar. So I think the services are less reverent, particularly in places where they have dancing and hand-clapping, and noisy pop music in some places. We used to have quiet prayer before the service started, you know, going back some years now, it's not the case now, any church you go to now almost you find that people are talking all the time before the service ... We used to come into church and kneel and prepare ourselves for the service, like pray for our preacher and congregation. And, when I left St Bede's there were only two of us who did any kneeling at all, and it was a bit embarrassing because people sort of looked sideways at you, and think you were trying to be holier than thou, because you're kneeling and nobody else troubles now, so that is a bit embarrassing these days in some places. And I think that people are afraid of formality these days, everything has to be done in rather the manner of the cabaret, you have the man at the front, acting as a kind of DJ.

Suzanne, a lapsed Roman Catholic student in Northern Ireland, voiced a deeply felt yearning for the atmosphere of the old Latin Mass.

Bring back Latin Masses, they're fun. I quite like Latin Mass, I think they have this whole air of mystery, I think the whole air of mystery has gone, I know it's very [popular], to bring more of the people, and none of them speak Latin, but I think that the Latin bits are very nice. I still think *Lumen Christi* is much better than 'light of Christ'. Have you tried to sing 'light of Christ'? That's just a personal choice, [but when] you hear it sung in English: it just sounds so crap!

Local church

The third theme focused on the changes that had taken place in the local church. Some church-leavers complained that they did not like the new style of worship, while others complained that they did not like the new style of teaching. Some church-leavers complained that they found it hard to adjust to a new priest, minister or pastor, while others complained that they did not like the new seating arrangement in church. John Ingram, a vicar interviewed to discover his perceptions of why people leave church, put his finger on a crucial insight when he began to consider why change in the local church can be so uncomfortable for some church members.

People [move] because the musical tradition changes, or because the hymn book changes, again because their reason for coming, I guess, is that they do things in a particular way. Some folk cope with change very, very badly . . . One of the things that strikes me about folk in the church, particularly those who've been around for a long time, is that, when you're someone like me, who floats in and says, 'oh, we'll have a new hymn book', or 'oh, well, we'll change the order of service', or 'oh, well, we'll do this or that', I'm not actually just tinkering with the periphery of people's lives, their entire life is bound up with what goes on in this church. You know, some of the old ladies here have been part of this church ever since it was built sixty years ago. And therefore for me to come in and say, 'oh, we'll do something different now', I'm not just changing something on the edge of their lives, I'm changing, or seeking to change something which is to do with their inmost being. And it is, therefore, no wonder that they get upset when that sort of thing happens. It's actually one of the reasons why I try not to do it. I don't succeed all the time, and we have, for example, as I say, changed this [service] book, and it took us two years to get to this. In full consultation with everyone, experimental periods, chopping it around, changing it, trying it out, consulting the bishop, you know this sort of thing, until we got something that we're happy with, and we've deliberately printed it on card which is going to fall apart in a couple of year's time, so that we can start all over again, and get something which is appropriate for then, rather than this which is actually appropriate now. I don't think anything should be set in stone, but to move people to that is quite difficult and some people fall out, you know fall off, fall away, because [of changes to] the things which they thought were set in stone, the things which have, they think, have always been with them. You know, the old joke about changing from the Authorised Version of the Bible, 'if it was good enough for St Paul, it's good enough for me', but people have left churches on that issue.

Listening to the statistics

A set of questions included in the survey set out to examine how much church-leavers cited these three themes concerned with problems with change as implicated in their own experience of leaving church. An overview of the findings is presented in Table 15, in the Appendix.

From these data it is clear that change had posed a major problem to one in every five church-leavers. Thus, 20% of church-leavers made it plain that they had not liked the changes that had happened in the church. A similar proportion (21%) put the matter another way and said that they had not liked the direction in which the church was going. One major source of change which church-leavers associated with their disengagement from church concerned the liturgy and worship. One in every five church-leavers pointed to change in this area as implicated in their own disengagement. Thus, 19% did not like the new hymns, 18% did not like the new service book and 18% did not like the new translations of the Bible.

Changes that take place in the local church can have far-reaching implications for the ways in which people feel about the church to which they may have belonged for some time. Of the four types of change experienced in many local churches, change in the style of worship was identified by the largest number of church-leavers as implicated in their disengagement from local church life. Thus, 16% of church-leavers said that they did not like the new style of worship. Second in order came teaching, with 11% of church-leavers saying that they did not like the new style of teaching. Third in order came the leader, with 10% of church-leavers saying that they found it hard to adjust to the new priest, minister or pastor. Fourth in order came the physical ordering of the church, with as many as 5% of church-leavers saying that they did not like the new seating arrangement in their church.

Sex differences

Problems with change is a factor that had a similar level of influence in the disengagement of both men and women from the church, and this applied across all three themes explored in this section. For example, one in ten of the women (10%) found it hard to adjust to the new minister, and so did 9% of the men.

Generational differences

Changes in the church presented a much greater problem among older church-leavers across all three themes explored in this section. Thus, 28% of those aged sixty or over complained that they did not like the changes that had happened in the church, compared with 19% of those in their forties or fifties and 12% of those under the age of forty.

In terms of worship and liturgy, 26% of those aged sixty or over disliked the new hymns, compared with 20% of those in their forties or fifties and 11% of those under the age of forty. New service books were disliked by 29% of those aged sixty or over, compared with 18% of those in their forties or fifties and 6% of those under the age of forty. New translations of the Bible were disliked by 31% of those aged sixty or over, compared with 17% of those in their fifties or sixties and 7% of those under the age of forty.

In terms of the local church, 25% of those aged sixty or over did not like the new style of worship, compared with 17% of those in their forties or fifties and 5% of those under the age of forty. The new style of teaching was disliked by 17% of those aged sixty or over, compared with 12% of those in their forties or fifties and 3% of those under the age of forty.

Cohort differences

In many ways problems with change is a factor that had a similar level of influence in the disengagement from church of those who left over twenty years ago and of those who left in the past twenty years. However, two items within this set of nine items recorded statistically significant differences between the two cohorts of church-leavers. These differences suggest ways in which problems with change may themselves be changing. First, the controversy over new translations of the Bible is lessening in significance. While 22% of those who left church over twenty years ago had left disliking the new translations of the Bible, the proportion fell to 15% among those who left within the past twenty years. Second, problems arising over adjusting to new ministers are gaining in significance. While just 7% of those who left church over twenty years ago had left finding it hard to adjust to the new minister, the proportion rose to 12% among those who left within the past twenty years.

Age at leaving

Problems with change is a factor that played a significantly more important role in disengagement from church during the later stages of life. This trend is seen clearly throughout all three themes explored in the present chapter. The straightforward complaint that they did not like the changes that had happened in the church was made by 27% of those who left after their fortieth birthday, compared with 21% of those who left in their twenties or thirties and 15% of those who left before their twentieth birthday.

Problems with changes to the service book and problems with

246

changes to the translations of the Bible were both more likely to be associated with church-leaving later in life. Thus, 26% of those who left after their fortieth birthday had disliked the new service book, compared with 12% of those who left in their twenties or thirties and 12% of those who left before their twentieth birthday. Similarly, 26% of those who left after their fortieth birthday had disliked the new translations of the Bible, compared with 20% of those who left in their twenties or thirties and 13% of those who left before their twentieth birthday.

Problems with changes within the local church were more likely to be associated with church-leaving in later life. Thus, 23% of those who left after their fortieth birthday had not liked the new style of worship, compared with 19% of those who left in their twenties or thirties and 10% of those who left before their twentieth birthday. Similarly, 17% of those who left after their fortieth birthday had not liked the new style of teaching, compared with 13% of those who left in their twenties or thirties and 8% of those who left before their twentieth birthday. Difficulty in adjusting to a new minister was associated with their disengagement from church by 17% of those who left after their fortieth birthday, compared with 10% of those who left in their twenties or thirties and 6% of those who left before their twentieth birthday.

Denomination

Problems with change are particularly symptomatic of the Anglican experience. For example, Anglican church-leavers are much more likely to link their disengagement from church with dislike of the new hymns, the new service book, or the new translations of the Bible. One in four Anglicans (25%) complained that they did not like the new hymns, compared with 10% of Roman Catholics and 12% of Free Church members. One in four Anglicans (24%) complained that they did not like the new service book, compared with 9% of Roman Catholics and 6% of

247

Free Church members. One in four Anglicans (24%) complained that they did not like the new translations of the Bible, compared with 9% of Roman Catholics and 7% of Free Church members.

Dislike of new styles of worship and dislike of new styles of teaching were also cited more often by Anglicans than by members of other denominations. Thus, 21% of Anglicans complained that they did not like the new style of worship, compared with 9% of Roman Catholics and 7% of Free Church members. Similarly, 14% of Anglicans complained that they did not like the new style of teaching, compared with 7% of Roman Catholics and 5% of Free Church members.

Sudden or gradual leaving

Problems with change is a factor which is almost equally reflected in sudden leaving and in gradual leaving. The one item within this set of nine items that recorded a statistically significant difference between the responses of sudden leavers and gradual leavers concerned adjustment to the new minister. Those who experienced difficulty in adjusting to the new minister were more likely to leave gradually than to leave suddenly. Just 7% of the sudden leavers had found it hard to adjust to the new minister, compared with 12% of the gradual leavers.

Likelihood of returning

Church-leavers who had disengaged following problems with change were as likely to place themselves among the potential returners as among the permanent disaffiliates. Thus, 21% of the potential returners and 19% of the permanent disaffiliates had left church disliking the changes that had been happening there.

Pastoral implications

At least one in every five church-leavers disengaged having experienced problems with change in the church. New hymns, new service books, new translations of the Bible and new styles of worship all contributed challenges and obstacles to church-goers who were uncomfortable with change. Even the arrival of a new minister brought with it the problem of change. Problems with change were particularly salient for older church-leavers and for those who left church later in life. Problems with change were particularly salient for Anglicans. Those who left church complaining about change are among those church-leavers who may change their minds and seek opportunities to come back. There are important pastoral implications that follow from such an analysis.

The promotion of church-leaving can hardly ever have been high on the conscious agenda of those who engineer change within the church, but church-leaving clearly emerges as a significant (unintended) by-product of many well-intended changes. Somehow the people who initiate the changes and the people who feel marginalised and excluded by the changes live in two very different worlds. The conceptualisation, initiation and management of change are issues that require thorough analysis and understanding at all levels of church leadership.

There are church leaders who see the initiation of change as crucial for the long-term development of the church, and who conceptualise those who resist change as enemies to the church's sustainability. Mishandled changes, however, can leave local churches not stronger but weaker, not more sustainable but less sustainable. Change should not be initiated without a proper long-term development plan and sufficient market research to test and to establish the viability of new developments. It is precisely in areas like this that business and commerce wisely invest in specialist consultancy and high quality negotiation. Such specialist resources need also to be available to local churches. If it is true that without change some churches will die, it may also be true that through change some churches will die.

One of the real strengths of the 'fresh expressions' movement is that it enables new forms of church life to grow up alongside established, traditional and secure expressions of church without demanding high levels of change within what already exists and what already works well for a more traditional constituency of church-goers. Good pastoral practice may wish to encourage several different forms of church life to flourish side by side.

According to the present statistical data, it is the Anglican Church which seems to have been most seriously damaged by church-goers turning into church-leavers in the face of changes to the services. New styles of service, new hymn books, and above all new service books have all taken their toll on faithful Anglican church-goers. The strength of the Prayer Book Society, for example, provides good evidence of ways in which Anglicans continue to organise themselves to make sense of (or to resist) change. Indeed, Anglican pastoral ministry still needs to seek ways to re-engage those who lost touch with their Anglican heritage when the Book of Common Prayer became relegated to the damp cupboard under the tower.

16

Problems with worship

Introduction

In many ways church services function as the 'shop window' to the church. What actually happens in the service is likely to be crucial to whether people stay or drift away. A number of strands of theory point to why different people may expect different things from church services. At the most obvious level young children and senior adults approach worship in different ways (see Francis and Astley, 2002). At a less visible level, the theory of faith development as proposed by Fowler (1981) and discussed by Astley and Francis (1992) suggests that two adults of the same age may display quite different stages (or styles) of faith. Drawing on a very different theoretical framework, Francis (2005a) suggested that preferred worship styles may be related to very basic and fundamental individual differences in personality. There may be many reasons why church services and worship may generate problems for church-goers and precipitate church-leaving. The present chapter seeks to examine the extent to which church-leavers themselves explain their distance from the church in terms of problems with worship. Our interviewees highlighted three main themes within the broad area of problems with worship. We described these three themes as: a matter of style, a matter of taste, and a matter of level.

A matter of style

The first theme focused on matters of style. Some church-leavers said simply that they disliked the church's style of worship without necessarily going on to define precisely what they disliked about the style. For some church-leavers the problem was that the worship style was too formal. For other church-leavers, however, the problem was that the worship style was too informal. Complaints against modern and informal worship were well expressed by Richard Elliott, a man in his sixties who had left an Anglican church.

> If they were to go back to a normal liturgy, and if they were to take some of the services such as the Communion service in the old Prayer Book, I'd be only too happy to go back, if that were the case . . . What I like about the Prayer Book is that the prayers are so lovely in a sense of how they're phrased, and they say exactly what you want to say without any, you know, for example, the prayers don't start off praying about the postman, and the policeman, then for the fire-brigade [laughter], and all the rest of them, as though God doesn't know that all these people need praying for. But it sets out the worship, to my mind, in the right way . . . Another thing I think is good, which has been discarded, somewhat, at St Bede's, and that is a lectionary, so the readings week-by-week take you through the Bible, the main themes of the Bible, so you don't miss anything. But now, very often, depending on the whims of that particular vicar we'll have a session on the Holy Spirit, or we'll have so many sermons on this or that, and during those weeks you're missing some readings which are set out in the lectionary, so we forget those things and go off at a tangent on something else.

It was not, however, only the more elderly church-leavers who complained about the modernisation of church services. Suzanne, a lapsed Roman Catholic student in Northern Ireland, also found it hard to accept ways in which the traditional Christmas carol service had undergone changes to make it more accessible to her generation.

> I sat through the carol service, and it was painful. I love Christmas carols, I love the whole idea of Christmas, and I was so happy and everyone's happy, everyone's full of goodwill, and I love the idea of Christmas, the idea of Jesus being born. I mean, it's lovely, but . . . I still have to work out why we had to have the 'Rivers of Babylon' twice, I don't know why, but the girl who sang it, was [part of a] clique. They're all too smiley, and they're all a bit too merry, and I think, 'what are they drinking? – there's more to that wine, than meets the eye!' . . . I don't know what it is, but there's definitely a clique with tambourines . . . which is very nice and well in Woolworth's when you're walking round getting your Christmas shopping, but it's not something I like. I like the old 'Good King Wenceslas', 'In Dulci Jubilo' and 'Adeste Fideles'. I can sing and sing and sing, but this didn't do that for me. I just don't fit into the mould I don't think.

A matter of taste

The second theme focused on matters of taste rather than matters of style. Some church-leavers had found worship to be too mechanical. Some had felt that there was too little sense of the presence of God in worship. Others complained that there was not enough variety in worship to suit different tastes. Sarah Johnson, a homemaker in her thirties who had left an Anglican church, provided an insightful description of how it is that worship can feel too mechanical in some churches.

> I felt that [the worship] was too structured, it becomes a routine, and although sometimes a routine is good, because it

keeps you doing things that you are meant to be doing or what-ever, like it's good to have a routine for when you're reading the Bible, or when you pray and things like that, but sometimes it can become just routine and not meaningful and I felt that's how we'd got. You know, it was quite easy to mentally switch off from the words that were coming out of my mouth, when we were saying the Creed, or when we were answering, doing all the different bits, and then my mind would be on what the children were doing next to me, or 'has the roast turned itself on by now?', and so yes, it had become a routine, and I don't think routine is always good.

For Sharon Chapman, a former Methodist in her thirties, the problem was rather that her own response to worship had become too mechanical.

When I went to church, I was just going through the motions, I was doing it because I had to, and I think, if anything, there was that block there, 'I'm not going to do anything, I'm not going to believe, you know, you're trying to force it down my throat', but now I feel I do want to start going and I do believe, but in my own time. And I think He understands that. I hope so. But, yes, that's what I think, and I don't feel you've got to go to church every week to have a relationship with God.

While he shows great respect for some of the faithful church-goers Arron Coates, a lapsed Roman Catholic postgraduate student, felt that the general atmosphere of his church did little to convey the sense of the presence of God in worship.

After the Mass, there are people [who] go kissing the feet of the statue of Mary, and I think, 'you show such faith and devotion that it sort of inspires me', and I'm in awe of it, because I think I'm far too . . . self-aware to go and kiss the feet of a statue, or to

254

kneel in front of a statue on the altar while there are people still milling about behind me, I just couldn't do that. So there are some people there that I'm really in awe of, but it doesn't come through in the ceremony, because they all seem bored and jaded, and really not interested, and like it's just not getting through, it's just not interesting them, or holding their attention or imagination. And kids are screaming, and kids are running around, and old people are falling asleep, and people are doing the rosary, and if you're doing the rosary you're not paying a blind bit of notice to the ceremony that is the Mass. And so I just sit there, I find it all distracting. And so I don't go at the moment.

A matter of level

The third theme focused on matters to do with the level on which the worship, in general, and the teaching in particular, were conducted. The problem for some church-leavers was that the teachings were pitched too high: the church's teaching seemed to go over their heads. The problem for other church-leavers was that the teachings were pitched too low: the church's teaching seemed too simplified and unchallenging. Peter Kendall, an ex-Methodist in his forties, had been brought up within the framework of clear Bible teaching and he had grown to find it all too simplistic.

I was brought up as a Methodist to believe very basic things: that there was a God, that God created the world, that He had a Son, and He sent His Son into the world, and that whoever believed in Him would have everlasting life. Then there was a virgin birth, and there was a crucifixion, and a resurrection, and that there was one God for all of man and womankind. And those were basic simplistic beliefs. And it took me a long time to begin to understand that monotheistic religions . . . were very, very simplistic religions. And didn't reflect the

255

spiritual dimension in the way that they should. And so, I think, when I became disillusioned with the church, I began to get disillusioned with that simplistic view of spirituality.

Taking a rather different perspective, Paul West, a civil servant in his forties who had left an Anglican church, had become irritated by the disjunction between critically informed understanding of the Bible and the apparently pre-critical assumptions of his local church.

I can't say I like it when people after the readings say, 'this is the word of the Lord', when we all know that it was written by somebody else, and most of the time we're reading from letters, such as Corinthians, or letters to the Philippians, or something like that, when it's not the word of the Lord, it's the word of somebody else [laughter]. It's just niggly things like that, that I must admit, I don't like.

Listening to the statistics

A set of questions included in the survey set out to examine how much church-leavers cited these three themes concerned with problems with worship as implicated in their own experience of leaving church. An overview of the findings is presented in Table 16, in the Appendix.

The data make it clear that at least one in every five church-leavers associated their disengagement from church with a reaction against the style of worship promoted by their church. Thus, 21% of church-leavers said quite simply that they disliked the church's style of worship. In terms of worship styles, formality in worship seems to have cost the church more members than informality in worship. One in ten church-leavers (10%) felt that the worship style they had left behind was too informal, compared with one in four church-leavers (26%) who felt that the worship style they had left behind was too formal.

Tastes in worship may vary considerably from one individual to another, but it may be most worthwhile to listen to the varied criticisms made by church-leavers. One in every three church-leavers (32%) felt that the worship they had left behind was too mechanical. One in every four church-leavers (25%) felt that there was too little sense of the presence of God in worship, and one in every five church-leavers (22%) felt that there was not enough variety in worship to suit different tastes.

One in every three church-leavers associated their disengagement from church with discontent regarding the level of teaching offered. The problem, however, is that the complaints are equally divided between those who felt that the level was too high and those who felt that the level was too low. For 16% of church-leavers, the church's teaching seemed to go 'over their head', while for another 17% of church-leavers the church's teaching was too simplified and unchallenging.

Sex differences

Problems with the worship is a factor that had a similar level of influence in the disengagement of both men and women from the church, and this applied across the three themes explored in this section. The one item within the set of eight items that recorded a statistically significant difference between the responses of men and women concerned attitude toward informality in worship. The female church-leavers were significantly more likely than the male church-leavers to dislike informal worship: 12% of the women felt that the worship was too informal, compared with 6% of the men.

Generational differences

Problems with worship were experienced by similar proportions of all three generational groups examined by the study. Around one in every five church-leavers across the age range had disliked the style of worship that they had left behind. Beneath this level of agreement, however, what was disliked about the style of worship shifted across the age range. The youngest age group voted more against formality, while the oldest age group voted more against informality. While just 3% of those under the age of forty had felt that the worship was too informal, the proportion who took this view rose to 10% among those in their forties or fifties and to 15% among those aged sixty or over. While 34% of those under the age of forty had felt that the worship was too formal, the proportion who took this view dropped to 24% among those in their forties or fifties and to 20% among those aged sixty or over.

Matters of taste hardly varied across the age range. For example, one-third of those under the age of forty (33%) felt that the worship was too mechanical, and so did 31% of those in their forties or fifties and 32% of those aged sixty or over. Also matters of level hardly varied across the age range. Between 17% and 18% of all three age groups had found the church's teaching was too simplified and unchallenging. Between 14% and 18% of all three age groups considered that the church's teaching seemed to go over their heads.

Cohort differences

Generally problems with worship is a factor that had a similar level of influence in the disengagement from church of those who left over twenty years ago and of those who left in the past twenty years. The one item within this set of eight items that recorded a statistically significant difference between the responses of the two cohorts of church-leavers concerned variety in worship. The case for variety in worship has become more salient within the past twenty years. While 18% of those who left over twenty years ago felt that there was not enough variety in worship to suit different tastes, the proportion rose to 26% among those who left in the past twenty years.

Age at leaving

Problems with worship is a factor that had a similar level of influence in the disengagement from church of those who left before their twentieth birthday, during their twenties or thirties, or after their fortieth birthday. Although similar proportions of all three age groups had disliked the style of worship that they had left behind, precisely what was disliked about the worship was clearly different. Among those who left before their twentieth birthday, 32% had judged the worship to be too formal and 3% to be too informal. Among those who left in their twenties or thirties, 23% judged the worship to be too formal and 12% to be too informal. Among those who left after their fortieth birthday, 18% judged the worship to be too formal and 18% to be too informal. On the other hand, complaints about the level of teaching provided by the church remained much more constant across the age of leaving.

Denomination

Problems with worship played a similar part in the process of disengagement from church across the three denominational groups. One item in this set of eight items, however, recorded a statistically significant difference between the responses of Free Church members, Roman Catholics and Anglicans, and this item concerned reaction against informality in worship. Anglicans were more likely to have become church-leavers reacting against informal worship. While 3% of Roman Catholics and 6% of Free

Church members complained that the worship was too informal, the proportion rose to 12% among Anglicans.

Sudden or gradual leaving

Generally problems with worship is a factor which is equally reflected in sudden leaving and in gradual leaving. The one item within this set of eight items that recorded a statistically significant difference between the responses of sudden leavers and gradual leavers concerned the criticism that the worship was too mechanical. Among the sudden leavers 36% had been critical of the worship as too mechanical, compared with 28% of the gradual leavers.

Likelihood of returning

Church-leavers who had disengaged following problems with worship were, overall, more likely to place themselves among the permanent disaffiliates than among the potential returners. For example, 25% of the permanent disaffiliates had disliked the church's style of worship, compared with 15% of the potential returners. Over one-third of the permanent disaffiliates (36%) had felt the worship to have been too mechanical, compared with 22% of the potential returners. In terms of teaching, 18% of the permanent disaffiliates had found the church's teaching to go over their heads, compared with 7% of the potential returners. In other words, those church-leavers who considered that they had had a bad experience of worship were less inclined to return to try again.

Pastoral implications

This section makes it clear that one-third of church-leavers had experienced problems with the style of worship offered (either too formal or too informal) or with the level of teaching offered (either too high or too low). Problems with worship seem to have been a constant issue with church-leavers over the years, and of equal importance to both sexes, and across the denominations. The only major variation is that formality in worship is a greater problem for younger people, and informality in worship is a greater problem for older people. Experiencing problems with worship is reflected both in gradual leaving and in sudden leaving. Those who leave church having experienced problems with the worship seem to be reluctant to return to try again. There are important pastoral implications that follow from this analysis.

The first crucial observation is that tastes in worship so clearly vary from one individual to another. Some despair of the church because of its formality, and others despair of the church because of its informality. Clearly one form of service is not going to woo back the church-leavers or even keep the loyalty of today's church-goers. One of the potential strengths of the different denominations is that different styles of worship may serve to forge links with different types of people. For such a view of the church to work, however, there need to be proper respect and co-operation between different churches, and church-goers need to be encouraged to step outside their own tradition to experience what is on offer elsewhere. While a major chain of supermarkets may regard losing a valued customer to a rival store as a failure, this may not be an appropriate model to be adopted by major denominations. Encouraging denominational switching may be preferable to condoning church-leaving.

Individual churches tackle the problem of trying to cater for a variety of tastes in worship in different ways. Some of these ways seem more successful than others. The problem may be particularly acute in those 'single church' areas where there is little or no choice between churches. Larger and better-staffed churches in such situations may be successful in operating multiple and distinctive congregations. This is something that Anglican churches may have been particularly successful at doing in an earlier generation (quiet early-morning Holy Communion, family Eucharist, sung Mattins, and Evensong), before the pressure came to merge highly distinctive congregations within one main service. Smaller churches sharing a minister with other smaller churches (often in rural areas) may try a rotating pattern of services to cater for a variety of tastes. This seems to work well for the highly committed who know which services to avoid, but considerably less well for the casual attenders who find it difficult to predict the time or type of service on any given Sunday.

The second crucial observation is that needs in teaching clearly vary from one person to another. Some find the teaching offered simply goes over their head, while others find it too simplified and unchallenging. In an age when the church can no longer assume that most people have been brought up with 'the Christian story' and are familiar with the basic themes and doctrines of the Christian tradition, real thought and care needs to be given to the broad range of education required to build up the local church. The Sunday morning sermon alone may not be adequate to the need.

Various educational programmes are now widely available for use by local churches both to introduce the Christian faith to new members and to nurture established members in their on-going Christian formation. Courses introducing the basics of the Christian faith like Alpha or Emmaus are well-established. The Exploring Faith programme, operated for example in North Wales, works through local education groups to provide a formal programme in 'education for discipleship' validated at the level of the certificate of higher education. The Theology Quest and Questions Course run by the Southern Theological Education and Training Scheme and Sarum College provides a weekly week-night course based in Salisbury and spread over two years, also validated at the level of the certificate of higher education.

17

Problems with leadership

Setting the scene

The public face of the church is often seen to be shaped by the leadership, at local, national and international levels. Different church leaders model very different kinds of leadership style, as demonstrated, for example, by Oswald and Kroeger (1988). There are introverted and extraverted styles of leadership. There are democratic and autocratic styles of leadership. There are leadership styles that proclaim the will of God and leadership styles that facilitate individual discernment of the will of God. There are leadership styles that include women and men as equals, and leadership styles that subordinate or exclude women. There may be many reasons why leadership issues generate problems for church-goers and precipitate church-leaving. The aim of the present chapter, therefore, is to examine the extent to which church-leavers themselves explain their distance from the church in terms of problems with leadership. Listening to our interviewees, three main themes emerged within the broad area of problems with leadership. We describe these themes as: a matter of style, a matter of status, and a matter of direction.

A matter of style

The first theme focused on styles of leadership as defined by the contrast between authoritarian leadership and democratic leadership. Some church-leavers ascribed their dissatisfaction to the fact that the leadership style of their church was too authoritarian. Other church-leavers ascribed their dissatisfaction to the fact that the leadership style of their church was too democratic. One example of problems caused by strong authoritarian leadership was provided by Charles Mason, who had left a charismatic Anglican church.

I remember one thing that particularly annoyed me was one speaker . . . a very powerful speaker, a very emotional speaker. At one stage, I can't remember how this came about, but he prayed for Josephine. Basically if I remember, it was near the end of the meeting. He put his hand on Josephine's head, and was calling down, invoking the power of the spirit, 'come through my hand, and fill Josephine', and really building up, and saying to Josephine, 'can you feel it, can you feel it, can you feel the power of the spirit', and I was thinking 'what am I listening to here? This is absolute bull. What is this guy going on about?' And I heard Josephine say 'yes, I can', and I thought 'come on'. And I asked her afterwards 'what was all that about?' And she said 'well, I just had to say yes, because, I mean, he was so forceful'. And I thought 'well, that's what this is all about, I'm sorry, this is just not real, this is manipulation, it's highly emotive, and I'm not interested'.

Another example of problems caused by strong authoritarian leadership was provided by Nicholas White who had left an independent Baptist church.

It was to do with the personality of the minister more than anything else, I think, and the way he had managed and manipulated that particular church and congregation. At the end of the day we felt that there were principles involved, and we battled with them too. I mean, they tried to say to us that we were not allowed, no one was allowed from the church to associate with us, they weren't allowed to come to our house . . . And we actually battled with him on the basis that, you know, he from that point said, 'that's it, end of story', and we went, 'no, it's not the end of story. You don't have the right to just lay the law down to people, and then they go away with their tail between their legs, and we're certainly not going to do that. So we would like to have a meeting with you, we would like to have a meeting with you where we bring a third party to it, and we discuss it with you, and we find out your reasons why you've taken these actions, and why you behave like you have, and we actually try and get to a point of understanding because you're not going to just lay the law down with us, and us go away.' And it took a long, long time before he agreed to do that, and eventually after a lot of discussion and argument, he agreed, and it took me and a friend of mine to go to the church after a service, and stand at the back of the church until he'd finished. He'd been warned we were going to come there if he hadn't given us a date to meet, and in front of the whole congregation he said, 'oh, I see Nicholas is here, he's obviously come to publicly apologise. Have you?', trying to sort of humiliate me, and I just said like, 'no, you know full well why I'm here. I asked you for a date to meet and you wouldn't give me one, and I promised you if you wouldn't do that I'd come down here tonight, and that's why I'm here.' And we stood there afterwards for an hour, with him and one of his elders, and him just being stubborn, and in the end he said, 'alright then, I'll give you a date'.

A matter of status

The second theme focused on issues of status involved in leadership. For some church-leavers the problem was a general one concerned with status: for them the church was too hierarchical and status-conscious. For other church-leavers the problem was specifically concerned with the status of women within the church: for them the church did not allow women their rightful place in decision-making. The general problem with status was illustrated by Arron Coates, a young postgraduate student who had left a Roman Catholic church. He found the status given to the choir unacceptable.

The choir are held up as being somehow better than everyone else. When they go for Communion they all get to line around the altar and they get to go before anyone else, so it's altar-boys, choir, you know, and they get to look down on everyone, and they get, and it just seems so pompous and stuck-up, and really goes against the grain of my understanding of what the Bible's about.

The problem of the role of women in leadership was brought up from an Evangelical Free Church perspective by Kate White, who had left an independent Baptist church.

They couldn't cope very much with . . . things like equality in the sexes or anything. There was one woman who was pretty talented, and she was a very good singer, but she was never allowed to lead worship, a man had to lead worship, and she would sing with the guy leading worship . . . It was all that sort of thing. Women don't really have a say, as though we're a bit weird.

The problem over refusal to recognise the role of women in leadership was also a very real issue to some Roman Catholics. The point was made by Arron Coates.

I think the church's treatment of women is pretty poor . . . I mean, I think it's outrageous, I think it's ridiculous . . . unless

267

they're ordaining women, unless women are seen to be taking a more active role in the decision of the church, and are being treated within equal terms in the church. You know, my church has still got the situation where there are women eucharistic ministers, and you see people avoiding them. There used to be a really, a sister of a friend of mine, a really attractive girl, blonde and blue eyes, and very pretty, giving out, she was a eucharistic minister, and nobody would go to her [laughter]. I don't know if they were intimidated by her, or they were scared of her, or because she was young and blonde and good-looking people didn't think she should be doing it, but nobody would go, and that's just ridiculous, completely stupid.

Another lapsed Roman Catholic, Suzanne, a student in Northern Ireland, made a similar point.

I still can't get the idea why they can't have women priests, I can't get that . . . I still can't work out why they can't. Granted I don't want to be a female priest, and I'm saying that here and now. Because, I remember we had a priest in, talking to us, and trying to be modern in school, and I just don't know, and the teacher said go and ask questions, and I asked, 'why can't there be women priests?' and I didn't think I was being so mad and off the wall. And the teacher said, 'you can't say that'. And of course, the priest tried to be funny, 'why, do you want to be one?' And I thought, 'don't be such a smarmy git'. And I said, 'no, I just think we ought to have the right to actually choose', and they sort of went, 'oh, right'.

A matter of direction

The third theme focused on the kind of direction given by the leadership. For some church-leavers the problem was that the church leadership was not giving a clear enough sense of direction. In particular, some church-leavers felt that their church had not taken enough account of church tradition. Other church-leavers felt that their church had not taken enough account of the will of God. Richard Elliott, a man in his sixties who had left an Anglican church, provided a very clear account regarding how, in his opinion, his local church had failed to give a clear enough sense of direction on what were, for him, unambiguous moral absolutes.

At St Bede's we had a case where two people living down the road, the lady had had three different partners, I don't think she was married to any of them, and children by each of these men. She then took up with another man and had a child, and the child was baptised, and shortly as a result of that they came into the church. After a while they persuaded the couple to get married, they got married, and shortly afterwards, twelve months, or eighteen months afterwards, the man, after professing conversion, ran off and set up home with a married woman from the congregation. Then the wife got a divorce eventually, went to live with her husband's brother, then came back to the vicar and said, 'would you marry us?' and he said, 'no, you go and get married at the register office or somewhere else, come back and I will bless the marriage', which seems completely ridiculous. And I felt at the time that, and we had other examples of people coming to the church who were divorced and got remarried, and I felt that it was inhibiting whoever was preaching. Because you see, how [are they] to stand up and preach about Christ's teaching regarding adultery? – 'And he who remarries is committing adultery' – when people sitting in [the congregation] have been encouraged to come into the church, told it's perfectly alright, and according to the Bible? My interpretation of what Christ said is that if you remarry you are in a permanent state of adultery, because all the time you are committing adultery, as long as you are living together. So it doesn't all add up, and you don't want to upset the couple, you can't tell them it's wrong, because the vicar says it's right, and they're being encouraged to come in, so the whole thing is nonsense. So you're going to get more and more people coming to the church [on false pretexts], unless the church tells people that it's wrong. They're all expected to be able to come into church, to be integrated into the church, and still maintain their own form of immorality.

Listening to the statistics

A set of questions included in the survey set out to examine how much church-leavers cited the three themes concerned with problems with leadership as implicated in their own experience of leaving church. An overview of the findings is presented in Table 17 in the Appendix.

The data made it clear that at least one in every four church-leavers associated their disengagement from church with problems with leadership. Thus, 27% of church-leavers commented on the leadership style. The real problem here concerns the reaction of church-leavers to what they describe as an authoritarian leadership style. The leadership style of the church was judged to be too authoritarian by 22% of church-leavers. By way of contrast, another 5% of church-leavers judged the leadership style in the church that they left to have been too democratic.

For one in every four church-leavers (25%) the church was considered to be too hierarchical and status-conscious. Within this hierarchical structure, a particular point of contention concerned the role of women. Thus, 22% of church-leavers felt that the church did not allow women their rightful place in decision-making.

For a number of church-leavers the problem with leadership focused on the way in which the leadership was or was not setting the kind of direction thought to be appropriate. One in every six church-leavers (17%) felt that the leadership was not giving a clear enough sense of direction. For 8% of church-leavers the problem with direction was that the leadership did not seem to take enough account of church tradition. For another 8% of church-leavers the problem with direction was that the leadership did not seem to take enough account of the will of God.

Sex differences

Certain problems with leadership were given more prominence by male church-leavers than by female church-leavers. Male church-leavers were more likely to emphasise problems with authoritarian leadership styles and with hierarchical structures. One in four of the male church-leavers (26%) complained that the leadership style of the church was too authoritarian, compared with 19% of the female church-leavers. Nearly one in every three of the male church-leavers (30%) complained that the church was too hierarchical and status-conscious, compared with 22% of the female church-leavers. In other respects, however, the assessments of the male and female church-leavers were more closely aligned.

Generational differences

Issues concerning the style and status of leadership held similar weight across the three generational groups of church-leavers. On the other hand, issues concerning the direction taken by leadership gained in significance with increasing age. While 12% of those under the age of forty complained that the church leadership was not giving a clear enough sense of direction, the proportions rose to 15% of those in their forties or fifties and to 25% of those aged sixty or over. While 3% of those under the age of forty complained that the church did not take enough account of

271

church tradition, the proportions rose to 6% among those in their forties or fifties and to 14% among those aged sixty or over. While 5% of those under the age of forty complained that the church did not take enough account of the will of God, the proportions rose to 8% among those in their forties or fifties and to 12% among those aged sixty or over.

Cohort differences

In many ways problems with leadership is a factor that had a similar level of influence in the disengagement from church of those who left over twenty years ago and of those who left in the past twenty years. The one item in this set of seven items that recorded a statistically significant difference between the responses of the two cohorts of church-leavers concerned the issue of an authoritarian leadership style. While 26% of those who left over twenty years ago complained that the leadership style of the church was too authoritarian, the proportion fell to 19% among those who left in the past twenty years. This finding may reflect an overall change in the leadership style projected by the churches in more recent years.

Age at leaving

Different aspects of problems with leadership come into greater prominence for those who disengage from church at different stages in life. For those who leave church later in life, matters to do with church tradition and with the perceived will of God carry greater weight. While just 3% of those who left before their twentieth birthday considered that the church did not take enough account of church tradition, the proportions rose to 10% among those who left in their twenties or thirties and to 13% among those who left after their fortieth birthday. While just 5% of those who left before their twentieth birthday considered that the church did not take enough account of the will of God, the proportion rose to 12% among those who left in their twenties or thirties and to 10% among those who left after their fortieth birthday.

On the other hand, for those who leave church earlier in life, matters to do with the leadership role of women in the church carry greater weight. While 15% of those who left after their fortieth birthday complained that the church did not allow women their rightful place in decision-making, the proportions rose to 20% among those who left in their twenties or thirties and to 27% among those who left before their twentieth birthday.

Denomination

Problems with leadership were given significantly more prominence by Roman Catholic church-leavers than by members of other denominations, specifically in terms of matters of style and matters of status. Roman Catholics were more likely to see the church that they had left behind as too authoritarian and as too hierarchical. Two out of every five Roman Catholics (40%) described the leadership style of the church they had left behind as too authoritarian, compared with 20% of Anglicans and 11% of Free Church members. More than one-third of Roman Catholics (36%) described the church that they had left behind as too hierarchical and status-conscious, compared with 25% of Anglicans and 20% of Free Church members.

It was the leadership of the Anglican Church, however, that was most likely to be criticised as lacking direction. One out of every five Anglicans (20%) described the leadership of the church that they had left behind as not giving a clear enough sense of direction, compared with 13% of Roman Catholics and 9% of Free Church members. In similar vein, 10% of Anglicans complained that the church they had left behind did not take enough account of church tradition, compared with 7% of Roman Catholics and 2% of Free Church members.

273

Sudden or gradual leaving

Some problems with leadership are reflected equally in sudden leaving and in gradual leaving. For example, 23% of those who left suddenly had gone believing that the leadership style of the church was too authoritarian, and so had 21% of those who left gradually. Other problems with leadership, however, tended to be reflected more frequently in sudden leaving, especially issues concerned with the status of women and with dislike for hierarchical structures. Thus, 26% of the sudden leavers complained that the church did not allow women their rightful place in decision-making compared with 18% of the gradual leavers. Among the sudden leavers, 29% had rejected the church as too hierarchical and status-conscious, compared with 23% of the gradual leavers.

Likelihood of returning

Some problems with leadership were more likely to encourage church-leavers to see themselves as permanent disaffiliates than as potential returners. Those who left church complaining about the authoritarian style of leadership, about the church being too hierarchical or status-conscious, or about the unfair treatment of women in leadership roles were less open to returning to church. Thus, 27% of the permanent disaffiliates complained that the leadership style of the church was too authoritarian, compared with 14% of the potential returners; 29% of the permanent disaffiliates complained that the church was too hierarchical and status-conscious, compared with 22% of the potential returners; and 29% of the permanent disaffiliates complained that the church did not allow women their rightful place in decision-making, compared with 15% of the potential returners. Other problems with leadership, however, were as likely to be given voice by the potential returners as by the permanent disaffiliates.

Pastoral implications

This section makes it clear that at least one in every four church-leavers associated their disengagement from church with problems with leadership. The two main problems with leadership concerned the complaint that the leadership style was too authoritarian and too hierarchical, and the struggle to accept the leadership role of women alongside men. Both problems were most salient among Roman Catholic church-leavers, while the distinctive cry of Anglican church-leavers was that the church leadership was not giving a clear enough sense of direction. In other words, Roman Catholics seemed to want less control and Anglicans seemed to want more control in the hands of church leaders. There are important implications that follow from this analysis.

Church leaders tend to remain caught in present society between being expected to give strong leadership and being criticised for doing so. Part of the social dynamic within some models of church life is to project authority on the church leader and subservience on the church member. Sometimes the very language of referring to the church leader as 'father' may (unintentionally) reinforce the self-image of church members as children from whom appropriate obedience and respect should be addressed to their father-like leader. Sometimes the very language of referring to the church leader as 'pastor' may (unintentionally) reinforce the self-image of church members as sheep from whom appropriate obedience and respect should be addressed to their shepherd-like leader. Psychodynamic theories may see such relationships as inherently unhealthy both for leaders and for those who are led. For those who lead the imagery may generate intolerable responsibility. In turn such a sense of responsibility may produce guilt (among those who feel that they fail to live up to the expectations) or delusions (among those who feel that they succeed in living up to the expectations).

Both psychological theories and sociological theories are able to provide important insights into the personal and social implications of the kind of leadership problems currently experienced within the churches. It may be increasingly important for church leaders to be properly equipped with the insights of such theories as a core part of their on-going continuing professional development. Such theories only really begin to make sense when clergy have had sufficient practical experience of leadership to recognise the symptoms and to anticipate the dangers. The benefits of such training should be reflected not only in the work-related psychological health of the leaders but also in the positive response of church members.

18

Problems with conservatism

Setting the scene

The balance between conservatism and liberalism is a perennial problem for the churches. Reading some analyses of church decline, the weight of criticism seems to be placed firmly on the failure of the churches to move with the times. The failure of the churches to revise their theological teaching to take modern perspectives into account is seen to precipitate church-leaving. In his account of *The Sheep that Got Away*, Michael J. Fanstone (1993: 69) drew attention to the church-leaver who argued that church teaching is 'contradicted by modern scientific knowledge'. The failure of the churches to revise their moral teaching to take modern perspectives into account is seen to precipitate church-leaving. The point is made, for example, by Alan Jamieson (2002: 37) when he relates Pam's struggle to escape from the moral teachings of a conservative evangelical church. The aim of the present chapter, therefore, is to examine the extent to which church-leavers themselves explain their distance from the church in terms of problems with conservatism. Listening to our interviewees, two main themes emerged within the broad area of problems with conservatism. We described these themes as: problems with theology, and problems with morality.

Problems with theology

The first theme focused on problems concerned with the view that the church's theological teaching was too conservative. Some church-leavers complained that the church's theological teachings were too narrow. Other church-leavers said that they were tired of being told what to believe by the church. Some saw theological conservatism reflected in the church's attitude toward the world and complained that the church was too negative toward the world outside. Others saw theological conservatism reflected in the church's attitude toward their own personal quest and complained that the church allowed them far too little space to explore ideas for themselves. Justine Sullivan, a young teacher brought up as an Anglican, had briefly joined a new Christian movement. She told us that the theological narrowness of this movement drove her to give up church-going altogether.

> They believed that only people within that church are the ones going to heaven. [When I left the church] I wrote a letter to them saying that I would be leaving, and I got a letter back saying that I'd lose my salvation and that of my friends and family. And wasn't that awful? And it was just horrific, you can imagine what it was like, somebody condemning you like that, and the people that you have been very close to for about six weeks, two months, you know. So they'd become quite a big part of my life. So I think that was probably the biggest reason why I felt dubious about churches, so if I was to look back and say why I left, it would be partly because of college, you know, questioning things, but I think mainly it was because of this awful experience I'd had in this church, and also because when I did start to go and look into [other] churches . . . they were still preaching, sort of the traditional understanding of heaven and hell.

A similar account was given by Matthew Williams, a freelance graphic designer who had left a New Church congregation.

> I don't believe in the exclusiveness of the Christian religion, I think. I can't believe that Christianity is about making some decision in your life, or that God is about making a decision in your life, and those who make the right decision are going to heaven, and those who didn't make the decision are going to go to hell, I just can't believe that anymore, I just think that's, it just can't be, it just doesn't make sense. I do believe that we are in a fallen world, and that the world is broken and that there is, I mean there's sin and evil, but I think we see it all back-to-front, I think there's more evil in the church than outside it sometimes, I don't know. I mean, I think there's a disintegration, a kind of collapse going on, and that's the closest I can get to understanding what evil is all about, it's like disintegration.

For Alison Matthews, a young social worker who had left a Roman Catholic church, the problem was to do with the way in which the church, through her parish priest, had tried to discourage her spiritual quest.

> I don't think, at this point when I was questioning, that I actually thought of leaving. It was very strange the way it happened . . . I'd been speaking to a priest about the fact that I was also seeing some people from the Ba'hai faith and I was praying with them as well, and I was going to go and visit them after Mass, and he'd been very against that idea, he'd spoken quite strongly against it, and I'd become quite angry. And then I went into Mass, and I was still feeling very angry as I went into Mass and as I sat through Mass, and suddenly the idea that I couldn't carry on going to church in this regular way, it hit me so suddenly . . . I think the biggest discovery that I've made, really, is that I was so concerned about whether Catholicism

was the right way, or Christianity was the right way to worship God, or whether the Ba'hai faith had all the answers, or whether the Muslim faith had all the answers, or whether Buddhism had all the answers, and all these things I was looking into, and I've come to the realisation that whatever God is, God is something far greater and far more wise than something that would be at all worried about how we pray to him, or how we love him.

Problems with morality

The second theme focused on problems concerned with the view that the church's moral teaching was too conservative. Some church-leavers complained that the church's moral teachings were too narrow. Others said that they were tired of being told how to behave by the church. Some church-leavers saw conservatism reflected in the church's attitudes toward moral certainties and complained that the church's approach to morality was far too 'black and white'. Others felt that the church's moral teachings restricted their own life-style and complained that the church was too conservative for them. For Sharon Chapman, an ex-Methodist in her thirties, it was her parents' moral conservatism, shaped by their church, that had really caused her to part company with the church.

[My parents are] anti-alcohol, obviously anti-smoking, they'll vet any television programme that's on . . . My friends from school didn't go to church, and they couldn't understand why I couldn't go [to a disco], and I would have liked that life as well, it didn't mean I was going to do anything that I shouldn't, but it would have been nice to have been allowed . . . My mum and dad and the church governed my life, that was what they said I had to do, and I don't believe that the church would say that you can't go out and enjoy yourself at a school disco, but that's the way they see it, 'it's not right, you shouldn't go to discos' . . . I would never have left if it had not been forced on me like that, I would have kept going and stayed with the friends I had, but it was because they got so strict with everything, that's why I stopped. And I think there's lots of parents out there who are the same, they've got this pre-conception that the church has these rigid rules, and you can't worship God unless you do this, that and the other, and there's no deviation.

Another of our interviewees, Gareth Wilkinson, a businessman in his forties who had left a Methodist church, was still reacting to the moral conservatism he had encountered in his Sunday school at the age of nine.

I subsequently came to regard the church to be very rigid, that particular Methodist church, or perhaps I mean the particular Sunday school teachers. I mean, we had this ludicrous business, when I think we were all about nine, and we were, it was very forcefully suggested to us that we should sign a pledge never to drink alcohol, which is just an amazing decision to try and impose on a nine-year-old, and it was very, very strongly and very, very forcibly put to us.

Listening to the statistics

A set of questions included in the survey set out to examine how much church-leavers cited the two themes concerned with problems with conservatism as implicated in their own experience of leaving church. An overview of the findings is presented in Table 18 in the Appendix.

The data make it clear that between one-fifth and one-third of church-leavers associated their disengagement from church with a growing sense of frustration with what they saw to be the church's conservative thinking and conservative practice. In this context roughly equal weight seems to have been given to problems with theological conservatism and to problems with moral conservatism.

In terms of theological conservatism, one in every five church-leavers (21%) considered that the church's theological teachings were too narrow. The proportion increased a little to 23% of church-leavers who maintained that the church was too negative toward 'the world outside'. The proportion increased further to 27% of church-leavers who felt that the church had allowed them too little space to explore ideas for themselves. The proportion increased even further to 32% of church-leavers who had become tired of being told what to believe by the church.

In terms of moral conservatism, one in every four church-leavers said simply that the church was too conservative for them (25%) or that they were tired of being told how to behave by the church (24%). The proportion increased a little to 28% of church-leavers who maintained that the church's moral teachings were too narrow. The proportion increased even further to 37% of church-leavers who argued that the church's approach to morality was too 'black and white'.

Sex differences

In a number of ways problems with conservatism carried equal weight among male church-leavers and among female church-leavers. In one respect, however, men voiced a more critical view than women concerning what they saw as the conservative and narrow stance of the church. While 18% of the women criticised the church's theological teachings as too narrow, the proportion rose to 24% among the men. While 25% of the women criticised the church's moral teachings as too narrow, the proportion rose to 32% among the men.

Generational differences

Similar proportions of all three generational groups shared the view that the church's theological teachings were too narrow. However, there were significant differences between the age groups concerning the aspects of theological conservatism that were more distasteful to them. Younger church-leavers were more likely to focus on dislike of being told what to believe, while older church-leavers were more likely to focus on the division between the church and the world. While 28% of those aged sixty or over and 30% of those in their forties or fifties complained that they were tired of being told what to believe by the church, the proportion rose to 40% among those under the age of forty. While 19% of those under the age of forty and 21% of those in their forties or fifties complained that the church was too negative toward 'the world outside', the proportion rose to 29% among those aged sixty or over.

Similar proportions of all three age groups shared the view that the church's moral teachings were too narrow. Once again, however, there were significant differences between the age groups concerning the aspects of moral conservatism that were more distasteful to them. Younger church-leavers were more likely to focus on distaste for being told how to behave by the church, and on distaste for clear-cut moral certainty. While 19% of those aged sixty or over and 23% of those in their forties or fifties complained that they were tired of being told how to behave by the church, the proportion rose to 31% among those under the age of forty. While 27% of those aged sixty or over complained that the church's approach to morality was too 'black and white', the proportion rose to 37% among those in their forties or fifties and to 47% among those under the age of forty.

The general complaint that the church was too conservative for them was voiced by one in every three of those under the age of forty (33%), compared with 21% of those in their forties or fifties and 22% of those aged sixty or over.

Cohort differences

Problems with conservatism is a factor that had a similar level of influence in the disengagement from church of those who left over twenty years ago and of those who left in the past twenty years. However, one item in this set of eight items recorded statistically significant differences between the two cohorts of church-leavers. This item suggests that complaints about the division between the church and the world were becoming less salient among church-leavers. While 28% of those who left over twenty years ago complained that the church was too negative toward 'the world outside', the proportion dropped to 19% among those who left in the past twenty years.

Age at leaving

Problems with conservatism played a significantly more important part in the process of disengagement from church among those who left before their twentieth birthday than among those who left later in life. In terms of theological conservatism, 42% of those who left before their twentieth birthday complained that they were tired of being told what to believe by the church, compared with 31% of those who left in their twenties or thirties and 15% of those who left after their fortieth birthday. One-third of those who left before their twentieth birthday (32%) felt that the church allowed them too little space to explore ideas for themselves, compared with 26% of those who left in their twenties or thirties and 17% of those who left after their fortieth birthday.

In terms of moral conservatism, 46% of those who left before their twentieth birthday felt that the church's approach to morality was too 'black and white', compared with 38% of those who left in their twenties or thirties and 18% of those who left after their fortieth birthday. Similarly, 29% of those who left before their twentieth birthday complained that they were tired of being told how to behave by the church, compared with 26% of those who left in their twenties or thirties and 9% of those who left after their fortieth birthday.

The general complaint that the church was too conservative for them was voiced by 32% of those who left before their twentieth birthday, compared with 21% of those who left in their twenties or thirties and 19% of those who left after their fortieth birthday.

Denomination

Problems with conservatism played a particularly salient role in the process of disengagement from church among Roman Catholics. Roman Catholics were more likely than members of the other denominations to cite problems with theological conservatism and with moral conservatism. Overall, 36% of Roman Catholics made the general complaint that the church was too conservative for them, compared with 23% of Anglicans and 23% of Free Church members.

In terms of theological conservatism, 33% of Roman Catholics said that the church's theological teachings were too narrow, compared with 19% of Anglicans and 17% of Free Church members. Half of the Roman Catholics (49%) had grown tired of being told what to believe by the church, compared with 28% of Anglicans and 32% of Free Church members.

In terms of moral conservatism, 42% of the Roman Catholics said that the church's moral teachings were too narrow, compared with 27% of the Anglicans and 23% of the Free Church members. Two-fifths of the Roman Catholics (42%) were tired of being told how to behave by the church, compared with 19% of the Anglicans and 25% of the Free Church members. For 63% of the Roman Catholics the church's approach to morality was too 'black and white', compared with 34% of the Anglicans and 28% of the Free Church members.

Sudden or gradual leaving

Problems with conservatism is a factor which in many ways is equally reflected in sudden leaving and in gradual leaving. The two items within this set of eight items that recorded a statistically significant difference between the responses of sudden leavers and gradual leavers concerned dislike for being told what to believe or what to do by the church. While 27% of gradual leavers were tired of being told what to believe by the church, the proportion rose to 38% among sudden leavers. While 21% of gradual leavers were tired of being told how to behave by the church, the proportion rose to 27% among sudden leavers.

Likelihood of returning

Church-leavers who had disengaged following problems with conservatism were much more likely to place themselves among the permanent disaffiliates than among the potential returners. In terms of theological conservatism, while 10% of the potential returners complained that the church's theological teachings were too narrow, the proportion rose to 25% among the permanent disaffiliates. Three times as many permanent disaffiliates as potential returners were tired of being told what to believe by the church (43% compared with 14%). Twice as many permanent disaffiliates as potential returners felt that the church was too negative toward 'the world outside' (28% compared with 15%). One in three of the permanent disaffiliates (33%) complained that the church allowed them too little space to explore ideas for themselves, compared with 12% of the potential returners.

In terms of moral conservatism, while 16% of the potential returners complained that the church's moral teachings were too narrow, the proportion rose to 34% among the permanent disaffiliates. Three times as many permanent disaffiliates as potential returners were tired of being told how to behave by the church (33% compared with 10%). Twice as many permanent disaffiliates as potential returners felt that the church's approach to morality was too 'black and white' (47% compared with 21%). While 16% of potential returners said that the church was too conservative for them, the proportion rose to 30% among the permanent disaffiliates.

Pastoral implications

This section makes it clear that between one-fifth and one-third of church-leavers associated their disengagement from church with a growing sense of frustration with what they saw to be the church's conservative thinking and conservative practice. They were increasingly tired of being told by the church what to believe and how to behave. Problems with conservatism were particularly salient for younger church-leavers and especially for those who disengaged before their twentieth birthday. Problems with conservatism played a significantly more prominent role among those church-leavers who left a Roman Catholic church. Moreover, those who left church complaining about problems with conservatism tend to be reluctant to explore ways back into participation in church life. There are important practical implications that follow from such an analysis.

The first implication concerns reflection on the content of what the church teaches. The impression that the church's theological teaching and that the church's moral teaching is too narrow may, in some cases, be little more than an unfortunate misapprehension based on inadequate presentation of potentially rich and broadly grounded streams within the Christian tradition.

The second implication concerns reflection on the manner in which the church teaches. The impression that the church tells people what to believe and tells people how to behave may, in some cases, be little more than an unfortunate misapprehension based on inappropriate presentation of the church's intentions and expectations.

The third implication concerns taking seriously the best available research-based information concerning ways in which different individuals process and deal with different styles of Christian teaching at different stages in their lives. While at certain stages in their Christian pilgrimage individuals may welcome the certainty of clear teaching and may welcome the clarity of being told what to believe and how to behave, at other stages in their Christian pilgrimage such certainty and such clarity may indeed become a barrier to faith rather than a facilitator of faith. When churches recognise individuals beginning to struggle with the clearly defined faith from which they formerly drew strength, they may be wise to help these individuals to reformulate their faith in more liberal categories. The empirical evidence suggests that the alternative may be to watch such individuals disengage from church life, disenchanted by what they conceptualise as the unacceptable conservatism of the church, and then remain at a distance from the church, reluctant to return.

19

Problems with liberalism

Setting the scene

While the previous chapter has concentrated on how some church-leavers trace their disengagement from church to problems with conservatism, the present chapter turns attention to the opposite perspective. Reading other analyses of church decline, the weight of criticism seems to be placed firmly on the failure of churches to stay more closely with the tradition. The tendency for the churches to revise their theological teaching to take modern perspectives into account is seen to precipitate church-leaving. For example, in their study of *Vanishing Boundaries*, Hoge, Johnson and Luidens (1994: 178) argue that the mainline churches 'have lost members because, over the years, beliefs have been changing'. The tendency for churches to revise their moral teaching to take modern perspectives into account is seen to precipitate church-leaving (Roof, 1999: 124). The aim of the present chapter, therefore, is to examine the extent to which church-leavers themselves explain their distance from the church in terms of problems with liberalism. Listening to our interviewees, two main themes emerged within the broad area of problems with liberalism. We describe these themes as: lack of clear boundaries, and lack of clear teaching.

Lack of clear boundaries

The first theme concerned with liberalism focused on the lack of clear boundaries that some church-leavers had desired to see more clearly drawn between the church and the world. Some church-leavers expressed this concern by saying that there should be a clearer line drawn between Christian values and the values of the 'outside world'. Others felt that this kind of liberalism resulted in a lack of clarity regarding what commitment to the church involved. Some church-leavers said that it was not worth staying with their liberal church because it did not seem to matter what people believed or did. Others complained that the church compromised its teachings to be acceptable to secular culture. For Richard Elliott, a man in his sixties who had left an Anglican church, the problem with liberalism was articulated in terms of the views expressed by some of the bishops.

> People outside . . . they will come to me and say, 'bishop so-and-so said this, he's questioning this, that or the other, well, what is this? You don't believe in anything, do you?' I mean, people outside the church are very aware of these things, they have nothing to do with the church, but they're quite good at realising that things don't add up when somebody makes a statement like that, and . . . you feel responsible for what they've said and people expect you to be of the same opinion, and because the bishop says this, then this is what the church believes, as a whole. And it makes it very difficult for me to say, 'well, the bishops say that, but we don't really believe that . . .'

Later on in the interview Richard Elliott blamed what he called the pressure groups as well as bishops.

> I think that very often God's word is compromised today because of pressure groups. We've got the gay Christians, we've got the feminist lobby, and it seems to me that they're giving in

to these pressure groups because they have certain influence outside the church. Well, the feminists have, obviously, and the gay people have now got a sort of standing in public affairs and people accept them, and accept what they're doing, and think it's perfectly alright and it's legal. So it seems to me that the church gives in to these groups, to accommodate these groups, after all they have got gay Christians within the church, and also feminists in the church.

For Russell Briggs, a computer salesman in his fifties, the real problem was with the liberal views of the new vicar.

This [new vicar] came in, and . . . he was a real eccentric . . . and he caused havoc in the church. The evangelicals know what they believe and they expect the person who's their vicar to know even more, but this guy didn't know what he believed, and he caused real havoc. We tried to oust him, but the bishop didn't want to know because there's no such thing as heresy in the Church of England [laughter], it's such a broad church. So the bishop left him there, and he caused devastation.

Lack of clear teaching

The second theme concerned with liberalism focused on lack of certainty that some church-leavers had desired to see more clearly preached in their church. Some church-leavers complained that the church's teaching did not give the certainty they were seeking. Others said that the church failed to provide a firm moral lead. Some church-leavers said that the church did not seem to take sin seriously enough. Others complained that the church was just too liberal for them. One of our interviewees, Richard Elliott, a man in his sixties who had left an Anglican church, had found the church's liberal attitude toward homosexuality and the sanctity of marriage just unacceptable.

291

A failure to tell the nation that the Bible says that homosexuality, homosexual activities, are sinful. Sodom and Gomorrah is a good example . . . I was worried by this issue for a long time. And it eventually boiled over because of all the talk about it, and all the discussion about it, and all the articles in magazines and newspapers, and particularly one example, we have an example here in X where a vicar was accused of homosexual activities in the [public] toilets and he was fined £100 and bound over to keep the peace. And the bishop didn't take any action on it at all, and the chap has now gone [away] but he carried on for some years after that as vicar of that parish. And also there was the case of another chap in [another] parish who had a live-in lover, a male lover, in the vicarage, and people complained about it, and the bishop took no action, and said, 'keep it quiet'. Well, this is all pretty sleazy, and it's not in accordance with what the Scripture says anyway, so that sort of disgusted me completely, those sort of examples . . . I mean, unless the church tells the nation or the people that what they are doing is wrong, they're going to think it's alright.

The church's liberal attitude toward homosexuality also proved to be the stumbling block for Wesley Harris, a computer analyst in his thirties who had left a Methodist church.

At the time they were going on about ordaining, you know, homosexual priests. Now it's like, now hold on, if you're trying to teach the word of God, surely you teach it all. You know, and you don't say, 'well, OK, these bits, even though it's a sin in the Bible, but hey, this is the twentieth century, so we should be able to accept these sort of people, but then we can't accept normal people doing this, that and the other'. So I'm, 'well, hold on guys, there's a contradiction here' . . . Ordaining homosexual priests, it's like, well, how can you have that if you're, you know, saying the Bible says that homosexuality is wrong. But the Bible also says that sex outside of marriage is wrong. But, hey, we can ordain homosexual priests but you guys can't have sex outside of marriage. So, you know, it's double standards.

Listening to the statistics

A set of questions included in the survey set out to examine how much church-leavers cited the two themes concerned with problems with liberalism as implicated in their own experience of leaving church. An overview of the findings is presented in Table 19 in the Appendix.

The data make it clear that fewer church-leavers associated their disengagement from church with problems concerning liberalism than associated their disengagement from church with problems concerning conservatism. While up to one-third of church-leavers mentioned problems concerning conservatism, those who mentioned problems concerning liberalism never reached one-quarter.

Between one in five and one in four church-leavers complained about the lack of clear boundaries between the church and the world: 22% felt that there should be a clearer line drawn between Christian values and the values of the 'outside world'. The proportion dropped a little to 18% who complained that it was unclear what commitment to the church involved. The proportion dropped further to 14% who complained that it was not worth staying because it did not matter what people believed or did, and to 13% who complained that the church compromised its teachings to be acceptable to secular culture.

Between one in five and one in four church-leavers complained about the lack of clear teaching and direction given by the church: 23% felt that the church's teaching did not give the certainty they were seeking. The proportion fell to 16% who complained that the church failed to provide a firm moral lead. The proportion then fell even further to 10% who complained that the church did not seem to take sin seriously enough, and to 7% of church-leavers who said quite simply that the church was just too liberal for them.

Sex differences

In a number of ways problems with liberalism carried equal weight among male church-leavers and among female church-leavers. For example, in terms of the blurred boundaries between the church and the world, similar proportions of the men (19%) and of the women (17%) felt that it was unclear what commitment to the church involved. On the other hand, a significantly higher proportion of the men than of the women made the clear statement that there should be a clearer line drawn between Christian values and the values of the 'outside world' (27% compared with 20%).

In terms of assessing the church's teaching, similar proportions of the men (24%) and of the women (22%) complained that the church's teaching did not give the certainty they were seeking. On the other hand, the male church-leavers were significantly more likely than the female church-leavers to complain about the liberalisation of the church's moral teaching. Thus, 20% of the men complained that the church failed to provide a firm moral lead, compared with 14% of the women. For 14% of the men the church did not seem to take sin seriously enough, compared with 8% of the women.

Generational differences

Problems with liberalism were significantly more troubling for the older church-leavers. In terms of complaining about what they saw as a lack of clear teaching, 30% of those aged sixty or over said that the church's teaching did not give them the certainty they were seeking, compared with 21% among those under the age of forty and 19% of those in their forties or fifties. Similarly, 29% of those aged sixty or over said that the church failed to provide a firm moral lead, compared with 10% of those under the age of forty and 12% of those in their forties or fifties. For 16% of those aged sixty or over, the church did not seem to take sin seriously enough, compared with 10% of those in their forties or fifties and 5% of those under the age of forty. For 12% of those aged sixty or over the church was described as too liberal compared with 6% of those in their forties or fifties and 3% of those under the age of forty.

In terms of complaining about what they saw as a lack of clear boundaries, 29% of those aged sixty or over said that there should be a clearer line drawn between Christian values and the values of the 'outside world', compared with 21% of those in their forties or fifties and 17% of those under the age of forty. Similarly, 19% of those aged sixty or over said that the church compromised its teachings to be acceptable to secular culture, compared with 14% of those in their forties or fifties and 8% of those under the age of forty.

Cohort differences

Problems with liberalism is a factor that had a similar level of influence in the disengagement from church among those who left over twenty years ago and among those who left in the past twenty years. For example, in terms of the lack of clear boundaries, 22% of those who left church over twenty years ago felt there should be a clearer line drawn between Christian values and the values of the 'outside world', and so did 23% of those who left in the past twenty years. In terms of the lack of clear teaching, among those who left church over twenty years ago 11% complained that the church did not seem to take sin seriously enough, and so did 10% of those who left in the past twenty years.

Age at leaving

Problems with liberalism tended to play a significantly more important part in the process of disengagement from church among those who left church later in life than among those who left before their twentieth birthday. In terms of the lack of clear boundaries, 28% of those who left church after their fortieth birthday felt that there should be a clearer line drawn between Christian values and the values of the 'outside world', compared with 19% of those who left before their twentieth birthday. One in five of those who left church after their fortieth birthday (19%) complained that the church compromised its teachings to be acceptable to secular culture, compared with 10% of those who left before their twentieth birthday.

In terms of a lack of clear teaching, 14% of those who left church after their fortieth birthday complained that the church was too liberal for them, compared with 3% who left before their twentieth birthday. Nearly one-quarter of those who left church after their fortieth birthday (23%) felt that the church failed to provide a firm moral lead, compared with 15% who left before their twentieth birthday. One in every six of those who left church after their fortieth birthday (17%) felt that the church did not take sin seriously enough, compared with 8% of those who left before their twentieth birthday.

Denomination

Overall, problems with liberalism played a similar role in disengagement from church across the three main denominational groups. For example, in terms of a lack of clear boundaries, 24% of Roman Catholics felt that there should be a clearer line drawn between Christian values and the values of the 'outside world', and so did 24% of Anglicans and 21% of Free Church members. In terms of a lack of clear teaching, 23% of Roman Catholics felt that the church's teaching did not give the certainty they were seeking, and so did 23% of Anglicans and 21% of Free Church members.

The one item within this set of eight items that recorded a statistically significant difference between the responses of the three denominational groups concerned the moral lead given by the church. In this case the Anglicans proved to be the most critical. Thus, 19% of Anglicans complained that the church failed to provide a firm moral lead, compared with 15% of Roman Catholics and 9% of Free Church members.

Sudden or gradual leaving

Problems with liberalism is a factor that is equally reflected in sudden leaving and in gradual leaving. For example, in terms of a lack of clear boundaries, 23% of those who left church suddenly felt that there should be a clearer line drawn between Christian values and the values of the 'outside world', and so did 23% of those who left church gradually. In terms of a lack of clear teaching, 16% of those who left church suddenly complained that the church failed to provide a firm moral lead, and so did 16% of those who left gradually.

Likelihood of returning

Overall, church-leavers who had disengaged following problems with liberalism were as likely to place themselves among the potential returners as among the permanent disaffiliates. However, two items within this set of eight items recorded a statistically significant difference between the responses of the potential returners and the responses of the permanent disaffiliates. Those who left church thinking that it was not worth staying because it did not matter what people believed or did were significantly more likely to be found among the permanent disaffiliates than among the potential returners (19% compared with 7%). Those who left church complaining that the church's teachings did not give the certainty they were seeking were also significantly more likely to be found among the permanent disaffiliates than among the potential returners (27% compared with 16%).

Pastoral implications

This section makes it clear that up to one-quarter of church-leavers associated their disengagement from church with a growing sense of frustration with what they saw to be the church's lack of clear teaching or the lack of clear boundaries separating the church from the world. They were frustrated by what they saw to be the liberalism of the church. They were frustrated by the church's failure to provide clear teaching or a firm moral lead. Problems with liberalism were particularly salient for older church-leavers and especially for those who disengaged after their fortieth birthday. Moreover, those who left church complaining that the church's teaching did not give the certainty they were seeking, or complaining that it was not worth staying because it did not matter what people believed or did, tended to be reluctant to explore ways back into church life. There are important practical implications that follow from such an analysis.

The main implication concerns assessing ways in which the more liberal and the more conservative streams within the Christian tradition relate one to another. The previous chapter demonstrated how one group of church-leavers attributed their disengagement from church to a growing sense of frustration with conservatism. Now the current chapter has demonstrated that a second group of church-leavers attributed their disengagement from church to a growing sense of frustration with liberalism. Given the breadth within the Christian tradition it seems highly unfortunate that there is not closer conversation between liberal churches and conservative churches. Church-goers who become frustrated with their conservative churches might surely be encouraged to seek participation within a more liberal congregation as preferable to joining the ranks of church-leavers. Church-goers who become frustrated with their liberal churches might surely be encouraged to seek participation within a more conservative congregation as preferable to joining the ranks of church-leavers.

This positive approach to church-switching presupposes a very special kind of relationship between different churches, whereby liberal churches can respect conservative churches and conservative churches can respect liberal churches. The fundamental assumption is that individual Christians should be free to savour and to assess the spectrum of the Christian tradition and, perhaps, within the course of their life to be nurtured by and contribute to several different streams within that tradition. Within this very special kind of relationship between different churches, each stream must continue to be highly committed to the unique value of its theological position, but at the same time and in proper humility acknowledge the divine presence and the divine grace within other theological positions.

20

Conclusion

Setting the scene

Having sifted through the rich resources of information made available both by our qualitative data provided by the interviews and our quantitative data provided by the questionnaires, we are now in a position to draw together the insights generated by our study. We propose to do so in four stages. First, we review the aims set out at the beginning of the book and assess how well these aims have been fulfilled. Second, we apply the findings from our study to help us understand the individual church-leaver. Third, we reflect on what this understanding of church-leavers and church-leaving means theologically. This theological reflection could provide an important platform from which to address one of the major problems facing the churches in the twenty-first century. We take the view that programmes and invitations to welcome new members to enter by the front door into church life remain unproductive and inadequate unless attempts are also made to review what is happening at the back door through which church-leavers exit. Rooted in a strong doctrine of creation and in a rich theology of individual differences, we propose the model of the multiplex church, and advocate church-switching as infinitely more preferable to church-leaving. Fourth, we return to the 15 reasons identified by our study as underpinning church-leaving and develop implications from these reasons for shaping our vision of the multiplex church.

Reviewing the aims

Gone for Good? set out to advance understanding of church-leaving in three ways. The first aim was to refine and to test a typology of reasons or motivations for disengagement from church. By building on and extending the typology proposed by our earlier book *Gone but not Forgotten*, we have identified 15 discrete themes from the myriad reasons given by church-leavers for their disengagement from church attendance. Set out sequentially in Chapters 5 through 19, these reasons or motivations were defined as: matters of belief and unbelief; growing up and changing; life transitions and life changes; alternative lives and alternative meanings; incompatible life-styles; not belonging and not fitting in; costs and benefits; disillusionment with the church; being let down by the church; problems with relevance; problems with change; problems with worship; problems with leadership; problems with conservatism; and problems with liberalism. Having set this typology to work in a systematic way, we remain convinced by its usefulness and by its ability to generate insight into the complex and diverse phenomenon of church-leaving. It is with confidence, therefore, that we invite other researchers to adopt our typology and to critique and to modify it in the light of further empirical evidence.

The second aim was to propose and to test the theory that, far from being a unified phenomenon, church-leaving would be characterised by identifiable patterns and trends. In order to test this general theory we identified a limited number of well-defined and discrete themes against which we could cross-tabulate the evidence analysed within the 15 core chapters. In this way the following seven themes were subjected to close scrutiny.

Are there discernible differences in the reasons underpinning church-leaving offered by men and by women? Are there discernible differences in the causes of church-leaving advanced by those under the age of forty, those in their forties or fifties, or those aged sixty or over? Are there discernible cohort differences in reasons for leaving church, comparing those who left over twenty years ago with those who left in the past twenty years? Are there discernible differences in reasons for leaving church at different stages in life, comparing those who left before their twentieth birthday, those who left in their twenties or thirties, and those who left aged forty or over? Are there discernible differences in reasons for leaving church offered by members of different denominations, comparing members of the Free Churches, the Roman Catholic Church, and the Anglican Church? Are there discernible differences between the reasons for church-leaving associated with sudden disengagement from church and the reasons for church-leaving associated with gradual disengagement from church? Are there discernible differences in reasons for leaving church between individuals who are likely to return to church and those who are more likely to stay away?

All seven themes proved to be illuminating in a variety of ways. Our broad hypothesis was supported. There are identifiable patterns and trends underpinning motivation for church-leaving. It is with confidence, therefore, that we invite other researchers to take such factors into account when new studies are designed to take research into church-leaving on to the next stage. Taking such factors into account, however, has important implications for the design and scale of future studies.

The third aim was to map the relationship between the motivation for church-leaving and the potential for returning. Are some reasons for leaving church associated either with greater openness to return or with greater resolution to remain at a distance from the church? The research evidence provided a very clear answer to this question. Some church-leavers are much more open than others to becoming potential returners, and willingness to return is clearly related to the reasons for leaving. In broad terms, the people most likely to return are those whose church-leaving was associated with life transitions and life changes, and alternative lives and alternative meanings. In broad terms, the people least likely to return are those whose church-leaving was associated with matters of belief and unbelief, growing up and changing, incompatible life-styles, costs and benefits, disillusionment with the church, problems with relevance, and problems with conservatism. It is with confidence, therefore, that we can recommend as good pastoral practice the close listening to church-leavers as they recount their reasons for maintaining distance from the church. Their story of disengagement offers clear insight into their potential for re-engagement.

Understanding church-leavers

The three aims of the present study reviewed above were all concerned with a high level of abstraction and with objective analysis. As a result we have been able to discern clear patterns and clear threads running through the phenomenon of church-leaving. It remains very important, however, not to lose sight of the complex individuals at the heart of our pastoral concern. It would be a serious mistake, for example, to imagine that the various reasons for church-leaving operate in clear isolation among different individuals. It would be unusual to identify a church-leaver whose disengagement from church was related solely to one of the 15 themes of our typology and to none of the others. For example, the church-leaver whose final disengagement from church was triggered by life transitions and life changes (say, moving house) may also have been influenced by incompatible life-styles (say, cohabiting outside marriage) or by problems with conservatism (say, feeling that the church's moral teachings were too narrow). The church-leaver whose final disengagement from church was triggered by being let down by the church (say, feeling that the church was not caring and supportive when such support was most needed) may also have been influenced by problems

303

with change (say, finding it hard to adjust to a new minister) or by disillusionment with the church (say, feeling that the church fails to live up to its ideals).

This complex interaction between the themes was made very clear to us by the initial in-depth interviews with which our study started. It is for this reason that we decided to draw so heavily on some of our interviewees to illustrate a range of the themes introduced in Chapters 5 through 19. The same voices re-emerged making different points in respect of different themes precisely to make clear the links and the connections running through individual and highly personal stories. Our statistical analyses of the questionnaire responses both confirmed and amplified this impression. To understand any one church-leaver it is necessary to listen to the whole story, to see how the threads were woven together and to try to identify the key precipitating factor that eventually tipped the balance and converted a church-goer into becoming a church-leaver.

Theological reflection

Gone for Good? was established as a research project located within the field of *empirical* theology (as discussed in Chapter 2). As a study in empirical theology the project drew on and applied high-quality research techniques pioneered within the social sciences, using both qualitative and quantitative methods. As a study in empirical *theology* the project was rooted in the theological and practical concerns of the church rather than in the somewhat more detached concerns of social scientific enquiry. It is for this reason that each of the 15 core chapters concluded with a section on pastoral implications.

The pastoral implications developed at the end of each chapter are offered as more than simple handy hints on how to work effectively among church-leavers, but they leave unfinished a more systematic discussion of the ecclesiological and theological implications of our findings. These findings were generated by a distinctive perspective in the social sciences (and especially in social psychology) characterised as the 'individual differences' approach. This approach has been reflected in the present study in two important ways. First, there was an attempt to define and to assess discrete strands, factors, or themes in church-leaving, and 15 such strands were identified. Second, there was an attempt to examine whether there were clear patterns within these 15 strands that could, to some extent, be predicted by other extraneous factors, and seven such factors were identified. This individual variability in the types and causes of church-leaving strongly suggests that the psychology of individual differences has something important to say in this area. It is also important, therefore, that an empirical theology that draws on the psychology of individual differences is supported by a systematic theology of individual differences.

Elsewhere Leslie J. Francis has sketched the clear foundations for a theology of individual differences rooted in a strong doctrine of creation (see, for example, Francis, 2005a). This biblically based doctrine of creation draws on Genesis 1.27.

So God created humankind in God's image,
in the image of God, God created them;
male and female God created them.

In this reading of the text it is not so much that men and women are each separately made in God's image, rather that the very distinction between men and women reflects something profound about the nature of a God whose unity exists in the presence of diversity. So this view of creation builds individual differences into the heart of the divine intentionality. Being created male and being created female implies fundamental difference, and it is this *diversity* that reflects the divine image. This diversity is expressed in the text of Genesis 1.27 through the difference of sex. Consequently, a church that takes seriously such a doctrine of creation will need to accord to men and to women equal respect and equal opportunity within the kingdom of God. A church that takes seriously such a doctrine of creation may also need to question generations of Christian teaching and practice which have been shaped by a very different view of male supremacy within the divinely designated order. A social science perspective that fully embraces this theologically driven imperative of equality between men and women may indeed learn something about the rich diversity within God when the empirical evidence identifies significant differences between men and women.

Diversity of sex in Genesis 1.27 acts as an analogy for other individual differences that may co-exist within the unity of God's people. When Paul expresses the importance of this unity in Galatians 3.28 he does not intend that the corresponding diversity is completely removed by unity in Christ. To say there is neither 'male nor female' is not to say that the divine imperative is for neutered human existence: it is recognising that the unity of God embraces the diversity that is innately human. Paul expands individual difference to include other differences such as ethnicity (neither Jew nor Gentile) and circumstances of life (neither slave nor free). This points back to the Genesis text as genuinely using sex as a metaphor for other human diversities. If divine intentionality created both male and female in the divine image, then it is reasonable to argue that differences of ethnicity may belong to a similar level. Reading Genesis 1.27 in the light of Galatians 3.28 implies a parallel revelation which may read as follows.

So God created humankind in God's image,
in the image of God, God created them;
black and white God created them.

A church that takes seriously such a doctrine of creation will need to accord to people of different ethnicities equal respect and equal opportunity within the kingdom of God. A church that takes seriously such a doctrine of creation may also need to question generations of Christian teaching and practice which has been shaped by a very different view of white supremacy within the divinely designated order.

Francis (2005a) extended this analysis of sex differences and ethnic differences as reflecting the rich diversity within the divine image to accord similar status to those fundamental personality differences that characterise the range of the normal human population. Drawing on Carl Jung's (1971) model of psychological type, as construed by the Myers-Briggs Type Indicator (Myers and McCaulley, 1985), such fundamental personality differences reflecting the rich diversity within the divine image may include at least the two orientations of extraversion and introversion, the two perceiving processes of sensing and intuition and the two judging processes of thinking and feeling. Surely an analogical reading of Genesis 1.27 implies a parallel revelation which may read as follows.

So God created humankind in God's image,
in the image of God, God created them;
introvert and extravert God created them.

A church that takes seriously such a doctrine of creation will need to accord people of different personality preferences equal respect and equal opportunity within the kingdom of God. It may also need to question generations of Christian teaching and practice which have (consciously or unconsciously) accorded higher value to some personality types over other types. For example, traditions in Christian spirituality that have emphasised the inward journey, silent retreat and inner exploration have supported the impression that introverts may be holier or more spiritual than extraverts. Traditions in Christian pastoral practice that have emphasised loving acceptance over critical judgement have supported the impression that feelers may be holier or more pastoral than thinkers.

Such a theology of individual differences grounded in a strong doctrine of creation carries important implications for our understanding of the church and for our understanding of the pastoral care of church-leavers. To begin with, a theology of individual differences that conceptualises human diversity as reflecting rich diversity within the creator God may need to develop an ecclesiology tolerant of diversity. Such an ecclesiology will hold to the vision of the one united transcendent Church (reflecting the unity of the Godhead) but positively welcome the rich diversity of ecclesial expressions within the local, national and international contexts. Just as men and women are different and allowed to emphasise and celebrate those differences precisely because both share and participate in the divine image, so should different expressions of church be seen as reflecting different aspects of the divine image these churches are called to express among God's people.

In other words, a theology of individual differences rooted in a strong doctrine of creation offers a distinctive vision for the ecumenical process in contemporary society. Just as a theology of individual differences rejoices, say, in the equality of men and of women within the kingdom of God, so this theological perspective rejoices in the rich and diverse expressions of church life. It is this approach to ecclesiology that offers some hope to church-leavers.

Our vision of the church of the future is that of the 'multiplex' church. The multiplex church offers different perspectives on the same faith, different perspectives on the same eternal truths. Seekers after the kingdom of God will be able to enter this multiplex church through many different doors and celebrate their participation within the kingdom of God in many different ways.

Just as there are many front doors into this multiplex church, so there are many back doors leading out of the many expressions of church. While some of these back doors properly lead directly into the 'outside world', others lead directly into different expressions of church. Our current study of church-leavers has suggested that within the current model of church many have searched for the back door away from their own congregation and have been, perhaps, surprised to find that this back door only leads away from church altogether. Some such church-leavers soon grow content living fulfilling lives and keeping their distance from the church. Others see themselves as potential returners, but nonetheless find it hard to discover the door that leads them back to the inside. Within the multiplex church, church-switching may begin to replace church-leaving.

Our multiplex church model is more ambitious than the 'multiple and midweek congregations' model outlined in *Mission-shaped Church* (Archbishops' Council, 2004: 59–62). Our model potentially embraces much more diversity and, unlike the 'multiple and midweek congregations' model, does not necessarily presuppose that the multiplex church occupies a single building. First and foremost, it is a new mindset that encourages churches to play to their strengths and to be aware of the niche markets for which they can, and cannot, cater. It encourages churches in a given locality to think of each other not as competitors but as collaborators, referring potential church-leavers on to other partner churches who can better meet their needs. We are taking the term 'multiplex' to mean: 'consisting of many elements in a complex relationship' (Soanes and Hawker, 2005). When used of a cinema, 'multiplex' refers to a number of separate 'screens' within a single building. But in a church context 'multiplex' can refer to a multiplicity of separate congregations within the same premises as well as a multiplicity of different styles of church in a given locality.

The multiplex church

Our systematic analysis of the different motivations underpinning church-leaving also helps to illuminate just how much the multiplex church may be able to help some who are tempted to become church-leavers to find doors that lead not away from the church but into other congregations. In order to test this theory, we will revisit the 15 themes in turn.

Chapter 5, which discussed matters of belief and unbelief, identified two different kinds of problems with Christian belief. The first kind of problem was characterised by two themes concerning losing faith and concerning the ways in which life experiences can undermine and undercut the bases on which faith has been built. Such issues may point incontrovertibly to the door leading to church-leaving. The second kind of problem was characterised by the two themes concerning problems with belief and concerning responding to doubt. Problems with belief included issues like reconciling the church's teaching with modern science or locating the distinctive claims of the Christian tradition within a theologically informed world-view that recognises the complexity of a multi-faith context. There are congregations in which such matters are handled as a matter of course. Problems with responding to doubt included complaining that a questioning faith did not seem acceptable to the church or feeling that the church did not allow people to discuss or disagree with its views. There are congregations in which such forms of religious quest are highly affirmed as central to the Christian tradition. Within the multiplex church there should be doors leading straight into such congregations.

Chapter 6, which discussed growing up and changing, identified two different kinds of issues. The first kind of issue was characterised by two themes concerning growing up and concerning the relationship between parents and children. Some congregations are clearly much better equipped than others to assist with developing Christian parenting and with nurturing discipleship through the transitions of childhood and adolescence. Here are highly specialised forms of ministry properly deserving quality resourcing at national and regional levels. Within the multiplex church such areas of strength should be well known and well signposted. The second kind of issue was characterised by ways in which individuals accepted responsibility for their own drifting away from church. A great number of church-leavers accounted for their disaffiliation simply in terms of getting out of the habit of going to church. Within the multiplex church there may be many ways of keeping in touch with those who are inclined to drift out, of helping them to find doors that lead into a variety of forms of church life.

Chapter 7, which discussed life transitions and life changes, identified two different kinds of changes. The first kind of changes concerned geographical transitions. Young people moved away from the parental home to enter higher education or to find work. Older people moved to new areas for a variety of reasons. Geographical movement of this nature severed established links with local churches and all too often new links were not made with churches in the new area. Within the multiplex church there need to be clear links not only with other congregations in the neighbourhood but across the globe. The multiplex church needs high visibility on the World Wide Web. The second kind of changes concerned personal transitions. Some individuals experienced new demands from growing children or from ageing parents. Other individuals experienced new difficulties from illness, bereavement or divorce. Within the multiplex church there need to be mechanisms for supporting individuals through such life transitions, and opportunities for engagement with church life in ways which are consistent with their life situation.

Chapter 8, which discussed alternative lives and alternative meanings, identified three different themes. The first theme examined ways in which the changing work schedule interfered with church attendance. Some individuals work on a Sunday and feel excluded from church life. Within the multiplex church there need to be doors leading from Sunday congregations to weekday congregations and meetings. The second theme examined ways in which tensions with relationships interfered with church attendance. Within the multiplex church there needs to be proper sensitivity toward the personal demands placed on members' lives and sufficient flexibility for the ways in which participation is expressed. The third theme concerned tensions with time. It is all too easy for church-goers to become attracted to and absorbed by other interests and activities which generate new circles of contacts. The danger then is that the new circle of friends remains completely isolated from church life. Within the multiplex church there needs to be a social network as well as a religious network through which church-goers' non-church-going friends can link with church-going friends.

Chapter 9, which discussed incompatible life-styles, identified a range of reasons for church-goers feeling that their life-style excluded them from continuing participation in church life. For some church-leavers, their judgement was probably well-grounded. For other church-leavers, however, their judgement may have been based on only a partial reading of the wide spectrum of life-style choices supported by the Christian community. Within the multiplex church there needs to be room for individuals created in the divine image to find acceptance and affirmation. For example, within the rich diversity in the Christian community, some congregations are likely to remain supportive of same-sex relationships and other congregations are likely to feel uncomfortable with this situation.

Chapter 10, which discussed not belonging and not fitting in, identified a range of reasons for church-goers feeling uncomfortable or out of place in their congregation. Somehow the chemistry just did not work; somehow the relationships just did not gel; somehow tensions managed to arise. Such issues are often inevitable in many social organisations. Within the multiplex church there need to be freedom and flexibility for individuals to get up, to walk away, and to settle down elsewhere.

Chapter 11, which discussed costs and benefits, recognised that some church-leavers gave up, feeling that their investment in church life was just not worthwhile. Often such decisions may be inevitable, but not always. For example, within the multiplex church the parents who leave saying that the church was failing to meet the needs of their children, might well benefit from knowing of congregations that provide a different form of ministry for children and young families. The multiplex church also needs to be aware of the danger of over-burdening some of its willing volunteers with too many demands. Within the multiplex church there need to be sufficient resources to sustain ministry without running the risk of burnout among professional staff or among lay volunteers.

Chapter 12 discussed disillusionment with the church, recognised that human institutions are unlikely to live up to all their ideals and aspirations. It is inevitable that some individuals will become disillusioned. Yet within the multiplex church it is crucial that there be room for idealism and for individual Christians to strive for the realisation of their ideals. Collectively, the multiplex church has its part to play in the struggles against racism, against social injustice, against sexism, against homophobia, against the abuse of power, and against materialism. It is reasonable, too, within the multiplex church for different congregations to espouse different causes and, thereby, to do so with professionalism and with expertise.

Chapter 13, which discussed being let down by the church, identified two different senses in which individuals may feel let down by the church. On the one hand, there is the sense in which some individuals feel that, for whatever reason, the church failed to be there for them when they needed it. Missed pastoral opportunities are always regrettable, but it is clearly impossible for all pastoral needs to be properly recognised and properly met. The diverse pastoral resources of the multiplex church need to be effectively and efficiently targeted. On the other hand, there is the sense in which some individuals feel themselves to be the victim of inappropriate pastoral practice. As long as church-leavers continue to give accounts of physical, psychological or sexual abuse at the hands of the church, professional standards and professional accountability remain seriously questioned. Professional standards need to be paramount within the multiplex church. Perhaps for the first time this model of church provides a powerful rationale for the development of a professional association of church leaders that transcends denominational structures. Such an association would make explicit the professional standards promoted by the multiplex church and make explicit who is licensed to practise within its jurisdiction. The general public deserves nothing less in the twenty-first century.

Chapter 14, which discussed problems with relevance, identified two major and quite different ways in which church-leavers questioned the relevance of the church in the twenty-first century. On the one hand, some church-leavers felt that the church was on 'another planet', largely old-fashioned, stuck in its views or irrelevant to everyday life. Within the multiplex church there is clearly room for 'new expressions' of church and for experimental ways to connect with contemporary issues and with contemporary life-styles. Indeed, the very doctrine of incarnation prevents the church of today resting content with relegation to another planet. On the other hand, other church-leavers were less concerned to question the relevance of church teaching, but more concerned to question the relevance of the institutional context for that teaching. Such individuals are characterised by the view that 'You do not need to go to church to be a Christian'. In an age that values loose networks alongside physical institutions, the multiplex church needs to embrace the virtual e-church as well as the visible congregation on the local street corner.

Chapter 15, which discussed problems with change, recognised the crucial tension in church life between respect for the established tradition and changes designed to link that tradition with developing world-views, changing life-styles and expanding knowledge. The psychology of individual differences makes it clear that some people are energised by change, while others are simply drained by it. Some people are anxious to pioneer innovation, while others are highly cautious about trusting new ideas. Within the multiplex church there needs to be room for both kinds of people to feel at home, and to extend proper respect for each other's position.

Chapter 16, which discussed problems with worship, distinguished between three issues defined as matters of style, matters of taste, and matters of level. Some church-leavers had disliked the worship because it was too formal, and others because it was too informal. Some church-leavers had disliked the teaching because it was too simple, and others because it was too difficult. Such contradictory problems are inevitable as long as each church lives in isolation and claims unique authority for its own preferences. The theology of the multiplex church provides the essential rationale for respect between and interchange among congregations. Within the multiplex church there is room for informality and for formality, room for basic foundational teaching and for advanced theological discussion.

Chapter 17, which discussed problems with leadership, revealed some fairly consistent criticisms of leadership styles prevalent within the church. Church leadership was criticised as too authoritarian, too hierarchical and too status-conscious. Within the multiplex church, proper attention needs to be given to leadership training and to leadership development. Too much is at stake not to take such issues seriously.

Chapters 18 and 19 concentrated on two contrasting issues: problems with conservatism and problems with liberalism. Both were issues causing discontent and discomfort among church-goers and leading to church-leaving. Within the multiplex church there must be room for liberals and there must be room for conservatives. Inclusivity of this nature breeds strengths, not weaknesses. A theology of individual differences supports diversity, but not uniformity.

Conclusion

By listening to the voices of a large number of church-leavers we have tried to listen also to the voice of God challenging the church to rethink the dominant model for being the people of God in twenty-first-century Britain. In response to this challenge, we have proposed the model of the multiplex church, rooted in a strong doctrine of creation and supported by a theology of individual differences. We commend continuing development and refinement of these ideas.

Appendix

Statistical tables

Table 5. Matters of belief and unbelief

	Yes (%)	? (%)	No (%)
Losing faith			
I doubted or questioned my faith.	43	15	42
I lost my faith.	32	19	50
Church had lost its meaning for me.	49	16	35
Life experience			
I felt God had let me down.	10	15	75
I could not reconcile my own suffering with my belief in God.	14	20	67
I could not reconcile others' suffering with my belief in God.	29	20	51
I became aware of alternative ways of thinking or living.	53	12	35
So many people fight each other in the name of religion.	66	10	25
Problems with belief			
Many of the church's teachings were illogical or nonsensical.	40	19	41
The church's teachings were difficult to reconcile with modern science.	42	20	38
It was increasingly difficult to believe Christianity is the only true faith.	48	17	35
Responding to doubt			
I felt nobody in the church would understand my doubts.	16	23	62
The church did not allow people to discuss or disagree with its views.	25	22	53
A questioning faith did not seem acceptable to the church.	29	25	47

Table 6. Growing up and changing

	Yes (%)	? (%)	No (%)
Growing up			
I grew up and started making decisions on my own.	54	7	39
The church was no longer helping me to grow.	29	20	51
Parents and children			
I associated church-going with my childhood and outgrew it.	39	12	50
I was made to go to church by my parents and it put me off.	25	11	64
Accepting responsibilities			
I changed – it wasn't the church's fault that I dropped off.	64	16	20
I got out of the habit of going to church.	69	7	24

Table 7. Life transitions and life changes

	Yes (%)	? (%)	No (%)
Going away from home			
I left home.	27	6	68
I went away to higher education.	16	6	78
Moving to a new area			
I moved to a new area.	33	7	60
I moved home and did not find a church I liked in my new area.	16	9	75
Growing family commitments			
I had increased family commitments.	33	7	60
My children needed me to provide transport on Sundays.	7	9	85
I needed to visit my (or my spouse's) parents on Sundays.	11	7	82
Changing status			
My marriage broke up.	8	6	85
I became ill.	7	5	88
I was bereaved.	10	6	84

Table 8. Alternative lives and alternative meanings

	Yes (%)	? (%)	No (%)
Tensions with work			
My work schedule interfered with attendance at church.	28	6	66
I had to work on Sundays.	25	7	69
Tensions with relationships			
My partner was not attending church.	32	13	55
My church-going was causing tension with my partner.	5	13	81
Tensions with time			
Most of my friends were not church-goers.	46	12	42
I found other interests and activities.	59	9	33
I was too busy.	52	11	37
I felt church-going was unfashionable.	14	14	72

Table 9. Incompatible life-styles

	Yes (%)	? (%)	No (%)
Growing self-awareness			
My church-going was hypocritical.	25	19	56
I was going to church for the wrong reasons.	31	16	53
I could not keep going to church and be true to myself.	29	16	55
I wanted to stop pretending to be someone I was not.	19	14	67
Clash of values			
I felt my life-style was not compatible with participation in the church.	39	15	46
I felt my values were not compatible with participation in the church.	33	16	51
The church did not give me room to be myself.	19	17	65
Clash of teaching			
I disagreed with the church's theological teachings.	20	28	53
I disagreed with the church's stance on key moral issues.	30	24	46
Specific life-style issues			
I was having sex outside marriage.	13	4	84
I was a practising homosexual/lesbian.	2	2	96
I was taking (illegal) drugs.	3	4	94

Table 10. Not belonging and not fitting in

	Yes (%)	? (%)	No (%)
Social exclusion			
I did not feel a part of the church.	45	13	42
There were cliques or 'in groups' from which I felt excluded.	25	14	61
The church did not value what I had to offer.	7	19	73
I was not allowed to play an active part in the church.	6	14	80
Personal marginalisation			
I felt powerless to bring about change within the church.	25	26	50
The church did not listen to me.	13	19	68
I felt pressured to join the church before I was ready.	13	11	77
I felt spiritually out of my depth.	14	14	72
Personal visibility			
There were not enough people of my age.	22	11	67
I felt there were not enough people in the congregation.	15	13	72
I was expected to do embarrassing things in the worship service.	9	10	81
I felt there were too many people in the congregation.	2	11	87
Tensions and conflicts			
There was tension between me and a church leader.	3	10	88
There was tension between me and a church member.	3	10	88
I had a clash of principles with the leadership of the church.	5	11	84
Relationships within the church had become soured.	6	13	81

Table 11. Costs and benefits

	Yes (%)	? (%)	No (%)
Not meeting my needs			
The church did not meet my needs.	40	19	40
The church was not meeting my child(ren)'s needs.	11	24	65
There was nothing in it for me.	29	19	52
My non-church-going friends did not seem to miss out on anything.	36	23	41
Not helping my spiritual growth			
The church was not helping me find meaning and purpose in my life.	38	17	45
The church was not meeting my spiritual needs.	36	19	44
The church was not providing me with enough teaching and guidance.	16	24	60
It was easy to drift in and out – my church did not expect strong commitment	32	24	44
Too many demands, too little return			
My participation in church had become a chore, with little enjoyment.	41	13	46
The church was making increasing demands on my time.	6	9	85
The church was making increasing demands on my money.	5	10	85

Table 12. Disillusionment with the church

	Yes (%)	? (%)	No (%)
The fragmented vision			
I was disillusioned by the church's failure to live up to its ideals.	32	20	48
The church lacked a sense of purpose and vision.	25	24	51
I was disillusioned by splits between church denominations.	31	21	49
The church was too much preoccupied with maintaining buildings.	17	22	62
The local church			
I was disillusioned by local factions within the church.	21	24	55
I disliked the hypocrisy I saw in other church-goers.	47	14	40
I felt other church-goers were not authentic Christians.	31	22	47
Issues of justice and power			
I was disillusioned by the church's materialism.	31	18	51
I was disillusioned by the church's abuse of power.	28	20	52
I was disillusioned by the church's lack of response to social injustice.	29	20	51
I was disillusioned by church-goers' racism.	21	18	62
Issues of sex and sexuality			
I was disillusioned by church-goers' attitudes to women.	24	18	59
I was disillusioned by church-goers' attitudes to homosexuals.	24	21	56
I was disillusioned by church-goers' attitudes to lesbians.	24	21	56

Table 13. Being let down by the church

	Yes (%)	? (%)	No (%)
Lack of care and support			
The church had failed me in some way.	14	19	67
I felt let down by the church at a time when I needed its support.	14	15	72
I did not find the church to be caring and supportive.	20	17	63
The clergy did not provide sufficient care for me.	14	21	65
Lack of professionalism			
I felt misdirected by the church when I needed its support.	10	22	69
The church's pastoral care to me was unprofessional.	4	11	85
The church's pastoral care to others was unprofessional.	5	14	81
Abuse of power			
The church's pastoral care was psychologically abusive to me.	4	10	87
The church's pastoral care was sexually abusive to me.	1	8	91
I was threatened with physical violence by a church leader.	1	5	94

Table 14. Problems with relevance

	Yes (%)	? (%)	No (%)
Irrelevance			
Sermons were irrelevant to my everyday life.	38	18	44
The church's teaching was irrelevant to my everyday life.	33	18	49
The church was stuck in its views.	33	20	47
The church was too old-fashioned.	26	19	55
Another planet			
The church failed to connect with the rest of my life.	46	19	35
I was not interested in the activities on offer.	43	16	40
I was bored.	39	17	44
Church felt like 'another planet'.	23	20	57
De-institutionalised faith			
I believed that you do not need to go to church to be a Christian.	75	12	13
People have God within them, so churches aren't really necessary.	40	27	32
I wanted to follow my own spiritual quest, without religious institutions.	36	16	49
I distrusted most institutions, including the church.	27	17	56

Table 15. Problems with change

	Yes (%)	? (%)	No (%)
The global direction			
I did not like the direction in which the church was going.	21	27	52
I did not like the changes that had happened in the church.	20	26	54
Worship and liturgy			
I did not like the new hymns.	19	17	63
I did not like the new service book.	18	20	62
I did not like the new translation of the Bible.	18	22	60
Local church			
I did not like the new style of worship.	16	22	63
I did not like the new style of teaching.	11	27	62
I found it hard to adjust to a new priest/minister/pastor.	10	18	73
I did not like the new seating arrangement in the church.	5	21	74

Table 16. Problems with worship

	Yes (%)	? (%)	No (%)
A matter of style			
I disliked the church's style of worship.	21	23	56
I felt that the worship was too formal.	26	22	52
I felt that the worship was too informal.	10	23	67
A matter of taste			
I felt the worship was too mechanical.	32	18	50
I felt that there was too little sense of the presence of God in worship.	25	23	53
I felt that there was not enough variety in worship to suit different tastes.	22	26	52
A matter of level			
The church's teaching seemed to go 'over my head'.	16	13	71
The church's teaching was too simplified and unchallenging.	17	15	68

329

Table 17. Problems with leadership

	Yes (%)	? (%)	No (%)
A matter of style			
The leadership style of the church was too authoritarian.	22	20	58
The church was too democratic.	5	24	71
A matter of status			
The church was too hierarchical and status-conscious.	25	24	51
The church did not allow women their rightful place in decision-making.	22	21	57
A matter of direction			
The church leadership was not giving a clear enough sense of direction.	17	28	55
The church did not take enough account of church tradition.	8	20	72
The church did not take enough account of the will of God.	8	28	64

Table 18. Problems with conservatism

	Yes (%)	? (%)	No (%)
Problems with theology			
The church's theological teachings were too narrow.	21	30	49
I was tired of being told what to believe by the church.	32	13	56
The church was too negative toward 'the world outside'.	23	24	53
The church allowed too little space to explore ideas for myself.	27	17	56
Problems with morality			
The church's moral teachings were too narrow.	28	23	49
I was tired of being told how to behave by the church.	24	11	66
The church's approach to morality was too 'black and white'.	37	14	49
The church was too conservative for me.	25	24	52

Table 19. Problems with liberalism

	Yes (%)	? (%)	No (%)
Lack of clear boundaries			
I felt there should be a clearer line drawn between Christian values and the values of the 'outside world'.	22	28	50
It was unclear what commitment to the church involved.	18	30	52
It was not worth staying because it didn't matter what people believed or did.	14	17	69
The church compromised its teachings to be acceptable to secular culture.	13	36	51
Lack of clear teaching			
The church's teaching did not give the certainty I was seeking.	23	18	60
The church failed to provide a firm moral lead.	16	23	61
The church did not seem to take sin seriously enough.	10	21	69
The church was too liberal for me.	7	21	73

References

Albrecht, S.L., Cornwall, M. and Cunningham, P.H. (1988), Religious leave-taking: disengagement and disaffiliation among Mormons, in David G. Bromley (ed.), *Falling from the Faith: causes and consequences of religious apostasy*, London, Sage, pp. 62–80.

Ainlay, S.C., Singleton Jr, R. and Swigert, V.L. (1992), Aging and religious participation: reconsidering the effects of health, *Journal for the Scientific Study of Religion*, 31 (2), 175–188.

Altemeyer, B. and Hunsberger, B. (1997), *Amazing Conversions: why some turn to faith and others abandon religion*, Amherst, New York, Prometheus Books.

Ammerman, N.T. (1998), Culture and identity in the congregation, in N.T. Ammerman, J.W. Carroll, C.S. Dudley and W. McKinney (eds), *Studying Congregations: a new handbook*, pp. 78–104, Nashville, Tennessee, Abingdon Press.

Ammerman, N.T. and Roof, W.C. (eds) (1995), *Work, Family and Religion in Contemporary Society*, London, Routledge.

Archbishops' Council (2004), *Mission-shaped Church: church planting and fresh expressions of church in a changing context*, London, Church House Publishing.

Argue, A.J., Johnson, D.R. and White, L.K. (1999), Age and religiosity: evidence from a three-wave panel analysis, *Journal for the Scientific Study of Religion*, 38 (3), 423–35.

Astley, J. and Francis, L.J. (eds) (1992), *Christian Perspectives on Faith Development: a reader*, Leominster, Gracewing.

Babinski, E.T. (1995), *Leaving the Fold: testimonies of former fundamentalists*, New York, Prometheus Books.

Bahr, H.M. (1970), Ageing and religious disaffiliation, *Social Forces*, 49 (1), 59–71.

Bailey, E.I. (1997), *Implicit Religion in Contemporary Society*, Kampen, Netherlands, Kok Pharos.

Barbour, J.D. (1994), *Versions of Deconversion: autobiography and the loss of faith*, Charlottesville, Virginia, University Press of Virginia.

Barker, E. (1998), The post-war generation and establishment religion in England, in W.C. Roof, J.W. Carroll and D.A. Roozen (eds), *The Post-war Generation and Establishment Religion: cross-cultural perspectives*, pp. 1–25, Oxford, Westview Press.

Bar-Lev, M., Leslau, A. and Ne'eman, N. (1997), Culture-specific factors which cause Jews in Israel to abandon religious practice, in M. Bar-Lev and W. Shaffir (eds), *Religion and the Social Order: leaving religion and religious life*, pp. 185–204, London, JAI Press.

Becker, P.E. and Hofmeister, H. (2001), Work, family, and religious involvement for men and women, *Journal for the Scientific Study of Religion*, 40 (4), 707–22.

Bibby, R.W. (1997), Going, going, gone: the impact of geographical mobility on religious involvement, *Review of Religious Research*, 38 (4), 289–307.

Black, A. (1928), London church and mission attendances, *The British Weekly*, 23 February; 1 March; 8 March.

Booth, C. (1902a), *Life and Labour of the People in London: third series: religious influences*, London, Macmillan.

Booth, C. (1902b), *Life and Labour of the People in London: third series: religious influences* (volume 7), London, Macmillan.

Booth, C. (1902c), *Life and Labour of the People in London: third series: religious influences* (volume 3), London, Macmillan.

Brierley, P. (ed.) (1991), *Prospects for the Nineties: all England*, London, MARC Europe.

Brierley, P. (2000), *The Tide is Running Out: what the English church attendance survey reveals*, Eltham, Christian Research.

Brierley, P. (2002), *Reaching and Keeping Tweenagers: analysis of the 2001 RAKES survey*, Eltham, Christian Research.

Brinkerhoff, M. B. and Mackie, M. M. (1993), Casting off the bonds of organised religion: a religious-careers approach to the study of apostasy, *Review of Religious Research*, 34 (3), 235–57.

Bromley, D.G. (ed.) (1988), *Falling from Faith: causes and consequences of religious apostasy*, London, Sage.

Bromley, D.G. (1997), Falling from the new faiths: toward an integrated model of religious affiliation/disaffiliation, in M. Bar-Lev and W. Shaffir (eds), *Religion and the Social Order: leaving religion and religious life*, pp. 31–60, London, JAI Press.

Bromley, D.G. (1998a), Linking social structure and the exit process in religious organizations: defectors, whistle-blowers, and apostates, *Journal for the Scientific Study of Religion*, 37, 145–160.

Bromley, D.G. (1998b), *The Politics of Religious Apostasy: the role of apostates in the transformation of religious movements*, Westport, Connecticut, Praeger.

Brown, C.G. (2001), *The Death of Christian Britain*, London, Routledge.

Brown, L.B. and Hunsberger, R.A. (1984), Religious socialization, apostasy, and the impact of family background, *Journal for the Scientific Study of Religion*, 23, 239–51.

Bruce, S. (1995), *Religion in Modern Britain*, Oxford, Oxford University Press.

Bruce, S. (1996), *Religion in the Modern World: from cathedrals to cults*, Oxford, Oxford University Press.

Bruce, S. (2002), *God is Dead: secularization in the west*, Oxford, Blackwell.

Bruce, S. and Glendinning, T. (2003), Religious beliefs and differences, in C. Bromley, J. Curtice, K. Hinds and A. Park (eds), *Devolution: Scottish answers to Scottish questions?* pp. 86–115, Edinburgh, Edinburgh University Press.

Butler, J.R. (1966), A sociological study of lapsed membership, *London Quarterly and Holborn Review*, 191, 236–44.

Cairns, D.S. (ed.) (1919), *The Army and Religion*, London, Macmillan.

Caplovitz, D. and Sherrow, F. (1977), *The Religious Dropouts: apostasy among college graduates*, Beverly Hills, California, Sage.

Carroll, J. and Roof, W.C. (1993), *Beyond Establishment: Protestant identity in a post-Protestant age*, Louisville, Kentucky, Westminster/John Knox Press.

Cartledge, M.J. (1999), Empirical theology: inter- or intra-disciplinary?, *Journal of Beliefs and Values*, 20, 98–104.

Chaves, M. (1991), Family structure and Protestant church attendance: the sociological basis of cohort and age effects, *Journal for the Scientific Study of Religion*, 30 (4), 501–14.

Church of England (1959), *Facts and Figures about the Church of England*, London, Church Information Office.

Church of England (2002), *Church Statistics: parochial membership, attendance and finance statistics, January to December 2000*, London, Church House Publishing.

Church of England (2006), *Church Statistics: parochial church attendance, membership and finance statistics together with statistics of licensed ministers for the Church of England 2004/5*, London, Church House Publishing.

Churches Information for Mission (2001), *Church Life Profile 2001: survey form*, London, Churches Information for Mission.

Clarke, R. (2001), Worshipping, in A.J. Jewell (ed.), *Older People and the Church*, pp. 62–79, Peterborough, Methodist Publishing House.

Coupland, D. (1995), 'Generation X'd', Details, June, p. 72 [obtainable via 'The Coupland File' – www.geocities.com/SoHo/Gallery/5560/index.html (accessed 19/8/02)].

Dart, J. (2000), Gender and churchgoing: men behaving badly, *Christian Century*, 117, 32, 1174–5.

Davie, G. (1994), *Religion in Britain Since 1945: believing without belonging*, Oxford, Blackwell.

Davie, G. (2002), Praying alone? Church-going in Britain and social capital: a reply to Steve Bruce, *Journal of Contemporary Religion*, 17, 329–34.

De Graff, N.D. and Need, A. (2000), Losing faith: is Britain alone? In R. Jowell, J. Curtice, A. Park, K. Thomson, L. Jarvis, C. Bromley and N. Stratford (eds), *British Social Attitudes: the seventeenth report*, pp. 119–36, London, Sage.

Dorsey, G. (1998), *Congregation: the journey back to church*, Cleveland, Ohio, Pilgrim.

Dudley, C.S. (1979), *Where Have All Our People Gone? New choices for old churches*, New York, Pilgrim Press.

Dudley, R.L. (1999), Youth religious commitment over time: a longitudinal study of retention, *Review of Religious Research*, 41, 109–120.

Ebaugh, H.R. (1988), Leaving Catholic convents: toward a theory of disengagement, in D.G. Bromley (ed.), *Falling from the Faith: causes and consequences of religious apostasy*, pp. 100–121, Newbury Park, Sage.

Fanstone, M.J. (1993), *The Sheep That Got Away: why do people leave the church?*, Tunbridge Wells, MARC.

Field, C.D. (2000), Joining and leaving British Methodism since the 1960s, in L.J. Francis and Y.J. Katz (eds), *Joining and Leaving Religion: research perspectives*, pp. 57–85, Leominster, Gracewing.

Firebaugh, G. and Harley, B. (1991), Trends in U.S. church attendance: secularization and revival, or merely lifecycle effects?, *Journal for the Scientific Study of Religion*, 30 (4), 487–500.

Flory, R.W. and Miller, D.E. (2000), *Gen X Religion*, London, Routledge.

Fowler, J.W. (1981), *Stages of Faith: the psychology of human development and the quest for meaning*, San Francisco, California, Harper & Row.

Francis, L.J. (1997), The psychology of gender differences in religion: a review of empirical research, *Religion*, 27, 81–96.

Francis, L.J. (2002), Personality theory and empirical theology, *Journal of Empirical Theology*, 15, 37–53.

Francis, L.J. (2005a), *Faith and Psychology: personality, religion and the individual*, London, Darton, Longman & Todd.

Francis, L.J. (2005b), Gender role orientation and attitude toward Christianity: a study among older men and women in the United Kingdom, *Journal of Psychology and Theology*, 33, 179–86.

Francis, L.J. and Astley, J. (eds) (2002), *Children, Churches and Christian Learning*, London, SPCK.

Francis, L.J. and Brierley, P.W. (1997), The changing face of the British churches: 1975–1995, in M. Bar-Lev and W. Shaffir (eds), *Leaving Religion and Religious Life*, pp. 159–184, Greenwich, Connecticut, JAI Press.

Francis, L. J. and Gibson, H.M. (1993), Parental influence and adolescent religiosity: a study of church attendance and attitude toward Christianity among adolescents 11 to 12 and 15 to 16 years old, *International Journal for the Psychology of Religion*, 3 (4), 241–53.

Francis, L.J., Robbins, M. and Astley, J. (2005), *Fragmented Faith? Exposing the fault-lines in the Church of England*, Carlisle, Paternoster.

Gallup, G. Jr. (1988), *The Unchurched American: ten years later*, Princeton, New Jersey, Princeton Religious Research Center.

Gallup, G. Jr. (1990), *Religion in America*, Princeton, New Jersey, Princeton Religious Research Center.

Gill, R. (1993), *The Myth of the Empty Church*, London, SPCK.

Gill, R. (1999), *Churchgoing and Christian Ethics*, Cambridge, Cambridge University Press.

Gill, R. (2002), *Changing Worlds: can the church respond?* Edinburgh, T & T Clark.

Gill, R. (2003a), *The 'Empty Church' Revisited*, Aldershot, Ashgate.

Gill, R. (2003b), Measuring church trends over time, in P. Avis (ed.), *Public Faith: the state of religious belief and practice in Britain*, pp. 19–27, London, SPCK.

Glendinning, T. and Bruce, S. (2006), New ways of believing or belonging: is religion giving way to spirituality?, *British Journal of Sociology*, 57, 399–414.

Greeley, A.M. (1992), Religion in Britain, Ireland and the USA, in R. Jowell, L. Brook, G. Prior and B. Taylor (eds), *British Social Attitudes: the 9th report*, pp. 51–70, Aldershot, Dartmouth Publishers.

Grotenhuis, M.T. and Scheepers, P. (2001), Churches in Dutch: causes of religious disaffiliation in the Netherlands, 1937–1995, *Journal for the Scientific Study of Religion*, 40 (4), 591–606.

Guest, M., Tusting, K. and Woodhead, L. (2004), *Congregational Studies in the UK*, Aldershot, Ashgate.

Hadaway, C.K. (1989), Identifying American apostates: a cluster analysis, *Journal for the Scientific Study of Religion*, 28, 201–15.

Hadaway, C.K. (1990a), *What Can We Do About Church Dropouts?* Nashville, Tennessee, Abingdon Press.

Hadaway, C.K. (1990b), Denominational defection: recent research on religious disaffiliation in America, in M.J. Coalter, J.M. Mulder and L.B. Weeks (eds), *The Mainstream Protestant 'Decline': the Presbyterian pattern*, pp. 102–21, Louisville, Kentucky, Westminster/ John Knox Press.

Hale, J.R. (1977), *Who are the Unchurched: an exploratory study*, Washington, DC, Glenmary Research Center.

Hale, J.R. (1980), *The Unchurched: who they are and why they stay away*, San Francisco, California, Harper & Row.

Hammond, G. and Treetops, J. (2001), Belonging, in A.J. Jewell (ed.), *Older People and the Church*, pp. 38–61, Peterborough, Methodist Publishing House.

Harris, M. (1998a), Religious congregations as nonprofit organizations: four English case studies, in N.J. Demerath III, P.D. Hall, T.

Schmitt and R.H. Williams (eds), *Sacred Companies: organizational aspects of religion and religious aspects of organizations*, pp. 307–20, Oxford, Oxford University Press.

Harris, M. (1998b), *Organizing God's Work: challenges for churches and synagogues*, Basingstoke, Macmillan.

Harris, J. (2001), Believing, in A.J. Jewell (ed.), *Older People and the Church*, pp. 80–102, Peterborough, Methodist Publishing House.

Hartman, W.J. (1976), *Membership Trends: a study of decline and growth in the United Methodist Church 1949–1975*, Nashville, Tennessee, Discipleship Resources.

Heelas, P. and Woodhead, L. (2005), *The Spiritual Revolution: why religion is giving way to spirituality*, Oxford, Blackwell.

Henkys, J. and Schweitzer, F. (1997), Atheism, religion and indifference in the two parts of Germany: before and after 1989, in M. Bar-Lev and W. Shaffir (eds), *Religion and the Social Order: leaving religion and religious life*, pp. 117–37, London, JAI Press.

Hoge, D.R. (1988), Why Catholics drop out, in D.G. Bromley (ed.), *Falling from the Faith: causes and consequences of religious apostasy*, pp. 81–99, Newbury Park, California, Sage.

Hoge, D.R., Johnson, B. and Luidens, D.A. (1993), Determinants of church involvement of young adults who grew up in Presbyterian churches, *Journal for the Scientific Study of Religion*, 32 (3), 242–55.

Hoge, D.R., Johnson, B. and Luidens, D.A. (1994), *Vanishing Boundaries: the religion of mainline Protestant baby boomers*, Louisville, Kentucky, Westminster/John Knox Press.

Hoge, D.R., Johnson, B. and Luidens, D.A. (1995), Congregational involvement of young adults who grew up in Protestant churches, in A.L. Sales and G.A. Tobin (eds), *Church and Synagogue Affiliation: theory, research, and practice*, pp. 59–76, London, Greenwood Press.

Hoge, D.R., McGuire, K. and Stratman, B.F. (1981), *Converts, Drop-outs, Returnees: a study of religious change among Catholics*, New York, Pilgrim Press.

Hornsby-Smith, M.P. (1992), Believing without belonging? The case of Roman Catholics in England, in B. Wilson (ed.), *Religion: Contemporary issues – the All Souls seminars in the sociology of religion*, pp. 125–134, London, Bellew Publishing.

Howard, R. (1996), *The Rise and Fall of the Nine O'Clock Service: a cult within the church*, London, Mowbray.

Hughes, P., Bellamy, J., Black, A. and Kaldor, P. (2000), Dropping out of church: the Australian experience, in L.J. Francis and Y.J. Katz (eds), *Joining and Leaving Religion: research perspectives*, pp. 167–94, Leominster, Gracewing.

Hunsberger, B. (1983), Apostasy: a social learning perspective, *Review of Religious Research*, 25 (1), 21–38.

Hunsberger, B. (2000), Swimming against the current: exceptional cases of apostates and converts, in L.J. Francis and Y.J. Katz (eds), *Joining and Leaving Religion: research perspectives*, pp. 233–48, Leominster, Gracewing.

Iannaccone, L. (1990), Religious practice: a human capital approach, *Journal for the Scientific Study of Religion*, 29 (3), 297–314.

Iannaccone, L. (1992), Religious markets and the economics of religion, *Social Compass*, 39, 123–31.

Iannaccone, L. (1994), Why strict churches are strong, *American Journal of Sociology*, 99, 1180–211.

Inglehart, R. (1990), *Culture Shift in Advanced Industrial Society*, Princeton, Princeton University Press.

Iversen, H.R. (1997), Leaving the distant church: the Danish experience, in M. Bar-Lev and W. Shaffir (eds), *Religion and the Social Order: leaving religion and religious life*, pp. 139–58, London, JAI Press.

Jamieson, A. (2002), *A Churchless Faith: faith journeys beyond the churches*, London, SPCK.

Jamieson, A. (2004), *Journeying in Faith: in and beyond the tough places*, London, SPCK.

Jewell, A.J. (ed.) (2001), *Older People and the Church*, Peterborough, Methodist Publishing House.

Jung, C.G. (1971), *Psychological Types: the collected works, volume 6*, London, Routledge & Kegan Paul.

Kay, W.K. (1981), Marital happiness and children's attitudes to religion, *British Journal of Religious Education*, 3, 102–5.

Kay, W.K. and Francis, L.J. (1996), *Drift from the Churches: attitude toward Christianity during childhood and adolescence*, Cardiff, University of Wales Press.

Lawton, L.E. and Bures, R. (2001), Parental divorce and the 'switching' of religious identity, *Journal for the Scientific Study of Religion*, 40 (1), 99–111.

Lofland, J. and Stark, R. (1965), Becoming a world-saver: a theory of conversion to a deviant perspective, *American Sociological Review*, 30, 862–75.

Louden, S.H. and Francis, L.J. (2003), *The Naked Parish Priest: what priests really think they're doing*, London, Continuum.

Lovat, T.J. (1997), Patterns of religious separation and adherence in contemporary Australia, in M. Bar-Lev and W. Shaffir (eds), *Religion and the Social Order: leaving religion and religious life*, pp. 97–116, London, JAI Press.

Lynch, G. (2002), *After Religion: "generation X" and the search for meaning*, London, Darton, Longman & Todd.

McGuire, M. (1987), *Religion: the social context*, Belmont, California, Wadsworth.

McTaggart, J.M. (1997), Organized humanism in Canada: an expression of secular reaffiliation, in M. Bar-Lev and W. Shaffir (eds), *Religion and the Social Order: leaving religion and religious life*, pp. 61–75, London, JAI Press.

Marler, P.L. (1995), Lost in the Fifties: the changing family and the nostalgic church, in N.T. Ammerman and W.C. Roof (eds), *Work, Family and Religion in Contemporary Society*, pp. 23–60, London, Routledge.

Methodist Church (1999), *The Methodist Worship Book*, Peterborough, Methodist Publishing House.

Miller, A.S. and Stark, R. (2002), Gender and religiousness: can socialization explanations be saved? *American Journal of Sociology*, 107, 1399–423.

Moffitt, L. (2001), Drifting, in A.J. Jewell (ed.), *Older People and the Church*, pp. 17–37, Peterborough, Methodist Publishing House.

Moser, F. (1999), *Les Croyants Non Pratiquants*, Geneva, Labor et Fides.

Myers, I.B. and McCaulley, M.H. (1985), *Manual: a guide to the development and use of the Myers-Briggs Type Indicator*, Palo Alto, California, Consulting Psychologists Press.

Newport, F. (1979), The religious switcher in the United States, *American Sociological Review*, 44, 528–552.

North, K. (2001), *An analysis of why young adults are not practising their faith within the Roman Catholic Church*, Unpublished MPhil dissertation, University of Surrey, Roehampton.

Oswald, R.M. and Kroeger, O. (1988), *Personality Type and Religious Leadership*, New York, Alban Institute.

Partridge, C. and Reid, H. (eds) (2006), *Finding and Losing Faith: studies in conversion*, London, Continuum.

Perry, E.L., Doyle, R.T., Davis, J.H. and Dyble, J.E. (1980), Toward a typology of unchurched Protestants, *Review of Religious Research*, 21 (4), 388–404.

Ploch, D.R. and Hastings, D.W. (1998), Effects of parental church attendance, current family status, and religious salience on church attendance, *Review of Religious Research*, 39 (4), 309–20.

Princeton Religion Research Center (1988), *The Unchurched American – 10 Years Later*, Princeton, New Jersey, Princeton Religion Research Center.

Reiff, J.T. (1996), Commitment in a congregation of 'cultural left' baby boomers, *Journal of Pastoral Theology*, 6, 93–118.

Richter, P. (1999), Church leaving in the late twentieth century: eschewing the double life, in L. J. Francis (ed.), *Sociology, Theology and the Curriculum*, pp. 175–86, London, Cassell.

Richter, P. (2000), Gone but not quite out of the frame: approaching some of the distinctive problems of researching religious disaffiliation, in L.J. Francis and Y.J. Katz (eds), *Joining and Leaving Religion: Jewish and Christian Perspectives*, pp. 21–31, Leominster, Gracewing.

Richter, P. (2002), *That Elusive Methodist Identity: a sociological perspective*, Epworth Review, 29 (1), 39–48.

Richter, P. (2004), Denominational cultures: the Cinderella of congregational studies?, in M. Guest, K. Tusting and L. Woodhead (eds), *Congregational Studies in the UK: Christianity in a post-Christian context*, pp. 169–84, Aldershot, Ashgate.

Richter, P. and Francis, L.J. (1998), *Gone but not Forgotten: church leaving and returning*, London, Darton, Longman & Todd.

Robbins, M. (2000), Leaving before adolescence: profiling the child no longer in the church, in L.J. Francis and Y.J. Katz (eds), *Joining and Leaving Religion: research perspectives*, pp. 103–28, Leominster, Gracewing.

Rohr, R. (2005), *From Wild Man to Wise Man: reflections on male spirituality*, Cincinnati, Ohio, St Anthony's Messenger Press.

Roof, W.C. (1993), *A Generation of Seekers: the spiritual journeys of the baby boom generation*, San Francisco, California, HarperSanFrancisco.

Roof, W.C. (1999), *Spiritual Marketplace: baby boomers and the remaking of American religion*, Princeton, New Jersey, Princeton University Press.

Roof, W.C., Carroll, J.W. and Roozen, D.A. (1998), *The Post-war Generation and Establishment Religion: cross-cultural perspectives*, Oxford, Westview Press.

Roof, W.C. and Gesch, L. (1995), Boomers and the culture of choice: changing patterns of work, family, and religion, in N.T. Ammerman and W.C. Roof (eds), *Work, Family and Religion in Contemporary Society*, pp. 61–79, London, Routledge.

Roof, W.C. and Landres, J.S. (1997), Defection, disengagement and dissent: the dynamics of religious change in the United States, in M. Bar-Lev and W. Shaffir (eds), *Religion and the Social Order: leaving religion and religious life*, pp. 77–95, London, JAI Press.

Roozen, D.A. (1978), *The Churched and the Unchurched in America: a comparative profile*, Washington, DC, Glenmary Research Center.

Roozen, D.A. (1980), Church dropouts: Changing patterns of disengagement and re-entry, *Review of Religious Research*, 21 (4), 427–50.

Roozen, D.A., Carroll, J.W. and Roof, W.C. (1998), Fifty years of religious change in the United States, in W.C. Roof, J.W. Carroll and D.A. Roozen (eds), *The Post-war Generation and Establishment Religion: cross-cultural perspectives*, pp. 59–85, Oxford, Westview Press.

Roozen, D.A. and McKinney, W. (1990), The 'big chill' generation warms to worship: a research note, *Review of Religious Research*, 31 (3), 314–22.

Ryerson, C.M. (1995), *Generation X: through the eyes of a gen-xer*, unpublished paper, Santa Barbara, University of California.

Sandomirsky, S. and Wilson, J. (1990), Processes of disaffiliation: religious mobility among men and women, *Social Forces*, 68 (4), 1211–1229.

Savage, J.S. (1976), *The Apathetic and Bored Church Member: psychological and theological implications*, New York, LEAD Consultants.

Shaffir, W. (1997), 'Introduction' in M. Bar-Lev and W. Shaffir (eds), *Leaving Religion and Religious Life*, pp. 1–15, Greenwich, Connecticut, JAI Press.

Sherkat, D.E. (1991), Leaving the faith: testing theories of religious switching using survival models, *Social Science Research*, 20, 171–87.

Sherkat, D.E. and Wilson, J. (1995), Preferences, constraints, and choices in religious markets: an examination of religious switching and apostasy, *Social Forces*, 73, 993–1026.

Skonovd, N. (1983), Leaving the 'cultic' religious milieu, in D.G. Bromley and J.T. Richardson (eds), *The Brainwashing/Deprogramming Controversy: sociological, psychological, legal and historical perspectives*, pp. 91–105, New York, Edwin Mellen Press.

Soanes, C. and Hawker, S. (eds) (2005), *Compact Oxford English Dictionary of Current English* (third edition), Oxford, Oxford University Press.

SPSS Inc (1988), *SPSSX User's Guide*, New York, McGraw-Hill.

Stark, R. (1996), Why religious movements succeed or fail: a revised general model, *Journal of Contemporary Religion*, 11 (2), 133–46.

Stark, R. (2002), Physiology and faith: addressing the 'universal' gender differences in religious commitment, *Journal for the Scientific Study of Religion*, 41, 495–507.

Stolzenberg, R.M., Blair-Loy, M. and Waite, L.J. (1995), Religious participation in early adulthood: age and family life cycle effects on church membership, *American Sociological Review*, 60, 84–103.

Tapia, A. (1994), Reaching the first post-Christian, *Christianity Today* (12 September 1994).

Thomas, A. and Finch, H. (1990), *On Volunteering: a qualitative study of images, motivations and experiences*, London, Volunteer Centre UK.

Thornton, A., Axinn, W.G. and Hill, D.H. (1992), Reciprocal effects of religiosity, cohabitation and marriage, *American Journal of Sociology*, 98 (3), 628–51.

Van der Ven, J.A. (1993), *Practical Theology: an empirical approach*, Kampen, Kok Pharos.

Van der Ven, J.A. (1998), *Education for Reflective Ministry*, Louvain, Peeters.

Walter, T. and Davie, G. (1998), The religiosity of women in the modern west, *British Journal of Sociology*, 49, 4, 640–60.

Wilson, J. and Sherkat, D.E. (1994), Returning to the fold, *Journal for the Scientific Study of Religion*, 33 (2), 148–61.

Wind, J.P. (1995), Afterword, in A.L. Sales and G.A. Tobin (eds), *Church and Synagogue Affiliation: theory, research, and practice*, pp. 177–81, London, Greenwood Press.

Winter, G. (1961), *The Suburban Captivity of the Churches: an analysis of Protestant responsibility in the expanding metropolis*, New York, Doubleday.

Wright, S.A. (1987), *Leaving Cults: the dynamics of defection*, Washington, DC, Society for the Scientific Study of Religion.

Wright, S.A. (1988), Leaving new religious movements: issues, theory, and research, in D.G. Bromley (ed.), *Falling from the Faith: causes and consequences of religious apostasy*, pp. 143–65, London, Sage.

Wuthnow, R. and Christiano, K. (1979), The effects of residential migration on church attendance in the United States, in R. Wuthnow (ed.), *The Religious Dimension: new directions in quantitative research*, pp. 257–76, New York, Academic Press.

Index of Subjects

Index of Names

357